Lives on the Boundary

Lives
on the
Boundary

—◆—

The Struggles and Achievements
of America's Underprepared

Mike Rose

THE FREE PRESS
A Division of Macmillan, Inc.
NEW YORK

Collier Macmillan Publishers
LONDON

The Free Press
A Division of Macmillan, Inc.
866 Third Avenue, New York, N.Y. 10022

Collier Macmillan Canada, Inc.

Printed in the United States of America

printing number
1 2 3 4 5 6 7 8 9 10

Library of Congress Cataloging-in-Publication Data

Rose, Mike.
    Lives on the boundary : the struggles and achievements of
America's underprepared / Mike Rose.
        p. cm.
    Bibliography: p.
    ISBN 0-02-926821-4
    1. Remedial teaching—United States. 2. Literacy—United States. I. Title.
LB1029.R4R58 1989
428.4'2—dc19   88-21469
                                                                              CIP

Permission Credits

*To my mother and
the memory of my father
and
to my many teachers
in and out of the classroom*

Contents

———◆———

Preface

◆

This is a hopeful book about those who fail. *Lives on the Boundary* concerns language and human connection, literacy and culture, and it focuses on those who have trouble reading and writing in the schools and the workplace. It is a book about the abilities hidden by class and cultural barriers. And it is a book about movement: about what happens as people who have failed begin to participate in the educational system that has seemed so harsh and distant to them. We are a nation obsessed with evaluating our children, with calibrating their exact distance from some ideal benchmark. In the name of excellence, we test and measure them—as individuals, as a group—and we rejoice or despair over the results. The sad thing is that though we strain to see, we miss so much. All students cringe under the scrutiny, but those most harshly affected, least successful in the competition, possess some of our greatest unperceived riches.

I've worked for twenty years with children and adults deemed slow or remedial or underprepared. And at one time in my own educational life, I was so labeled. But I was lucky. I managed to get redefined. The people I've tutored and taught and the people whose lives I've studied—working-class children, poorly educated Vietnam veterans, underprepared college students, adults in a literacy program—they, for the most part, hadn't been so fortunate. They lived for many of their years in an educational underclass. In trying to present the cognitive and social reality of such a life—the brains as well as the heart of it—I have written a personal book. The stories of my work with literacy interweave with the story of my own engagement with language. *Lives on the Boundary* is both vignette and commentary, reflection and analysis. I didn't know how else to get it right.

Acknowledgments

◆

The stories in this book would have never been woven together without the help of Luther Nichols, who initiated the project; John Wright, who joyously hawked it; and Joyce Seltzer, who saw it through to careful completion.

David Bartholomae, Sheridan Blau, Lauren Cammack, Catherine Ciraulo, Kevin Fitzsimmons, Linda Flower, Tim Flower, Glynda Hull, Arthur Kovacks, Sheri Repp, Jacqueline Royster, Lillian Roybal-Rose, Tracey Thompson, and Michael Ventura read and generously commented on large portions of the manuscript. They helped shape and focus the writing, offered fresh ideas, pointed out again and again where the narrative failed. Also of great help were those who read and commented on particular sections: Benigno Campos, Kenyon Chan, Gary Colombo, Terry Curtis, Steve Duarte, Joan Feinberg, Sarah Freedman, Mike Gustin, Michael Havens, Bonnie Lisle, Donald McQuade, Mariolina Salvatori, Paul Smith, Nancy Spivey, David Tyack, and Donald Wasson. Gratitude as well to Edmundo Cardenas and Ed Frankel for journeys through the neighborhoods; to Margot Dashiell, Bruce Jacobs, Peter Simon, and Smokey Wilson for invitations to the classroom; and to Sheri Repp for superintending periods of scribal madness. Recognition is due to two of the people who typed the many drafts of this manuscript: Lourdes Everett slipped encouragement between the pages, and Antonia Turman, my longtime overseer of style and grace, saved the reader from many a flat line. Finally, my deep thanks to Edith Lewis and Sue Llewellyn, the people at The Free Press who, at the end, fixed the book in the many places where fixing was needed.

A number of people had a hand in shaping the way I think about education and, particularly, the study of writing. The bibliography at the end of the book lists some of those I know only through their publications. Let me now thank the others for the early, formative conversations: Chip Anderson, David Bartholomae, Patricia Bizzell, Kenyon Chan, Charles Cooper, Robert Connors, Linda Flower, Anne Ruggles Gere, Marcella Graffin, Annette Gromfin, Patrick Hartwell, Barbara Hayes-Roth, Morris Holland, Richard Lanham, Ruth Mitchell, Sondra Perl, Nancy Sommers, Richard Shavelson, Garth Sorenson, Mary Taylor, Joseph Williams, Stephen Witte, Merlin Wittrock. Our ideas come from engagement with the ideas of others; I am grateful to these people for making my ideas possible.

1

◆

Our Schools
and Our Children

Her name is Laura, and she was born in the poor section of Tijuana, the Mexican border city directly south of San Diego. Her father was a food vendor, and her memories of him and his chipped white cart come back to her in easy recollection: the odor of frying meat, the feel of tortillas damp with grease, and the serpentine path across the city; rolling the cart through dust, watching her father smile and haggle and curse—hawking burritos and sugar water to old women with armloads of blouses and figurines, to blond American teenagers, wild with freedom, drunk and loud and brawny. She came to the United States when she was six, and by dint of remarkable effort—on her parents' part and hers—she now sits in classes at UCLA among those blond apparitions.

She has signed up for and dropped the course I'm teaching, remedial English, *four* times during this, her freshman year: twice in the summer before she officially started, once in each of the quarters preceding this one. This is her fifth try. She is with me in my office, and she is scared to death: ''I get in there, and everything seems okay. But as soon as we start writing, I freeze up. I'm a crummy writer, I know it. I know I'm gonna make lots of mistakes and look stupid. I panic. And I stop coming.''

The Middle Ages envisioned the goddess of grammar, Grammatica, as an old woman. In one later incarnation, she is depicted as severe, with a scalpel and a large pair of pincers. Her right hand, which is by her side, grasps a bird by its neck, its mouth open as if in a gasp or a squawk. All this was emblematic, meant as a memory aid for the budding grammarian. But, Lord, how fitting the choices of emblem were—the living thing being strangled, beak open but silent, muted by the goddess Grammatica. And the scalpel, the pincers, are reminders to the teacher to be vigilant for error, to cut it out with the coldest tool. Laura has never seen the obscure book that holds my illustration of Grammatica, but she knows the goddess intimately, the squinting figure who breathes up to her side whenever she sits down to write.

It is the first week of fall quarter, and I am observing a section of English A, UCLA's most basic writing course, the course that students and many professors have come to call "bonehead." English A students vex universities like UCLA. By the various criteria the institutions use, the students deserve admission—have earned their way—but they are considered marginal, "high risk" or "at risk" in current administrative parlance. "The truly illiterate among us," was how one dean described them.

Dr. Gunner is a particularly gifted teacher of English A. She refuses to see her students as marginal and has, with a colleague, developed a writing course on topics in Western intellectual history. As I watch her, she is introducing her class to the first item on her syllabus, classical mythology. She has situated the Golden Age of Athens on a time line on the blackboard, and she is encouraging her students to tell her what they already know about Greek culture. Someone mentions Aristotle; someone else says "Oedipus Rex . . . and the Oedipus complex." "Who wrote about the Oedipus complex?" asks Dr. Gunner. "Freud," offers a soft voice from the end of the table.

One boy is slouched down in his chair, wearing a baseball cap, the bill turned backward. Two or three others are leaning forward: One is resting his head on his folded arms and looking sideways at Dr. Gunner. A girl by me has set out neatly in front of her two pencils, an eraser, a tiny stapler, and a pencil sharpener encased in a little plastic egg. Talismans, I think. Magical objects. The girl sitting next to her is somber and watches the teacher suspiciously. At the end of the table two other girls sit up straight and watch Dr. Gunner walk back and forth in front of the board. One plays with her bracelet. "Narcissus," says Dr. Gunner.

"Narcissus. Who was Narcissus?" "A guy who fell in love with himself," says the boy with his head on his arms.

The hour goes on, the class warms up, students let down their defenses, discussion drifts back and forth along the time line. Someone asks about a book he read in high school called *The Stranger*. Another knows that *renaissance* "means rebirth in the French language." Socrates and Plato get mentioned, as do Mars and Apollo. Dr. Gunner's first name is Eugenia; she writes it on the board and asks the class what Greek word it looks like: "Gene," says the girl with the sharpener and stapler. A halting "genetics" comes from the wary girl. "Eugenia, eugen . . . ," says the boy with the baseball cap, shifting in his chair. "Hey, that means something like race or good race." "Race control," says the boy with his head on his arms.

These are the truly illiterate among us.

It hits you most forcefully at lunchtime: the affluence of the place, the attention to dress and carriage, but the size, too—vast and impersonal, a labyrinth of corridors and classrooms and libraries; you're also struck by the wild intersection of cultures, spectacular diversity, compressed by a thousand social forces. I'm sitting under a canopy of purple jacarandas with Bobby, for Bobby is in a jam. Students are rushing to food lines or dormitories or sororities, running for elevators or taking stairs two at a time. Others "blow it off" and relax, mingling in twos and threes. Fifties fashion is everywhere: baggy pants, thin ties, crew cuts, retro ponytails—but so are incipient Yuppiedom and cautious punk, and this month's incarnation of the nuevo wavo. Palm trees sway on the backs of countless cotton shirts. A fellow who looks Pakistani zooms by on a skateboard. A Korean boy whose accent is still very strong introduces himself as Skip. Two Middle Eastern girls walk by in miniskirts and heels. Sometimes I think I'm teaching in a film by Ridley Scott.

I first met Bobby when he enrolled in a summer program I had developed for underprepared students. I was visiting the American social history course we offered, listening to the lecturer discuss the role of working women in the late-nineteenth-century mercantile economy. It was an organized, nicely paced presentation. The professor provided a broad overview of the issues and paused to dwell on particularly revealing cases, reading from editorials of the time and from a rich collection of letters written by those women. I was sitting in the back, watching the eighty or so students, trying to get a sense of their involvement, when I noticed this young man down the aisle to my left. He was watching the professor intently. His notebook was open in front of him. His pen was poised. But he wasn't writing. Nothing. I'd look back during the hour: still attentive but still no notes. I caught up with him after class—he knew me from our orientation—and asked how he liked the lecture. "Interesting," he said. So I asked him why he wasn't taking any notes. "Oh, well, 'cause the teacher was just talking about people and reading letters and such. She didn't cover anything important."

For Bobby, and for lots of other freshmen in lots of other colleges, history is a chronicle. History is dates and facts: Who invaded whom? When? With how many men? And Bobby could memorize this sort of thing like a demon. But *social* history, the history of moods and movements and ordinary people's lives, left Bobby without a clue. He was a star in his inner-city school, and he developed a set of expectations about subjects like history (history is lists of facts) and had appropriated a powerful strategy that fit his expectations (he memorized the lists). Social history was as unfamiliar to him as a Bahamian folktale.

So I sit under the jacarandas with Bobby. His girlfriend joins us. She is having a rough time, too. Both have been at UCLA for about three months now. They completed the summer program, and they are now in the fourth week of fall term. Bobby is talking animatedly about his linguistics course. It is all diagrams and mathematics and glottal stops. It was not what he expected from a course about the study of language. "They're asking me to do things I don't know how to do. All the time. Sometimes I sit in the library and wonder if I'm gonna make it. I mean I don't know, I really don't know." He pauses, looks out across the food lines, looks back at me. He gestures to himself and his girlfriend: "We don't belong at UCLA, do we?"

Students are everywhere. A girl squeals "Vanessa!" and runs over to hug a friend. A big guy with a backpack cuts into the food line. I shift down the bench to make room for a girl with a knee brace. Palm trees swaying on cotton shirts, Pakistanis on skateboards. History woven from letters, language converted to mathematics. A young man who never failed, failing. It's easy to forget what a strange place this is.

———◆———

The back-to-basics movement got a lot of press, fueled as it was by fears of growing illiteracy and cultural demise. The movement raked in all sorts of evidence of decline: test scores, snippets of misspelled prose, enrollments in remedial courses in our finest schools. Guardians of culture were called on to pronounce and diagnose, and they did. Poets, historians, philologists, and literary scholars were ominously cited in *Newsweek's* highly influential article, *Why Johnny Can't Write.** Among the many, many children, adolescents, and young adults who became the focus of this national panic were college freshmen like Laura, Bobby, and the members of Eugenia Gunner's English A. People with low SATs; people who wrote poorly. The back-to-basics advocates suggested—and many university faculty members solemnly agreed—that what was needed here was a return to the fundamentals: drills on parts of speech, grammar, rules of punctuation, spelling, usage. All of that. Diagraming sentences too. We've gotten soft. Images of the stern grammarian were resurrected from a misty past: gray, pointer in hand, rows of boys and girls, orderly as syntax, reflected in the flat lenses of his spectacles.

The more things change, the more they remain the same. In 1841 the president of Brown complained that "students frequently enter college almost wholly unacquainted with English grammar." In the mid-1870s, Harvard professor Adams Sherman Hill assessed the writing of students after four years at America's oldest college: "Every year Harvard graduates a certain number of men—some of them high scholars—whose manuscripts would disgrace a boy of twelve." In 1896, *The Nation* ran an article entitled "The Growing Illiteracy of American Boys," which reported on another Harvard study. The authors of this one lamented the spending of "much time, energy, and money" teaching students "what they ought to have learnt already." There was "no conceivable justification," noted a rankled professor named Good-

---

* The sources of titles, quotations, and statistics are listed in the back of the book by page number.

win, to use precious revenues "in an attempt to enlighten the Egyptian darkness in which no small portion of Harvard's undergraduates were sitting." In 1898 the University of California instituted the Subject A Examination (the forerunner of the writing test that landed Laura, Bobby, and Dr. Gunner's crew in English A) and was soon designating about 30 to 40 percent of those who took it as not proficient in English, a percentage that has remained fairly stable to this day. Another development was this: In 1906 an educational researcher named Franklyn Hoyt conducted the first empirical study to determine if traditional instruction in grammar would improve the quality of writing. His results were not encouraging. Neither were the majority of the results of such studies carried out over the next eighty years. Whatever that stern grammarian was doing to his charges, it didn't seem to affect large numbers of them, historically or experimentally. There is one thing, though, we can say with certainty: He wasn't teaching the earlier incarnations of Laura, Bobby, and most of those in English A. Women, immigrants, children of the working class, blacks, and Latinos occupied but a few of the desks at Brown, Harvard, and the other elite colleges. Those disgraceful students were males from the upper crust.

Statistics are often used to demonstrate educational decay, but let's consider our literacy crisis through the perspective provided by another set of numbers. In 1890, 6.7 percent of America's fourteen- to seventeen-year-olds were attending high school; by 1978 that number had risen to 94.1 percent. In 1890, 3.5 percent of all seventeen-year-olds graduated from high school; by 1970 the number was 75.6 percent. In the 1930s "functional literacy" was defined by the Civilian Conservation Corps as a state of having three or more years of schooling; during World War II the army set the fourth grade as a standard; in 1947 the Census Bureau defined functional illiterates as those having fewer than five years of schooling; in 1952 the bureau raised the criterion to the sixth grade; by 1960 the Office of Education was setting the eighth grade as a benchmark; and by the late 1970s some authorities were suggesting that completion of high school should be the defining criterion of functional literacy. In the United States just over 75 percent of our young people complete high school; in Sweden 45 to 50 percent complete the gymnasium (grades 11 to 12); in the Federal Republic of Germany about 15 percent are enrolled in the *Oberprima* (grade 13). In 1900 about 4 percent of American eighteen- to twenty- two-year-olds attended college; by the late 1960s, 50 percent of eighteen- to nineteen-year-olds were entering some form of postsecondary education. Is this an educational system on the decline, or is it a system attempting to honor—through wrenching change—the many demands of a pluralistic democracy?

It would be an act of hollow and evil optimism to downplay the problems of American schools—the way they're structured and financed, the unevenness of their curricula, the low status of their teachers, their dreary record with the poor and disenfranchised. But what a curious thing it is that when we do criticize our schools, we tend to frame our indictments in terms of decline, a harsh, laced-with-doom assault stripped of the historical and social realities of American education—of its struggle to broaden rather than narrow access, of the increasing social as well as cognitive demands made on it, of our complex, ever-changing definitions of what it means to be literate and what a citizenry should know. How worthy of reflection it is that our policy is driven so often by a yearning for a mythic past or by apples-and-oranges comparisons to countries, past or present, less diverse and less educationally accessible than ours.

"The schools," write social historians David Cohen and Barbara Neufeld, "are a great theater in which we play out [the] conflicts in the culture." And it's our cultural fears—of internal decay, of loss of order, of diminishment—that weave into our assessments of literacy and scholastic achievement. The fact is that the literacy crisis has been with us for some time, that our schools have always been populated with students who don't meet some academic standard. It seems that whenever we let ourselves realize that, we do so with a hard or fearful heart. We figure that things were once different, that we've lost something, that somehow a virulent intellectual blight has spread among us. So we look to a past—one that never existed—for the effective, no-nonsense pedagogy we assume that past must have had. We half find and half create a curriculum and deploy it in a way that blinds us to the true difficulties and inequities in the ways we educate our children. Our purpose, finally, is to root out disease—and, too often, to punish. We write reductive prescriptions for excellence—that seductive, sentimental buzzword—and we are doing it in the late eighties with a flourish. What gets lost in all this are the real needs of children and adults working to make written language their own.

Every day in our schools and colleges, young people confront reading and writing tasks that seem hard or unusual, that confuse them, that they fail. But if you can get close enough to their failure, you'll find knowledge that the assignment didn't tap, ineffective rules and strategies that have a logic of their own; you'll find clues, as well, to the complex ties between literacy and culture, to the tremendous difficulties our children face as they attempt to find their places in the American educational system. Some, like Laura, are struck dumb by the fear of making a mistake; others, like Bobby, feel estranged because familiar cognitive landscapes have shifted, because once-effective strategies have been rendered obsolete; and still others are like the young men and women in Dr. Gunner's classroom: They know more than their tests reveal but haven't been taught how to weave that knowledge into coherent patterns. For Laura, Bobby, and the others the pronouncement of deficiency came late, but for many it comes as early as the first grade. Kids find themselves sitting on the threatening boundaries of the classroom. Marginal. Designated as "slow learners" or "remedial" or, eventually, "vocational."

I started this book as an account of my own journey from the high school vocational track up through the latticework of the American university. At first I tried brief sketches: a description of the storefront commerce that surrounded my house in South Los Angeles, a reminiscence about language lessons in grammar school and the teachers I had in Voc. Ed., some thoughts on my first disorienting year in college. But as I wrote, the landscapes and inhabitants of the sketches began to intersect with other places, other people: schools I had worked in, children and adults I had taught. It seemed fruitful to articulate, to probe and carefully render the overlay of my scholastic past and my working present. The sketches grew into a book that, of necessity, mixed genres. Autobiography, case study, commentary—it was all of a piece.

This is not to say that I see my life as an emblem. Representative men are often overblown characters; they end up distorting their own lives and reducing the complexity of the lives they claim to represent. But there are some things about my early life, I see now, that are reflected in other working-class lives I've encountered: the isolation of neighborhoods, information poverty, the limited means of protecting children from family disaster, the predominance of such disaster, the resilience of imagination, the intellectual curiosity and literate enticements that remain hidden from the schools, the feelings of scholastic inadequacy, the dislocations that come from crossing educational boundaries. This book begins, then, with autobiography—with my parents' immigration, my neighborhood, and my classrooms—but moves outward to communities beyond mine, to new encounters with schooling, to struggles to participate in the life of the mind. Those who are the focus of our national panic reveal themselves here, and what we see and hear is, simultaneously, cause for anger and cause for great hope.

2

"I Just Wanna Be Average"

Between 1880 and 1920, well over four million Southern Italian peasants immigrated to America. Their poverty was extreme and hopeless—twelve hours of farm labor would get you one lira, about twenty cents—so increasing numbers of desperate people booked passage for the United States, the country where, the steamship companies claimed, prosperity was a way of life. My father left Naples before the turn of the century; my mother came with her mother from Calabria in 1921. They met in Altoona, Pennsylvania at the lunch counter of Tom and Joe's, a steamy diner with twangy-voiced waitresses and graveyard stew.

For my mother, life in America was not what the promoters had told her father it would be. She grew up very poor. She slept with her parents and brothers and sisters in one room. She had to quit school in the seventh grade to care for her sickly younger brothers. When her father lost his leg in a railroad accident, she began working in a garment factory where women sat crowded at their stations, solitary as penitents in a cloister. She stayed there until her marriage. My father had found a freer route. He was closemouthed about his past, but I know that he had been a salesman, a tailor, and a gambler; he knew people in the mob and had, my uncles whisper, done time in Chicago. He went through a year or two of Italian elementary school and could write a few words—those necessary to scribble measurements for a suit—and over the years developed a quiet urbanity, a persistence, and a slowly debilitating arteriosclerosis.

When my father proposed to my mother, he decided to open a

spaghetti house, a venture that lasted through the war and my early years. The restaurant collapsed in bankruptcy in 1951 when Altoona's major industry, the Pennsylvania Railroad, had to shut down its shops. My parents managed to salvage seven hundred dollars and, on the advice of the family doctor, headed to California, where the winters would be mild and where I, their seven-year-old son, would have the possibility of a brighter future.

At first we lived in a seedy hotel on Spring Street in downtown Los Angeles, but my mother soon found an ad in the *Times* for cheap property on the south side of town. My parents contacted a woman named Mrs. Jolly, used my mother's engagement ring as a down payment, and moved to 9116 South Vermont Avenue, a house about one and one-half miles northwest of Watts. The neighborhood was poor, and it was in transition. Some old white folks had lived there for decades and were retired. Younger black families were moving up from Watts and settling by working-class white families newly arrived from the South and the Midwest. Immigrant Mexican families were coming in from Baja. Any such demographic mix is potentially volatile, and as the fifties wore on, the neighborhood would be marked by outbursts of violence.

I have many particular memories of this time, but in general these early years seem a peculiar mix of physical warmth and barrenness: a gnarled lemon tree, thin rugs, a dirt alley, concrete in the sun. My uncles visited a few times, and we went to the beach or to orange groves. The return home, however, left the waves and spray, the thick leaves and split pulp far in the distance. I was aware of my parents watching their money and got the sense from their conversations that things could quickly take a turn for the worse. I started taping pennies to the bottom of a shelf in the kitchen.

My father's health was bad, and he had few readily marketable skills. Poker and pinochle brought in a little money, and he tried out an idea that had worked in Altoona during the war: He started a ''suit club.'' The few customers he could scare up would pay two dollars a week on a tailor-made suit. He would take the measurements and send them to a shop back East and hope for the best. My mother took a job at a café in downtown Los Angeles, a split shift 9:00 to 12:00 and 5:00 to 9:00, but her tips were totaling sixty cents a day, so she quit for a night shift at Coffee

Dan's. This got her to the bus stop at one in the morning, waiting on the same street where drunks were urinating and hookers were catching the last of the bar crowd. She made friends with a Filipino cook who would scare off the advances of old men aflame with the closeness of taxi dancers. In a couple of years, Coffee Dan's would award her a day job at the counter. Once every few weeks my father and I would take a bus downtown and visit with her, sitting at stools by the window, watching the animated but silent mix of faces beyond the glass.

My father had moved to California with faint hopes about health and a belief in his child's future, drawn by that far edge of America where the sun descends into green water. What he found was a city that was warm, verdant, vast, and indifferent as a starlet in a sports car. Altoona receded quickly, and my parents must have felt isolated and deceived. They had fallen into the abyss of paradise—two more poor settlers trying to make a go of it in the City of the Angels.

Let me tell you about our house. If you entered the front door and turned right you'd see a small living room with a couch along the east wall and one along the west wall—one couch was purple, the other tan, both bought used and both well worn. A television set was placed at the end of the purple couch, right at arm level. An old Philco radio sat next to the TV, its speaker covered with gold lamé. There was a small coffee table in the center of the room on which sat a murky fishbowl occupied by two listless guppies. If, on entering, you turned left you would see a green Formica dinner table with four chairs, a cedar chest given as a wedding present to my mother by her mother, a painted statue of the Blessed Virgin Mary, and a black trunk. I also had a plastic chaise longue between the door and the table. I would lie on this and watch television.

A short hallway leading to the bathroom opened on one side to the kitchen and, on the other, to the bedroom. The bedroom had two beds, one for me and one for my parents, a bureau with a mirror, and a chest of drawers on which we piled old shirt boxes and stacks of folded clothes. The kitchen held a refrigerator and a stove, small older models that we got when our earlier (and newer) models were repossessed by two silent men. There was one white wooden chair in the corner beneath wall cabinets. You could walk in and through a tiny pantry to the backyard and to four one-room rentals. My father got most of our furniture from a secondhand store on the next block; he would tend the store two or three hours a day as payment on our account.

As I remember it, the house was pretty dark. My mother kept the blinds in the bedroom drawn—there were no curtains there—and the venetian blinds in the living room were, often as not, left closed. The walls were bare except for a faded picture of Jesus and a calendar from the *Altoona Mirror*. Some paper carnations bent out of a white vase on the television. There was a window on the north side of the kitchen that had no blinds or curtains, so the sink got good light. My father would methodically roll up his sleeves and show me how to prepare a sweet potato or avocado seed so it would sprout. We kept a row of them on the sill above the sink, their shoots and vines rising and curling in the morning sun.

The house was on a piece of land that rose about four feet up from heavily trafficked Vermont Avenue. The yard sloped down to the street, and three steps and a short walkway led up the middle of the grass to our front door. There was a similar house immediately to the south of us. Next to it was Carmen's Barber Shop. Carmen was a short, quiet Italian who, rumor had it, had committed his first wife to the crazy house to get her money. In the afternoons, Carmen could be found in the lot behind his shop playing solitary catch, flinging a tennis ball high into the air and running under it. One day the police arrested Carmen on charges of child molesting. He was released but became furtive and suspicious. I never saw him in the lot again. Next to Carmen's was a junk store where, one summer, I made a little money polishing brass and rewiring old lamps. Then came a dilapidated real estate office, a Mexican restaurant, an empty lot, and an appliance store owned by the father of Keith Grateful, the streetwise, chubby boy who would become my best friend.

Right to the north of us was a record shop, a barber shop presided over by old Mr. Graff, Walt's Malts, a shoe repair shop with a big Cat's Paw decal in the window, a third barber shop, and a brake shop. It's as I write this that I realize for the first time that three gray men could have had a go at your hair before you left our street.

Behind our house was an unpaved alley that passed, just to the north, a power plant the length of a city block. Massive coils atop the building hissed and cracked through the day, but the doors never opened. I used to think it was abandoned—feeding itself on its own wild arcs—until one sweltering afternoon a man was electrocuted on the roof. The air was thick and still as two firemen—the only men present—brought down a charred and limp body without saying a word.

The north and south traffic on Vermont was separated by tracks for the old yellow trolley cars, long since defunct. Across the street was a huge garage, a tiny hot dog stand run by a myopic and reclusive man named Freddie, and my dreamland, the Vermont Bowl. Distant and distorted behind thick lenses, Freddie's eyes never met yours; he would look down when he took your order and give you your change with a mumble. Freddie slept on a cot in the back of his grill and died there one night, leaving tens of thousands of dollars stuffed in the mattress.

My father would buy me a chili dog at Freddie's, and then we would walk over to the bowling alley where Dad would sit at the lunch counter and drink coffee while I had a great time with pinball machines, electric shooting galleries, and an ill-kept dispenser of cheese corn. There was a small, dark bar abutting the lanes, and it called to me. I would devise reasons to walk through it: "'Scuse me, is the bathroom in here?" or "Anyone see my dad?" though I can never remember my father having a drink. It was dark and people were drinking and I figured all sorts of mysterious things were being whispered. Next to the Vermont Bowl was a large vacant lot overgrown with foxtails and dotted with car parts, bottles, and rotting cardboard. One day Keith heard that the police had found a human head in the brush. After that we explored the lot periodically, coming home with stickers all the way up to our waists. But we didn't find a thing. Not even a kneecap.

When I wasn't with Keith or in school, I would spend most of my day with my father or with the men who were renting the one-room apartments behind our house. Dad and I whiled away the hours in the bowling alley, watching TV, or planting a vegetable garden that never seemed to take. When he was still mobile, he would walk the four blocks down to St. Regina's Grammar School to take me home to my favorite lunch of boiled wieners and chocolate milk. There I'd sit, dunking my hot dog in a jar of mayonnaise and drinking my milk while Sheriff John tuned up the calliope music on his "Lunch Brigade." Though he never complained to me, I could sense that my father's health was failing, and I began devising child's ways to make him better. We had a box of rolled cotton in the bathroom, and I would go in and peel off a long strip and tape it around my jaw. Then I'd rummage through the closet, find a sweater of my father's, put on one of his hats—and sneak around to the back door. I'd knock loudly and wait. It would take him a while to get there. Finally, he'd open the door, look down, and quietly say, "Yes, Michael?" I was disappointed. Every time. Somehow I thought I could fool him. And, I guess, if he had been fooled, I would have succeeded in redefining things: I would have been the old one, he much younger, more agile, with strength in his legs.

The men who lived in the back were either retired or didn't work that much, so one of them was usually around. They proved to be, over the years, an unusual set of companions for a young boy. Ed Gionotti was the youngest of the lot, a handsome man whose wife had run off and who spoke softly and never smiled. Bud Hall and Lee McGuire were two out-of-work plumbers who lived in adjacent units and who weekly drank themselves silly, proclaiming in front of God and everyone their undying friendship or their unequivocal hatred. Old Cheech was a lame Italian who used to hobble along grabbing his testicles and rolling his eyes while he talked about the women he claimed to have on a string. There was Lester, the toothless cabbie, who several times made overtures to me and who, when he moved, left behind a drawer full of syringes and burnt spoons. Mr. Smith was a rambunctious retiree who lost his nose to an untended skin cancer. And there was Mr. Berryman, a sweet and gentle man who eventually left for a retirement hotel only to be burned alive in an electrical fire.

Except for Keith, there were no children on my block and only one or two on the immediate side streets. Most of the people I saw day to day were over fifty. People in their twenties and thirties working in the shoe shop or the garages didn't say a lot; their work and much of what they were working for drained their spirits. There were gang members who sauntered up from Hoover Avenue, three blocks to the east, and occasionally I would get shoved around, but they had little interest in me either as member or victim. I was a skinny, bespectacled kid and had neither the coloring nor the style of dress or carriage that marked me as a rival. On the whole, the days were quiet, lazy, lonely. The heat shimmering over the asphalt had no snap to it; time drifted by. I would lie on the couch at night and listen to the music from the record store or from Walt's Malts. It was new and quick paced, exciting, a little dangerous (the church had condemned Buddy Knox's "Party Doll"), and I heard in it a deep rhythmic need to be made whole with love, or marked as special, or released in some rebellious way. Even the songs about lost love—and there were plenty of them—lifted me right out of my socks with their melodious longing:

> Came the dawn,
> and my heart and her love and the night
> were gone.
> But I know I'll never forget
> her kiss in the moonlight Oooo . . .
> such a kiss Oooo Oooo such a night . . .

In the midst of the heat and slow time the music brought the promise of its origins, a promise of deliverance, a promise that, if only for a moment, life could be stirring and dreamy.

But the anger and frustration of South Vermont could prove too strong for music's illusion; then it was violence that provided deliverance of a different order. One night I watched as a guy sprinted from Walt's to toss something on our lawn. The police were right behind, and a cop tackled him, smashing his face into the sidewalk. I ducked out to find the packet: a dozen glassine bags of heroin. Another night, one August midnight, an argument outside the record store ended with a man being shot to death. And the occasional gang forays brought with them some fated kid who would fumble his moves and catch a knife.

It's popular these days to claim you grew up on the streets. Men tell violent tales and romanticize the lessons violence brings. But, though it was occasionally violent, it wasn't the violence in South L.A. that marked me, for sometimes you can shake that ugliness off. What finally affected me was subtler, but more pervasive: I cannot recall a young person who was crazy in love or lost in work or one old person who was passionate about a cause or an idea. I'm not talking about an absence of energy—the street toughs and, for that fact, old Cheech had energy. And I'm not talking about an absence of decency, for my father was a thoughtful man. The people I grew up with were retired from jobs that rub away the heart or were working hard at jobs to keep their lives from caving in or were anchorless and in between jobs and spouses or were diving headlong into a barren tomorrow: junkies, alcoholics, and mean kids walking along Vermont looking to throw a punch. I developed a picture of human existence that rendered it short and brutish or sad and aimless or long and quiet with rewards like afternoon naps, the evening newspaper, walks around the block, occasional letters from children in other states. When, years later, I was introduced to humanistic psychologists like Abraham Maslow and Carl Rogers, with their visions of self-actualization, or even Freud with his sober dictum about love and work, it all sounded like a glorious fairy tale, a magical account of a world full of possibility, full of hope and empowerment. Sindbad and Cinderella couldn't have been more fanciful.

Some people who manage to write their way out of the working class describe the classroom as an oasis of possibility. It became their intellectual playground, their competitive arena. Given the richness of my memories of this time, it's funny how scant are my recollections of school. I remember the red brick building of St. Regina's itself, and the topography of the playground: the swings and basketball courts and peeling benches. There are images of a few students: Erwin Petschaur, a muscular German boy with a strong accent; Dave Sanchez, who was good in math; and Sheila Wilkes, everyone's curly-haired heartthrob. And there are two nuns: Sister Monica, the third-grade teacher with beautiful hands for whom I carried a candle and who, to my dismay, had wedded herself to Christ; and Sister Beatrice, a woman truly crazed, who would sweep into class, eyes wide, to tell us about the Apocalypse.

All the hours in class tend to blend into one long, vague stretch of time. What I remember best, strangely enough, are the two things I couldn't understand and over the years grew to hate: grammar lessons and mathematics. I would sit there watching a teacher draw her long horizontal line and her short, oblique lines and break up sentences and put adjectives here and adverbs there and just not get it, couldn't see the reason for it, turned off to it.

I would hide by slumping down in my seat and page through my reader, carried along by the flow of sentences in a story. She would test us, and I would dread that, for I always got Cs and Ds. Mathematics was a bit different. For whatever reasons, I didn't learn early math very well, so when it came time for more complicated operations, I couldn't keep up and started day-dreaming to avoid my inadequacy. This was a strategy I would rely on as I grew older. I fell further and further behind. A memory: The teacher is faceless and seems very far away. The voice is faint and is discussing an equation written on the board. It is raining, and I am watching the streams of water form patterns on the windows.

I realize now how consistently I defended myself against the lessons I couldn't understand and the people and events of South L.A. that were too strange to view head-on. I got very good at watching a blackboard with minimum awareness. And I drifted more and more into a variety of protective fantasies. I was lucky in that although my parents didn't read or write very much and had no more than a few books around the house, they never de-bunked my pursuits. And when they could, they bought me what I needed to spin my web.

One early Christmas they got me a small chemistry set. My fa-ther brought home an old card table from the secondhand store, and on that table I spread out my test tubes, my beaker, my Erlen-meyer flask, and my gas-generating apparatus. The set came equipped with chemicals, minerals, and various treated papers— all in little square bottles. You could send away to someplace in Maryland for more, and I did, saving pennies and nickels to get the substances that were too exotic for my set, the Junior Chem-craft: Congo red paper, azurite, glycerine, chrome alum, cochi-neal—this from female insects!—tartaric acid, chameleon paper, logwood. I would sit before my laboratory and play for hours. My father rested on the purple couch in front of me watching wrestling or *Gunsmoke* while I measured powders or heated crys-tals or blew into solutions that my breath would turn red or pink. I was taken by the blends of names and by the colors that swirled through the beaker. My equations were visual and phonetic. I would hold a flask up to the hall light, imagining the veils of a million atoms dancing. Sulfur and alcohol hung in the air. I wanted to shake down the house.

One day my mother came home from Coffee Dan's with an awful story. The teenage brother of one of her waitress friends was in the hospital. He had been fooling around with explosives in his garage "where his mother couldn't see him," and something happened, and "he blew away part of his throat. For God's sake, be careful," my mother said. "Remember poor Ada's brother." Wow! I thought. How neat! Why couldn't my experiments be that dangerous? I really lost heart when I realized that you could probably eat the chemicals spread across my table.

I knew what I had to do. I saved my money for a week and then walked with firm resolve past Walt's Malts, past the brake shop, across Ninetieth Street, and into Palazolla's market. I bought a little bottle of Alka-Seltzer and ran home. I chipped up the wafers and mixed them into a jar of white crystals. When my mother came home, dog tired, and sat down on the edge of the couch to tell me and Dad about her day, I gravely poured my concoction into a beaker of water, cried something about the unexpected, and ran out from behind my table. The beaker foamed ominously. My father swore in Italian. The second time I tried it, I got something milder—in English. And by my third near-miss with death, my parents were calling my behavior cute. Cute! Who wanted cute? I wanted to toy with the disaster that befell Ada Pendleton's brother. I wanted all those wonderful colors to collide in ways that could blow your voice box right off.

But I was limited by the real. The best I could do was create a toxic antacid. I loved my chemistry set—its glassware and its intriguing labels—but it wouldn't allow me to do the things I wanted to do. St. Regina's had an all-purpose room, one wall of which was lined with old books—and one of those shelves held a row of plastic-covered space novels. The sheen of their covers was gone, and their futuristic portraits were dotted with erasures and grease spots like a meteor shower of the everyday. I remember the rockets best. Long cylinders outfitted at the base with three slick fins, tapering at the other end to a perfect conical point, ready to pierce out of the stratosphere and into my imagination: X-fifteens and Mach 1, the dark side of the moon, the Red Planet, Jupiter's Great Red Spot, Saturn's rings—and beyond the solar system to swirling wisps of galaxies, to stardust.

I would check out my books two at a time and take them home to curl up with a blanket on my chaise longue, reading, sometimes, through the weekend, my back aching, my thoughts lost between galaxies. I became the hero of a thousand adventures, all with intricate plots and the triumph of good over evil, all many dimensions removed from the dim walls of the living room. We were given time to draw in school, so, before long, all this worked itself onto paper. The stories I was reading were reshaping themselves into pictures. My father got me some butcher paper from Palazolla's, and I continued to draw at home. My collected works rendered the Horsehead Nebula, goofy space cruisers, robots, and Saturn. Each had its crayon, a particular waxy pencil with mood and meaning: rust and burnt sienna for Mars, yellow for the Sun, lime and rose for Saturn's rings, and bright red for the Jovian spot. I had a little sharpener to keep the points just right. I didn't write any stories; I just read and drew. I wouldn't care much about writing until late in high school.

The summer before the sixth grade, I got a couple of jobs. The first was at a pet store a block or so away from my house. Since I was still small, I could maneuver around in breeder cages, scraping the heaps of parakeet crap from the tin floor, cleaning the water troughs and seed trays. It was pretty awful. I would go home after work and fill the tub and soak until all the fleas and bird mites came floating to the surface, little Xs in their multiple eyes. When I heard about a job selling strawberries door-to-door, I jumped at it. I went to work for a white-haired Chicano named Frank. He would carry four or five kids and dozens of crates of strawberries in his ramshackle truck up and down the avenues of the better neighborhoods: houses with mowed lawns and petunia beds. We'd work all day for seventy-five cents, Frank dropping pairs of us off with two crates each, then picking us up at preassigned corners. We spent lots of time together, bouncing around on the truck bed redolent with strawberries or sitting on a corner, cold, listening for the sputter of Frank's muffler. I started telling the other kids about my books, and soon it was my job to fill up that time with stories.

Reading opened up the world. There I was, a skinny bookworm drawing the attention of street kids who, in any other circumstances, would have had me for breakfast. Like an epic tale-teller, I developed the stories as I went along, relying on a flexible plot line and a repository of heroic events. I had a great time. I sketched out trajectories with my finger on Frank's dusty truck bed. And I stretched out each story's climax, creating cliff-hangers like the ones I saw in the Saturday serials. These stories created for me a temporary community.

It was around this time that fiction started leading me circuitously to a child's version of science. In addition to the space novels, St. Regina's library also had half a dozen books on astronomy—*The Golden Book of the Planets* and stuff like that—so I checked out a few of them. I liked what I read and wheedled enough change out of my father to enable me to take the bus to the public library. I discovered star maps, maps of lunar seas, charts upon charts of the solar system and the planetary moons: Rhea, Europa, Callisto, Miranda, Io. I didn't know that most of these moons were named for women—I didn't know classical mythology—but I would say their names to myself as though they had a woman's power to protect: Europa, Miranda, Io . . . The distances between stars fascinated me, as did the sizes of the big telescopes. I sent away for catalogs. Then prices fascinated me too. I wanted to drape my arm over a thousand-dollar scope and hear its motor drive whirr. I conjured a twelve-year-old's life of the astronomer: sitting up all night with potato chips and the stars, tracking the sky for supernovas, humming "Earth Angel" with the Penguins. What was my mother to do but save her tips and buy me a telescope?!

It was a little reflecting job, and I solemnly used to carry it out to the front of the house on warm summer nights, to find Venus or Alpha Centauri or trace the stars in Orion or lock onto the moon. I would lay out my star maps on the concrete, more for their magic than anything else, for I had trouble figuring them out. I was no geometer of the constellations; I was their balladeer. Those nights were very peaceful. I was far enough away from the front door and up enough from the sidewalk to make it seem as if I rested on a mound of dark silence, a mountain in Arizona, perhaps, watching the sky alive with points of light. Poor Freddie, toothless Lester whispering promises about making me feel good, the flat days, the gang fights—all this receded, for it was now me, the star child, lost in an eyepiece focused on a reflecting mirror that cradled, in its center, a shimmering moon.

The loneliness in Los Angeles fosters strange arrangements. Lou Minton was a wiry man with gaunt, chiseled features and prematurely gray hair, combed straight back. He had gone to college in the South for a year or two and kicked around the country for many more before settling in L.A. He lived in a small downtown apartment with a single window and met my mother at the counter of Coffee Dan's. He had been alone too long and eventually came to our house and became part of the family. Lou repaired washing machines, and he had a car, and he would take me to the vast, echoing library just west of Pershing Square and to the Museum of Science and Industry in Exposition Park. He bought me astronomy books, taught me how to use tools, and helped me build model airplanes from balsa wood and rice paper. As my father's health got worse, Lou took care of him.

My rhapsodic and prescientific astronomy carried me into my teens, consumed me right up till high school, losing out finally, and only, to the siren call of pubescence—that endocrine hoodoo that transmogrifies nice boys into gawky flesh fiends. My mother used to bring home *Confidential* magazine, a peep-show rag specializing in the sins of the stars, and it beckoned me mercilessly: Jayne Mansfield's cleavage, Gina Lollobrigida's eyes, innuendos about deviant sexuality, ads for Frederick's of Hollywood—spiked heels, lacy brassieres, the epiphany of silk panties on a mannequin's hips. Along with Phil Everly, I was through with counting the stars above.

Budding manhood. Only adults talk about adolescence budding. Kids have no choice but to talk in extremes; they're being wrenched and buffeted, rabbit-punched from inside by systemic thugs. Nothing sweet and pastoral here. Kids become ridiculous and touching at one and the same time: passionate about the trivial, fixed before the mirror, yet traversing one of the most important rites of passage in their lives—liminal people, silly and profoundly human. Given my own expertise, I fantasized about concocting the fail-safe aphrodisiac that would bring Marianne Bilpusch, the cloakroom monitor, rushing into my arms or about commanding a squadron of bosomy, linguistically mysterious astronauts like Zsa Zsa Gabor. My parents used to say that their son would have the best education they could afford. Maybe I would be a doctor. There was a public school in our neighborhood and several Catholic schools to the west. They had heard that quality schooling meant private, Catholic schooling, so they somehow got the money together to send me to Our Lady of Mercy, fifteen or so miles southwest of Ninety-first and Vermont.

So much for my fantasies. Most Catholic secondary schools then were separated by gender.

It took two buses to get to Our Lady of Mercy. The first started deep in South Los Angeles and caught me at midpoint. The second drifted through neighborhoods with trees, parks, big lawns, and lots of flowers. The rides were long but were livened up by a group of South L.A. veterans whose parents also thought that Hope had set up shop in the west end of the county. There was Christy Biggars, who, at sixteen, was dealing and was, according to rumor, a pimp as well. There were Bill Cobb and Johnny Gonzales, grease-pencil artists extraordinaire, who left Nembutal-enhanced swirls of ''Cobb'' and ''Johnny'' on the corrugated walls of the bus. And then there was Tyrrell Wilson. Tyrrell was the coolest kid I knew. He ran the dozens like a metric halfback, laid down a rap that outrhymed and outpointed Cobb, whose rap was good but not great—the curse of a moderately soulful kid trapped in white skin. But it was Cobb who would sneak a radio onto the bus, and thus underwrote his patter with Little Richard, Fats Domino, Chuck Berry, the Coasters, and Ernie K. Doe's mother-in-law, an awful woman who was ''sent from down below.'' And so it was that Christy and Cobb and Johnny G. and Tyrrell and I and assorted others picked up along the way passed our days in the back of the bus, a funny mix brought together by geography and parental desire.

Entrance to school brings with it forms and releases and assessments. Mercy relied on a series of tests, mostly the Stanford-Binet, for placement, and somehow the results of my tests got confused with those of another student named Rose. The other Rose apparently didn't do very well, for I was placed in the vocational track, a euphemism for the bottom level. Neither I nor my parents realized what this meant. We had no sense that Business Math, Typing, and English–Level D were dead ends. The current spate of reports on the schools criticizes parents for not involving themselves in the education of their children. But how would someone like Tommy Rose, with his two years of Italian schooling, know what to ask? And what sort of pressure could an exhausted waitress apply? The error went undetected, and I remained in the vocational track for two years. What a place.

My homeroom was supervised by Brother Dill, a troubled and unstable man who also taught freshman English. When his class drifted away from him, which was often, his voice would rise in paranoid accusations, and occasionally he would lose control and shake or smack us. I hadn't been there two months when one of his brisk, face-turning slaps had my glasses sliding down the aisle. Physical education was also pretty harsh. Our teacher was a stubby ex-lineman who had played old-time pro ball in the Midwest. He routinely had us grabbing our ankles to receive his stinging paddle across our butts. He did that, he said, to make men of us. "Rose," he bellowed on our first encounter; me standing geeky in line in my baggy shorts. "'Rose'? What the hell kind of name is that?"

"Italian, sir," I squeaked.

"Italian! Ho. Rose, do you know the sound a bag of shit makes when it hits the wall?"

"No, sir."

"Wop!"

Sophomore English was taught by Mr. Mitropetros. He was a large, bejeweled man who managed the parking lot at the Shrine Auditorium. He would crow and preen and list for us the stars he'd brushed against. We'd ask questions and glance knowingly and snicker, and all that fueled the poor guy to brag some more. Parking cars was his night job. He had little training in English, so his lesson plan for his day work had us reading the district's required text, *Julius Caesar*, aloud for the semester. We'd finish the play way before the twenty weeks was up, so he'd have us switch parts again and again and start again: Dave Snyder, the fastest guy at Mercy, muscling through Caesar to the breathless squeals of Calpurnia, as interpreted by Steve Fusco, a surfer who owned the school's most envied paneled wagon. Week ten and Dave and Steve would take on new roles, as would we all, and render a water-logged Cassius and a Brutus that are beyond my powers of description.

Spanish I—taken in the second year—fell into the hands of a new recruit. Mr. Montez was a tiny man, slight, five foot six at the most, soft-spoken and delicate. Spanish was a particularly rowdy class, and Mr. Montez was as prepared for it as a doily maker at a hammer throw. He would tap his pencil to a room in which Steve Fusco was propelling spitballs from his heavy lips, in which Mike Dweetz was taunting Billy Hawk, a half-Indian, half-Spanish, reed-thin, quietly explosive boy. The vocational track at Our Lady of Mercy mixed kids traveling in from South L.A. with South Bay surfers and a few Slavs and Chicanos from the harbors of San Pedro. This was a dangerous miscellany: surfers and hodads and South-Central blacks all ablaze to the metronomic tapping of Hector Montez's pencil.

One day Billy lost it. Out of the corner of my eye I saw him strike out with his right arm and catch Dweetz across the neck. Quick as a spasm, Dweetz was out of his seat, scattering desks, cracking Billy on the side of the head, right behind the eye. Snyder and Fusco and others broke it up, but the room felt hot and close and naked. Mr. Montez's tenuous authority was finally ripped to shreds, and I think everyone felt a little strange about that. The charade was over, and when it came down to it, I don't think any of the kids really wanted it to end this way. They had pushed and pushed and bullied their way into a freedom that both scared and embarrassed them.

Students will float to the mark you set. I and the others in the vocational classes were bobbing in pretty shallow water. Vocational education has aimed at increasing the economic opportunities of students who do not do well in our schools. Some serious programs succeed in doing that, and through exceptional teachers—like Mr. Gross in *Horace's Compromise*—students learn to develop hypotheses and troubleshoot, reason through a problem, and communicate effectively—the true job skills. The vocational track, however, is most often a place for those who are just not making it, a dumping ground for the disaffected. There were a few teachers who worked hard at education; young Brother Slattery, for example, combined a stern voice with weekly quizzes to try to pass along to us a skeletal outline of world history. But mostly the teachers had no idea of how to engage the imaginations of us kids who were scuttling along at the bottom of the pond.

And the teachers would have needed some inventiveness, for none of us was groomed for the classroom. It wasn't just that I didn't know things—didn't know how to simplify algebraic fractions, couldn't identify different kinds of clauses, bungled Spanish translations—but that I had developed various faulty and inadequate ways of doing algebra and making sense of Spanish. Worse yet, the years of defensive tuning out in elementary school had given me a way to escape quickly while seeming at least half alert. During my time in Voc. Ed., I developed further into a mediocre student and a somnambulant problem solver, and that affected the subjects I did have the wherewithal to handle: I detested Shakespeare; I got bored with history. My attention flitted here and there. I fooled around in class and read my books indifferently—the intellectual equivalent of playing with your food. I did what I had to do to get by, and I did it with half a mind.

But I did learn things about people and eventually came into my own socially. I liked the guys in Voc. Ed. Growing up where I did, I understood and admired physical prowess, and there was an abundance of muscle here. There was Dave Snyder, a sprinter and halfback of true quality. Dave's ability and his quick wit gave him a natural appeal, and he was welcome in any clique, though he always kept a little independent. He enjoyed acting the fool and could care less about studies, but he possessed a certain maturity and never caused the faculty much trouble. It was a testament to his independence that he included me among his friends—I eventually went out for track, but I was no jock. Owing to the Latin alphabet and a dearth of Rs and Ss, Snyder sat behind Rose, and we started exchanging one-liners and became friends.

There was Ted Richard, a much-touted Little League pitcher. He was chunky and had a baby face and came to Our Lady of Mercy as a seasoned street fighter. Ted was quick to laugh and he had a loud, jolly laugh, but when he got angry he'd smile a little smile, the kind that simply raises the corner of the mouth a quarter of an inch. For those who knew, it was an eerie signal. Those who didn't found themselves in big trouble, for Ted was very quick. He loved to carry on what we would come to call philosophical discussions: What is courage? Does God exist? He also loved words, enjoyed picking up big ones like *salubrious* and *equivocal* and using them in our conversations—laughing at himself as the word hit a chuckhole rolling off his tongue. Ted didn't do all that well in school—baseball and parties and testing the courage he'd speculated about took up his time. His textbooks were *Argosy* and *Field and Stream*, whatever newspapers he'd find on the bus stop—from *the Daily Worker* to pornography—conversations with uncles or hobos or businessmen he'd meet in a coffee shop, *The Old Man and the Sea*. With hindsight, I can see that Ted was developing into one of those rough-hewn intellectuals whose

sources are a mix of the learned and the apocryphal, whose discussions are both assured and sad.

And then there was Ken Harvey. Ken was good-looking in a
puffy way and had a full and oily ducktail and was a car enthusiast . . . a hodad. One day in religion class, he said the sentence
that turned out to be one of the most memorable of the hundreds
of thousands I heard in those Voc. Ed. years. We were talking
about the parable of the talents, about achievement, working
hard, doing the best you can do, blah-blah-blah, when the
teacher called on the restive Ken Harvey for an opinion. Ken
thought about it, but just for a second, and said (with studied,
minimal affect), "I just wanna be average." That woke me up.
Average?! Who wants to be average? Then the athletes chimed in
with the clichés that make you want to laryngectomize them, and
the exchange became a platitudinous melee. At the time, I
thought Ken's assertion was stupid, and I wrote him off. But his
sentence has stayed with me all these years, and I think I am
finally coming to understand it.

Ken Harvey was gasping for air. School can be a tremendously
disorienting place. No matter how bad the school, you're going
to encounter notions that don't fit with the assumptions and beliefs that you grew up with—maybe you'll hear these dissonant
notions from teachers, maybe from the other students, and
maybe you'll read them. You'll also be thrown in with all kinds
of kids from all kinds of backgrounds, and that can be unsettling—this is especially true in places of rich ethnic and linguistic
mix, like the L.A. basin. You'll see a handful of students far excel
you in courses that sound exotic and that are only in the curriculum of the elite: French, physics, trigonometry. And all this is
happening while you're trying to shape an identity, your body is
changing, and your emotions are running wild. If you're a
working-class kid in the vocational track, the options you'll have
to deal with this will be constrained in certain ways: You're defined by your school as "slow"; you're placed in a curriculum
that isn't designed to liberate you but to occupy you, or, if you're
lucky, train you, though the training is for work the society does
not esteem; other students are picking up the cues from your
school and your curriculum and interacting with you in particular
ways. If you're a kid like Ted Richard, you turn your back on all
this and let your mind roam where it may. But youngsters like

Ted are rare. What Ken and so many others do is protect themselves from such suffocating madness by taking on with a vengeance the identity implied in the vocational track. Reject the confusion and frustration by openly defining yourself as the Common Joe. Champion the average. Rely on your own good sense. Fuck this bullshit. Bullshit, of course, is everything you—and the others—fear is beyond you: books, essays, tests, academic scrambling, complexity, scientific reasoning, philosophical inquiry.

The tragedy is that you have to twist the knife in your own gray matter to make this defense work. You'll have to shut down, have to reject intellectual stimuli or diffuse them with sarcasm, have to cultivate stupidity, have to convert boredom from a malady into a way of confronting the world. Keep your vocabulary simple, act stoned when you're not or act more stoned than you are, flaunt ignorance, materialize your dreams. It is a powerful and effective defense—it neutralizes the insult and the frustration of being a vocational kid and, when perfected, it drives teachers up the wall, a delightful secondary effect. But like all strong magic, it exacts a price.

My own deliverance from the Voc. Ed. world began with sophomore biology. Every student, college prep to vocational, had to take biology, and unlike the other courses, the same person taught all sections. When teaching the vocational group, Brother Clint probably slowed down a bit or omitted a little of the fundamental biochemistry, but he used the same book and more or less the same syllabus across the board. If one class got tough, he could get tougher. He was young and powerful and very handsome, and looks and physical strength were high currency. No one gave him any trouble.

I was pretty bad at the dissecting table, but the lectures and the textbook were interesting: plastic overlays that, with each turned page, peeled away skin, then veins and muscle, then organs, down to the very bones that Brother Clint, pointer in hand, would tap out on our hanging skeleton. Dave Snyder was in big trouble, for the study of life—versus the living of it—was sticking in his craw. We worked out a code for our multiple-choice exams. He'd poke me in the back: once for the answer under *A*, twice for *B*, and so on; and when he'd hit the right one, I'd look up to the ceiling as though I were lost in thought. Poke: cytoplasm. Poke, poke: methane. Poke, poke, poke: William Harvey. Poke, poke, poke,poke: islets of Langerhans. This didn't work out perfectly, but Dave passed the course, and I mastered the dreamy look of a guy on a record jacket. And something else happened. Brother Clint puzzled over this Voc. Ed. kid who was racking up 98s and 99s on his tests. He checked the school's records and discovered the error. He recommended that I begin my junior year in the College Prep program. According to all I've read since, such a shift, as one report put it, is virtually impossible. Kids at that level rarely cross tracks. The telling thing is how chancy both my placement into and exit from Voc. Ed. was; neither I nor my parents had anything to do with it. I lived in one world during spring semester, and when I came back to school in the fall, I was living in another.

Switching to College Prep was a mixed blessing. I was an erratic student. I was undisciplined. And I hadn't caught onto the rules of the game: Why work hard in a class that didn't grab my fancy? I was also hopelessly behind in math. Chemistry was hard; toying with my chemistry set years before hadn't prepared me for the chemist's equations. Fortunately, the priest who taught both chemistry and second-year algebra was also the school's athletic director. Membership on the track team covered me; I knew I wouldn't get lower than a C. U.S. history was taught pretty well, and I did okay. But civics was taken over by a football coach who had trouble reading the textbook aloud—and reading aloud was the centerpiece of his pedagogy. College Prep at Mercy was certainly an improvement over the vocational program—at least it carried some status—but the social science curriculum was weak, and the mathematics and physical sciences were simply beyond me. I had a miserable quantitative background and ended up copying some assignments and finessing the rest as best I could. Let me try to explain how it feels to see again and again material you should once have learned but didn't.

You are given a problem. It requires you to simplify algebraic fractions or to multiply expressions containing square roots. You know this is pretty basic material because you've seen it for years. Once a teacher took some time with you, and you learned how to carry out these operations. Simple versions, anyway. But that was a year or two or more in the past, and these are more complex versions, and now you're not sure. And this, you keep telling yourself, is ninth- or even eighth-grade stuff.

Next it's a word problem. This is also old hat. The basic elements are as familiar as story characters: trains speeding so many miles per hour or shadows of buildings angling so many degrees. Maybe you know enough, have sat through enough explanations, to be able to begin setting up the problem: "If one train is going this fast . . ." or "This shadow is really one line of a triangle . . . ." Then: "Let's see . . ." "How did Jones do this?" "Hmmmm." "No." "No, that won't work." Your attention wavers. You wonder about other things: a football game, a dance, that cute new checker at the market. You try to focus on the problem again. You scribble on paper for a while, but the tension wins out and your attention flits elsewhere. You crumple the paper and begin daydreaming to ease the frustration.

The particulars will vary, but in essence this is what a number of students go through, especially those in so-called remedial classes. They open their textbooks and see once again the familiar and impenetrable formulas and diagrams and terms that have stumped them for years. There is no excitement here. *No* excitement. Regardless of what the teacher says, this is not a new challenge. There is, rather, embarrassment and frustration and, not surprisingly, some anger in being reminded once again of long-standing inadequacies. No wonder so many students finally attribute their difficulties to something inborn, organic: "That part of my brain just doesn't work." Given the troubling histories many of these students have, it's miraculous that any of them can lift the shroud of hopelessness sufficiently to make deliverance from these classes possible.

Through this entire period, my father's health was deteriorating with cruel momentum. His arteriosclerosis progressed to the point where a simple nick on his shin wouldn't heal. Eventually it ulcerated and widened. Lou Minton would come by daily to change the dressing. We tried renting an oscillating bed—which we placed in the front room—to force blood through the constricted arteries in my father's legs. The bed hummed through the night, moving in place to ward off the inevitable. The ulcer continued to spread, and the doctors finally had to amputate. My grandfather had lost his leg in a stockyard accident. Now my father too was crippled. His convalescence was slow but steady, and the doctors placed him in the Santa Monica Rehabilitation Center, a sun-bleached building that opened out onto the warm spray of the Pacific. The place gave him some strength and some color and some training in walking with an artificial leg. He did pretty well for a year or so until he slipped and broke his hip. He was confined to a wheelchair after that, and the confinement contributed to the diminishing of his body and spirit.

I am holding a picture of him. He is sitting in his wheelchair and smiling at the camera. The smile appears forced, unsteady, seems to quaver, though it is frozen in silver nitrate. He is in his mid-sixties and looks eighty. Late in my junior year, he had a stroke and never came out of the resulting coma. After that, I would see him only in dreams, and to this day that is how I join him. Sometimes the dreams are sad and grisly and primal: my father lying in a bed soaked with his suppuration, holding me, rocking me. But sometimes the dreams bring him back to me healthy: him talking to me on an empty street, or buying some pictures to decorate our old house, or transformed somehow into someone strong and adept with tools and the physical.

Jack MacFarland couldn't have come into my life at a better time. My father was dead, and I had logged up too many years of scholastic indifference. Mr. MacFarland had a master's degree from Columbia and decided, at twenty-six, to find a little school and teach his heart out. He never took any credentialing courses, couldn't bear to, he said, so he had to find employment in a private system. He ended up at Our Lady of Mercy teaching five sections of senior English. He was a beatnik who was born too late. His teeth were stained, he tucked his sorry tie in between the third and fourth buttons of his shirt, and his pants were chronically wrinkled. At first, we couldn't believe this guy, thought he slept in his car. But within no time, he had us so startled with work that we didn't much worry about where he slept or if he slept at all. We wrote three or four essays a month. We read a book every two to three weeks, starting with the *Iliad* and ending up with Hemingway. He gave us a quiz on the reading every other day. He brought a prep school curriculum to Mercy High.

MacFarland's lectures were crafted, and as he delivered them he would pace the room jiggling a piece of chalk in his cupped hand, using it to scribble on the board the names of all the writers and philosophers and plays and novels he was weaving into his discussion. He asked questions often, raised everything from Zeno's paradox to the repeated last line of Frost's "Stopping by Woods on a Snowy Evening." He slowly and carefully built up our knowledge of Western intellectual history—with facts, with connections, with speculations. We learned about Greek philosophy, about Dante, the Elizabethan world view, the Age of Reason, existentialism. He analyzed poems with us, had us reading sections from John Ciardi's *How Does a Poem Mean?*, making a potentially difficult book accessible with his own explanations. We gave oral reports on poems Ciardi didn't cover. We imitated the styles of Conrad, Hemingway, and *Time* magazine. We wrote and talked, wrote and talked. The man immersed us in language.

Even MacFarland's barbs were literary. If Jim Fitzsimmons, hung over and irritable, tried to smart-ass him, he'd rejoin with a flourish that would spark the indomitable Skip Madison— who'd lost his front teeth in a hapless tackle—to flick his tongue through the gap and opine, "good chop," drawing out the single "o" in stinging indictment. Jack MacFarland, this tobacco-stained intellectual, brandished linguistic weapons of a kind I hadn't encountered before. Here was this *egghead*, for God's sake, keeping some pretty difficult people in line. And from what I heard, Mike Dweetz and Steve Fusco and all the notorious Voc. Ed. crowd settled down as well when MacFarland took the podium. Though a lot of guys groused in the schoolyard, it just seemed that giving trouble to this particular teacher was a silly thing to do. Tomfoolery, not to mention assault, had no place in the world he was trying to create for us, and instinctively everyone knew that. If nothing else, we all recognized MacFarland's considerable intelligence and respected the hours he put into his work. It came to this: The troublemaker would look foolish rather than daring. Even Jim Fitzsimmons was reading *On the Road* and turning his incipient alcoholism to literary ends.

There were some lives that were already beyond Jack MacFarland's ministrations, but mine was not. I started reading again as I hadn't since elementary school. I would go into our gloomy little bedroom or sit at the dinner table while, on the television, Danny McShane was paralyzing Mr. Moto with the atomic drop, and work slowly back through *Heart of Darkness*, trying to catch the words in Conrad's sentences. I certainly was not MacFarland's best student; most of the other guys in College Prep, even my fellow slackers, had better backgrounds than I did. But I worked very hard, for MacFarland had hooked me. He tapped my old interest in reading and creating stories. He gave me a way to feel special by using my mind. And he provided a role model that wasn't shaped on physical prowess alone, and something inside me that I wasn't quite aware of responded to that. Jack MacFarland established a literacy club, to borrow a phrase of Frank Smith's, and invited me—invited all of us—to join.

There's been a good deal of research and speculation suggesting that the acknowledgment of school performance with extrinsic rewards—smiling faces, stars, numbers, grades—diminishes the intrinsic satisfaction children experience by engaging in reading or writing or problem solving. While it's certainly true that we've created an educational system that encourages our best and brightest to become cynical grade collectors and, in general, have developed an obsession with evaluation and assessment, I must tell you that venal though it may have been, I loved getting good grades from MacFarland. I now know how subjective grades can be, but then they came tucked in the back of essays like bits of scientific data, some sort of spectroscopic readout that said, objectively and publicly, that I had made something of value. I suppose I'd been mediocre for too long and enjoyed a public redefinition. And I suppose the workings of my mind, such as they were, had been private for too long. My linguistic play moved into the world; like the intergalactic stories I told years before on Frank's berry-splattered truck bed, these papers with their circled, red B-pluses and A-minuses linked my mind to something outside it. I carried them around like a club emblem.

One day in the December of my senior year, Mr. MacFarland asked me where I was going to go to college. I hadn't thought much about it. Many of the students I teach today spent their last year in high school with a physics text in one hand and the Stanford catalog in the other, but I wasn't even aware of what "entrance requirements" were. My folks would say that they wanted me to go to college and be a doctor, but I don't know how seriously I ever took that; it seemed a sweet thing to say, a bit of supportive family chatter, like telling a gangly daughter she's graceful. The reality of higher education wasn't in my scheme of things: No one in the family had gone to college; only two of my uncles had completed high school. I figured I'd get a night job and go to the local junior college because I knew that Snyder and Company were going there to play ball. But I hadn't even prepared for that. When I finally said, "I don't know," MacFarland looked down at me—I was seated in his office—and said, "Listen, you can write."

My grades stank. I had A's in biology and a handful of B's in a few English and social science classes. All the rest were C's—or worse. MacFarland said I would do well in his class and laid down the law about doing well in the others. Still, the record for my first three years wouldn't have been acceptable to any four-year school. To nobody's surprise, I was turned down flat by USC and UCLA. But Jack MacFarland was on the case. He had received his bachelor's degree from Loyola University, so he made calls to old professors and talked to somebody in admissions and wrote me a strong letter. Loyola finally accepted me as a probationary student. I would be on trial for the first year, and if I did Okay, I would be granted regular status. MacFarland also intervened to get me a loan, for I could never have afforded a private college without it. Four more years of religion classes and four more years of boys at one school, girls at another. But at least I was going to college. Amazing.

In my last semester of high school, I elected a special English course fashioned by Mr. MacFarland, and it was through this elective that there arouse at Mercy a fledgling literati. Art Mitz, the editor of the school newspaper and a very smart guy, was the kingpin. He was joined by me and by Mark Dever, a quiet boy who wrote beautifully and who would die before he was forty. MacFarland occasionally invited us to his apartment, and those visits became the high point of our apprenticeship: We'd clamp on our training wheels and drive to his salon.

He lived in a cramped and cluttered place near the airport, tucked away in the kind of building that architectural critic Reyner Banham calls a *dingbat*. Books were all over: stacked, piled, tossed, and crated, underlined and dog eared, well worn and new. Cigarette ashes crusted with coffee in saucers or spilled over the sides of motel ashtrays. The little bedroom had, along two of its walls, bricks and boards loaded with notes, magazines, and oversized books. The kitchen joined the living room, and there was a stack of German newspapers under the sink. I had never seen anything like it: a great flophouse of language furnished by City Lights and Café le Metro. I read every title. I flipped through paperbacks and scanned jackets and memorized names: Gogol, *Finnegan's Wake*, Djuna Barnes, Jackson Pollock, *A Coney Island of the Mind*, F. O. Matthiessen's *American Renaissance*, all sorts of Freud, *Troubled Sleep*, Man Ray, *The Education of Henry Adams*, Richard Wright, *Film as Art*, William Butler Yeats, Marguerite Duras, *Redburn*, *A Season in Hell*, *Kapital*. On the cover of Alain-Fournier's *The Wanderer* was an Edward Gorey drawing of a young man on a road winding into dark trees. By the hotplate sat a strange Kafka novel called *Amerika*, in which an adolescent hero crosses the Atlantic to find the Nature Theater of Oklahoma. Art and Mark would be talking about a movie or the school newspaper, and I would be consuming my English teacher's library. It was heady stuff. I felt like a Pop Warner athlete on steroids.

Art, Mark, and I would buy stogies and triangulate from MacFarland's apartment to the Cinema, which now shows X-rated films but was then L.A.'s premiere art theater, and then to the musty Cherokee Bookstore in Hollywood to hobnob with beatnik homosexuals—smoking, drinking bourbon and coffee, and trying out awkward phrases we'd gleaned from our mentor's bookshelves. I was happy and precocious and a little scared as well, for Hollywood Boulevard was thick with a kind of decadence that was foreign to the South Side. After the Cherokee, we would head back to the security of MacFarland's apartment, slaphappy with hipness.

Let me be the first to admit that there was a good deal of adolescent passion in this embrace of the avant-garde: self-absorption, sexually charged pedantry, an elevation of the odd and abandoned. Still it was a time during which I absorbed an awful lot of information: long lists of titles, images from expressionist paintings, new wave shibboleths, snippets of philosophy, and names that read like Steve Fusco's misspellings—Goethe, Nietzsche, Kierkegaard. Now this is hardly the stuff of deep understanding. But it was an introduction, a phrase book, a Baedeker to a vocabulary of ideas, and it felt good at the time to know all these words. With hindsight I realize how layered and important that knowledge was.

It enabled me to do things in the world. I could browse bohemian bookstores in far-off, mysterious Hollywood; I could go to the Cinema and see events through the lenses of European directors; and, most of all, I could share an evening, talk that talk, with Jack MacFarland, the man I most admired at the time. Knowledge was becoming a bonding agent. Within a year or two, the persona of the disaffected hipster would prove too cynical, too alienated to last. But for a time it was new and exciting: It provided a critical perspective on society, and it allowed me to act as though I were living beyond the limiting boundaries of South Vermont.

3

◆

Entering
the Conversation

If you walked out the back door of 9116 South Vermont and across our narrow yard, you would run smack into those four single-room rentals and, alongside them, an old wooden house-trailer. The trailer had belonged to Mrs. Jolly, the woman who sold us the property. It was locked and empty, and its tires were flat and fused into the asphalt driveway. Rusted dairy cases had been wedged in along its sides and four corners to keep it balanced. Two of its eight windows were broken, the frames were warped, and the door stuck. I was getting way too old to continue sharing a room with my mother, so I began to eye that trailer. I decided to refurbish it. It was time to have a room of my own.

Lou Minton had, by now, moved in with us, and he and I fixed the windows and realigned the door. I painted the inside by combining what I could find in our old shed with what I could afford to buy: The ceiling became orange, the walls yellow, the rim along the windows flat black. Lou redid the wiring and put in three new sockets. I got an old record player from the second-hand store for five dollars. I had Roy Herweck, the illustrator of our high school annual, draw women in mesh stockings and other objets d'redneck art on the yellow walls, and I put empty Smirnoff and Canadian Club bottles on the ledges above the windows. I turned the old trailer into the kind of bachelor digs a seventeen-year-old in South L.A. would fancy. My friends from high school began congregating there. When she could, my mother would make us a pot of spaghetti or pasta fasul'. And there was a clerk across the street at Marty's Liquor who would sell to us: We would run back across Vermont Avenue laughing and clutching our bags and seal ourselves up in the trailer. We spun fantasies about the waitress at the Mexican restaurant and mimicked our teachers and caught touchdown passes and, in general, dreamed our way through adolescence. It was a terrible time for rock 'n' roll—Connie Francis and Bobby Rydell were headliners in 1961—so we found rhythm and blues on L.A.'s one black station, played the backroom ballads of troubadour Oscar Brand, and discovered Delta and Chicago blues on Pacifica's KPFK:

> I'm a man
> I'm a full-grown man

As I fell increasingly under Mr. MacFarland's spell, books began replacing the liquor bottles above the windows: *The Trial* and *Waiting for Godot* and *No Exit* and *The Stranger*. Roy sketched a copy of the back cover of *Exile and the Kingdom,* and so the pensive face of Albert Camus now looked down from that patch of wall on which a cartoon had once pressed her crossed legs. My mother found a quilt that my grandmother had sewn from my father's fabric samples. It was dark and heavy, and I would lie under it and read Rimbaud and not understand him and feel very connected to the life I imagined Jack MacFarland's life to be: a subterranean ramble through Bebop and breathless poetry and back-alley revelations.

In 1962, John Connor moved into dank, old Apartment 1. John had also grown up in South L.A., and he and I had become best friends. His parents moved to Oregon, and John—who was a good black-top basketball player and an excellent student—wanted to stay in Los Angeles and go to college. So he rented an apartment for forty dollars a month, and we established a community of two. Some nights, John and I and Roy the artist and a wild kid named Gaspo would drive into downtown L.A.—down to where my mother had waited fearfully for a bus years before—and roam the streets and feel the excitement of the tenderloin: the flashing arrows, the blue-and-orange beer neon, the burlesque houses, the faded stairwell of Roseland—which we would inch up and then run down—brushing past the photos of taxi dancers, glossy and smiling in a glass display. Cops would tell us to go home, and that intensified this bohemian romance all the more.

About four months after John moved in, we both entered Loyola University. Loyola is now coeducational; its student center houses an Asian Pacific Students Association, Black Student Alliance, and Chicano Resource Center; and its radio station, KXLU, plays the most untamed rock 'n' roll in Los Angeles. But in the early sixties, Loyola was pretty much a school for white males from the middle and upper middle class. It was a sleepy little campus—its undergraduate enrollment was under two thousand—and it prided itself on providing spiritual as well as intellectual guidance for its students: Religion and Christian philosophy courses were a required part of the curriculum. It defined itself as a Catholic intellectual community—promotional brochures relied on phrases like "the social, intellectual, and spiritual aspects of our students"—and made available to its charges small classes, a campus ministry, and thirty-six clubs (the Chess Club, Economics Society, Fine Arts Circle, Debate Squad, and more). There were also six fraternities and a sports program that included basketball, baseball, volleyball, rugby, soccer, and crew. Loyola men, it was assumed, shared a fairly common set of social and religious values, and the university provided multiple opportunities for them to develop their minds, their spirits, and their social networks. I imagine that parents sent their boys to Loyola with a sigh of relief: God and man strolled together out of St. Robert Bellarmine Hall and veered left to Sacred Heart Chapel. There was an occasional wild party at one of the off-campus fraternity houses, but, well, a pair of panties in the koi pond was not on a par with crises of faith and violence against the state.

John and I rattled to college in his '53 Plymouth. Loyola Boulevard was lined with elms and maples, and as we entered the campus we could see the chapel tower rising in the distance. The chapel and all the early buildings had been constructed in the 1920s and were white and separated by broad sweeps of very green grass. Palm trees and stone pines grew in rows and clumps close to the buildings, and long concrete walkways curved and angled and crossed to connect everything, proving that God, as Plato suspected, is always doing geometry.

Most freshman courses were required, and I took most of mine in St. Robert Bellarmine Hall. Saint Robert was a father of the church who wrote on papal power and censored Galileo: The ceiling in his hallway was high, and dim lights hung down from it.

The walls were beige up to about waist level, then turned off-white. The wood trim was dark and worn. The floor combined brown linoleum with brown and black tile. Even with a rush of students, the building maintained its dignity. We moved through it, and its old, clanking radiators warmed us as we did, but it was not a warmth that got to the bone. I remember a dream in which I climbed up beyond the third floor—up thin, narrow stairs to a bell tower that held a small, dusky room in which a priest was playing church music to a class of shadows.

My first semester classes included the obligatory theology and ROTC and a series of requirements: biology, psychology, speech, logic, and a language. I went to class and usually met John for lunch: We'd bring sandwiches to his car and play the radio while we ate. Then it was back to class, or the library, or the student union for a Coke. This was the next step in Jack MacFarland's plan for me—and I did okay for a while. I had learned enough routines in high school to act like a fairly typical student, but—except for the historical sketch I received in Senior English—there wasn't a solid center of knowledge and assurance to all this. When I look back through notes and papers and various photographs and memorabilia, I begin to remember what a disengaged, half-awake time it really was. I'll describe two of the notebooks I found. The one from English is a small book, eight by seven, and only eleven pages of it are filled. The notes I did write consist of book titles, dates of publication, names of characters, pointless summaries of books that were not on our syllabus and that I had never read ("*The Alexandria Quartet*: 5 or 6 characters seen by different people in different stages of life"), and quotations from the teacher ("Perception can bring sorrow.") The notes are a series of separate entries. I can't see any coherence. My biology lab notes are written on green-tint quadrille. They, too, are sparse. There is an occasional poorly executed sketch of a tiny organism or of a bone and muscle structure. Some of the formulas and molecular models sit isolated on the page, bare of any explanatory discussion. The lecture notes are fragmented; a fair number of sentences remain incomplete.

By the end of the second semester my grades were close to dipping below a C average, and since I had been admitted provisionally, that would have been that. Jack MacFarland had oriented me to Western intellectual history and had helped me develop my writing, but he had worked with me for only a year, and I needed more than twelve months of his kind of instruction. Speech and Introductory Psychology presented no big problems. General Biology had midterm and final examinations that required a good deal of memorizing, and I could do that, but the textbook—particularly the chapters covered in the second semester—was much, much harder than what I read in high school, and I was so ill-adept in the laboratory that I failed that portion of the class. We had to set up and pursue biological problems, not just memorize—and at the first sign of doing rather than memorizing, I would automatically assume the problem was beyond me and distance myself from it. Logic, another requirement, spooked me with its syllogisms and Venn diagrams—they were just a step away from more formal mathematics—so I memorized what I could and squirmed around the rest. Theology was god-awful; ROTC was worse. And Latin, the language I elected on the strength of Jack MacFarland's one piece of bad advice, had me suffocating under the dust of a dead civilization. Freshman English was taught by a frustrated novelist with glittering eyes who had us, among other things, describing the consumption of our last evening's meal using the images of the battlefield.

I was out of my league.

Faculty would announce office hours. If I had had the sense, I would have gone, but they struck me as aloof and somber men, and I felt stupid telling them I was . . . well—stupid. I drifted through the required courses, thinking that as soon as these requirements were over, I'd never have to face anything even vaguely quantitative again. Or anything to do with foreign languages. Or ROTC. I fortified myself with defiance: I worked up an imitation of the old priest who was my Latin teacher, and I kept my ROTC uniform crumpled in the greasy trunk of John's Plymouth.

Many of my classmates came from and lived in a world very different from my own. The campus literary magazine would publish excerpts from the journals of upperclassmen traveling across Europe, standing before the Berlin Wall or hiking through olive groves toward Delphi. With the exception of one train trip back to Altoona, I had never been out of Southern California, and this translated, for me, into some personal inadequacy. Fraternities seemed exclusive and a little strange. I'm not sure why I didn't join any of Loyola's three dozen societies and clubs, though I do know that things like the Debate Squad were way too competitive. Posters and flyers and squibs in the campus newspaper gave testament to a lot of connecting activity, but John and I pretty much kept to ourselves, ragging on the "Loyola man," reading the literary magazine aloud with a French accent, simultaneously feeling contempt for and exclusion from a social life that seemed to work with the mystery and enclosure of the clockwork in a music box.

It is an unfortunate fact of our psychic lives that the images that surround us as we grow up—no matter how much we may scorn them later—give shape to our deepest needs and longings. Every year Loyola men elected a homecoming queen. The queen and her princesses were students at the Catholic sister schools: Marymount, Mount St. Mary's, St. Vincent's. They had names like Corinne and Cathy, and they came from the Sullivan family or the Mitchells or the Ryans. They were taught to stand with toe to heel, their smiles were inviting, and the photographer's flash illuminated their eyes. Loyola men met them at fraternity parties and mixers and "CoEd Day," met them according to rules of manner and affiliation and parental connection as elaborate as a Balinese dance. John and I drew mustaches on their photographs, but something about them reached far back into my life.

Growing up in South L.A. was certainly not a conscious misery. My neighborhood had its diversions and its mysteries, and I felt loved and needed at home. But all in all there was a dreary impotence to the years, and isolation, and a deep sadness about my father. I protected myself from the harsher side of it all through a life of the mind. And while that interior life included spaceships and pink chemicals and music and the planetary moons, it also held the myriad television images of the good life that were piped into my home: Robert Young sitting down to dinner, Ozzie Nelson tossing the football with his sons, the blond in a Prell commercial turning toward the camera. The images couldn't have been more trivial—all sentimental phosphorescence—but as a child tucked away on South Vermont, they were just about the only images I had of what life would be without illness and dead ends. I didn't realize how completely their message had seeped into my being, what loneliness and sorrow was being held at bay—didn't realize it until I found myself in the middle of Loyola's social life without a guidebook, feeling just beyond the superficial touch of the queen and her princesses, those smiling incarnations of a television promise. I scorned the whole silly show and ached to be embraced by one of these mythic females under the muted light of a paper moon.

So I went to school and sat in class and memorized more than understood and whistled past the academic graveyard. I vacillated between the false potency of scorn and feelings of ineptitude. John and I would get in his car and enjoy the warmth of each other and laugh and head down the long strip of Manchester Boulevard, away from Loyola, away from the palms and green, green lawns, back to South L.A. We'd throw the ball in the alley or lag pennies on Vermont or hit Marty's Liquor. We'd leave much later for a movie or a football game at Mercy High or the terrible safety of downtown Los Angeles. Walking, then, past the *discotecas* and pawnshops, past the windows full of fried chicken and yellow lamps, past the New Follies, walking through hustlers and lost drunks and prostitutes and transvestites with rouge the color of bacon—stopping, finally, before the musty opening of a bar where two silhouettes moved around a pool table as though they were underwater.

I don't know what I would have found if the flow of events hadn't changed dramatically. Two things happened. Jack MacFarland privately influenced my course of study at Loyola, and death once again ripped through our small family.

The coterie of MacFarland's students—Art Mitz, Mark Dever, and me—were still visiting our rumpled mentor. We would stop by his office or his apartment to mock our classes and the teachers and all that " 'Loyola man' bullshit." Nobody had more appreciation for burlesque than Jack MacFarland, but I suppose he saw beneath our caustic performances and knew we were headed for trouble. Without telling us, he started making phone calls to some of his old teachers at Loyola—primarily to Dr. Frank Carothers, the chairman of the English Department—and, I guess, explained that these kids needed to be slapped alongside the head with a good novel. Dr. Carothers volunteered to look out for us and agreed to some special studies courses that we could substitute for a few of the more traditional requirements, courses that would enable us to read and write a lot under the close supervi-

sion of a faculty member. In fact, what he promised were tutorials—and that was exceptional, even for a small college. All this
would start up when we returned from summer vacation. Our
sophomore year, Jack MacFarland finally revealed, would be different.

When Lou Minton rewired the trailer, he rigged a phone line
from the front house: A few digits and we could call each other.
One night during the summer after my freshman year, the phone
rang while I was reading. It was my mother and she was screaming. I ran into the house to find her standing in the kitchen hys-
terical—both hands pressed to her face—and all I could make out
was Lou's name. I didn't see him in the front of the house, so I
ran back through the kitchen to the bedroom. He had fallen back
across the bed, a hole right at his sideburn, his jaw still quivering.
They had a fight, and some ugly depth of pain convulsed within
him. He left the table and walked to the bedroom. My mother
heard the light slam of a .22. Nothing more.

That summer seems vague and distant. I can't remember any
specifics, though I had to take care of my mother and handle the
affairs of the house. I probably made do by blunting a good deal
of what I saw and navigating with intuitive quadrants. But
though I cannot remember details, I do recall feelings and recog-
nitions: Lou's suicide came to represent the sadness and dead
time I had protected myself against, the personal as well as public
oppressiveness of life in South Los Angeles. I began to see that
my escape to the trailer and my isolationist fantasies of the demi-
monde would yield another kind of death, a surrender to the culture's lost core. An alternative was somehow starting to take
shape around school and knowledge. Knowledge seemed . . .
was it empowering? No, that's a word I would use now. Then I
felt freed, as if I were untying fetters. There simply were times
when the pain and confusion of that summer would give way to
something I felt more than I knew: a lightness to my body, an
ease in breathing. Three or four months later I took an art history
course, and one day during a slide show on Gothic architecture
I felt myself rising up within the interior light of Mont-Saint-
Michel. I wanted to be released from the despair that surrounded
me on South Vermont and from my own troubled sense of exclusion.

Jack MacFarland had saved me at one juncture—caught my

fancy and revitalized my mind—what I felt now was something further, some tentative recognition that an engagement with ideas could foster competence and lead me out into the world. But all this was very new and fragile, and given what I know now, I realize how easily it could have been crushed. My mother, for as long as I can remember, always added onto any statement of intention—hers or others'—the phrase *se vuol Dio*, if God wants it. The fulfillment of desire, no matter how trivial, required the blessing of the gods, for the world was filled with threat. "I'll plant the seeds this weekend," I might say. "Se vuol Dio," she would add. *Se vuol Dio*. The phrase expressed several lifetimes of ravaged hope: my grandfather's lost leg, the failure of the Rose Spaghetti House, my father laid low, Lou Minton, the landscapes of South L.A. *Se vuol Dio*. For those who live their lives on South Vermont, tomorrow doesn't beckon to be defined from a benign future. It's up to the gods, not you, if any old thing turns out right. I carried within me no history of assurances that what I was feeling would lead to anything.

Because of its size and because of the kind of teacher who is drawn to small liberal arts colleges, Loyola would turn out to be a very good place for me. For even with MacFarland's yearlong tour through ideas and language, I was unprepared. English prose written before the twentieth century was difficult, sometimes impossible, for me to comprehend. The kind of reasoning I found in logic was very foreign. My writing was okay, but I couldn't hold a candle to Art Mitz or Mark Dever or to those boys who came from good schools. And my fears about science and mathematics prevailed: Pereira Hall, the Math and Engineering Building, was only forty to fifty yards from the rear entrance to the English Department but seemed an unfriendly mirage, a malevolent castle floating in the haze of a mescaline dream.

We live, in America, with so many platitudes about motivation and self-reliance and individualism—and myths spun from them, like those of Horatio Alger—that we find it hard to accept the fact that they are serious nonsense. To live your early life on the streets of South L.A.—or Homewood or Spanish Harlem or Chicago's South Side or any one of hundreds of other depressed communities—and to journey up through the top levels of the American educational system will call for support and guidance at many, many points along the way. You'll need people to guide you into conversations that seem foreign and threatening. You'll need models, lots of them, to show you how to get at what you don't know. You'll need people to help you center yourself in your own developing ideas. You'll need people to watch out for you. There is much talk these days about the value of a classical humanistic education, a call for an immersion in the humanities, a return to the great books. These appeals raise lots of suspicions, for such curricula have traditionally served to exclude working-class people from the classroom. It doesn't, of necessity, have to be that way. The teachers that fate and Jack MacFarland's crisis intervention sent my way worked at making the humanities truly human. What transpired between us was the essence of humane liberal education, and it enabled me to move far beyond the cognitive charade of my freshman year.

———◆———

From the midpoint of their freshman year, Loyola students had to take one philosophy course per semester: Logic, Philosophy of Nature, Philosophy of Man, General Ethics, Natural Theology, and so on. Logic was the first in the series, and I had barely gotten a C. The rest of the courses looked like a book fair of medieval scholasticism with the mold scraped off the bindings, and I dreaded their advent. But I was beginning my sophomore year at a time when the best and brightest of the Jesuit community were calling for an intellectually panoramic, socially progressive Catholicism, and while this lasted, I reaped the benefits. Sections of the next three courses I had to take would be taught by a young man who was studying for the priesthood and who was, himself, attempting to develop a personal philosophy that incorporated the mind and the body as well as the spirit.

Mr. Johnson could have strolled off a Wheaties box. Still in his twenties and a casting director's vision of those good looks thought to be all-American, Don Johnson had committed his very considerable intelligence to the study and teaching of philosophy. Jack MacFarland had introduced me to the Greeks, to Christian scholasticism, eighteenth-century deism, and French existentialism, but it was truly an introduction, a curtsy to that realm of the heavens where the philosophers dwell. Mr. Johnson provided a fuller course. He was methodical and spoke with vibrance and made connections between ancients and moderns with care. He did for philosophy what Mr. MacFarland had done for literary history: He gave me a directory of key names and notions.

We started in a traditional way with the Greek philosophers who preceded Socrates—Thales, Heraclitus, Empedocles—and worked our way down to Kant and Hegel. We read a little Aquinas, but we also read E. A. Burtt's *The Metaphysical Foundations of Modern Science*, and that gave me entry to Kepler, Copernicus, Galileo (which I was then spelling *Galelao*), and Newton. As he laid out his history of ideas, Mr. Johnson would consider aloud the particular philosophical issue involved, so we didn't, for example, simply get an outline of what Hegel believed, but we watched and listened as Don Johnson reasoned like Hegel and then raised his own questions about the Hegelian scheme. He was a working philosopher, and he was thinking out loud in front of us.

The Metaphysical Foundations of Modern Science was very tough going. It assumed not only a familiarity with Western thought but, as well, a sophistication in reading a theoretically rich argument. It was, in other words, the kind of book you encounter with increased frequency as you move through college. It combined the history of mathematics and science with philosophical investigation, and when I tried to read it, I'd end up rescanning the same sentences over and over, not understanding them, and, finally, slamming the book down on the desk—swearing at this golden boy Johnson and angry with myself. Here's a typical passage, one of the many I marked as being hopeless:

> We begin now to glimpse the tremendous significance of what these fathers of modern science were doing, but let us continue with our questions. What further specific metaphysical doctrines was Kepler led to adopt as a consequence of this notion of what constitutes the real world? For one thing, it led him to appropriate in his own way the distinction between primary and secondary qualities, which had been noted in the ancient world by the atomist and skeptical schools, and which was being revived in the sixteenth century in varied form by such miscellaneous thinkers as Vives, Sanchez, Montaigne, and Campanella. Knowledge as it is immediately offered the mind through the

senses is obscure, confused, contradictory, and hence untrustworthy; only those features of the world in terms of which we get certain and consistent knowledge open before us what is indubitably and permanently real. Other qualities are not real qualities of things, but only signs of them. For Kepler, of course, the real qualities are those caught up in this mathematical harmony underlying the world of the senses, and which, therefore, have a causal relation to the latter. *The real world is a world of quantitative characteristics only; its differences are differences of number alone.*

I couldn't get the distinction that was being made between primary and secondary qualities, and I certainly didn't have the background that would enable me to make sense of Burtt's brief historical survey: from "atomist and skeptical schools [to] . . . Campanella." It is clear from the author's italics that the last sentence of the passage is important, so I underlined it, but because Burtt's discussion is built on a rich intellectual history that I didn't know, I was reading words but not understanding text. I was the human incarnation of language-recognition computer programs: able to record the dictionary meanings of individual words but unable to generate any meaning out of them.

"What," I asked in class, "are primary and secondary qualities? I don't get it." And here Don Johnson was very good. "The answer," he said, "can be found in the passage itself. I'll go back through it with you. Let's start with primary and secondary qualities. If some qualities are primary and others secondary, which do you think would be most important?"

"Primary?"

"Right. Primary qualities. Whatever they are. Now let's turn to Kepler, since Kepler's the subject of this passage. What is it that's more important to Kepler?"

I pause and say tentatively, "Math." Another student speaks up, reading from the book: "Quantitative characteristics."

"All right. So primary qualities, for Kepler, are mathematical, quantitative. But we still don't know what this primary and secondary opposition really refers to, do we? Look right in the middle of the paragraph. Burtt is comparing mathematical knowledge to the immediate knowledge provided by—what?"

My light bulb goes on: "The senses."

"There it is. The primary-secondary opposition is the opposition between knowledge gained by pure mathematical reasoning versus knowledge gained through our five senses."

We worked with *The Metaphysical Foundations of Modern Science* for some time, and I made my way slowly through it. Mr. Johnson was helping me develop an ability to read difficult texts—I was learning how to reread critically, how to tease out definitions and basic arguments. And I was also gaining confidence that if I stayed with material long enough and kept asking questions, I would get it. That assurance proved to be more valuable than any particular body of knowledge I learned that year.

For my second semester, I had to take Philosophy of Man, and it was during that course that Mr. Johnson delivered his second gift. We read Gabriel Marcel and Erich Fromm, learning about phenomenology and social criticism. We considered the human animal from an anthropological as well as philosophical perspective. And we read humanistic psychologist Abraham Maslow's *Toward a Psychology of Being*. Maslow wrote about "the 'will to health,' the urge to grow, the pressure of self-actualization, the quest for one's identity." The book had a profound effect on me. Six months before, Lou Minton's jaw quivered as if to speak the race's deepest sorrow, and through the rest of that summer I could only feel in my legs and chest some fleeting assurance that the world wasn't a thin mask stretched over nothingness. Now I was reading an articulation of that vague, hopeful feeling. Maslow was giving voice to some delicate possibility within me, and I was powerfully drawn to it. Every person is, in part, "'his own project' and makes himself." I had to know more, so I called Mr. Johnson up and asked if I could visit with him. "Sure," he said, and invited me to campus. So one Saturday morning I took a series of early buses and headed west.

Mr. Johnson and the other initiates to the priesthood lived in an old white residence hall on the grassy east edge of campus, and the long walk up Loyola Boulevard was quiet and meditative: Birds were flying tree to tree and a light breeze was coming in off Playa del Rey. I walked up around the gym, back behind Math-Engineering to his quarters, a simple one-story building with those Spanish curves that seem simultaneously thick and weightless. The sun had warmed the stucco. A window by the door was open, and a curtain had fluttered out. I rang the bell and heard steps on a hardwood floor. Mr. Johnson opened the door and stepped out. He was smiling and his eyes were attentive in the light . . . present . . . there. They said, "Come, let's talk."

Dr. Frank Carothers taught what is generally called the sophomore survey, a yearlong sequence of courses that introduces the neophyte English major to the key works in English literary history. Dr. Carothers was tall and robust. He wore thick glasses and a checkered bow tie and his hairline was male Botticelli, picking up somewhere back beyond his brow. As the year progressed, he spread English literary history out in slow time across the board, and I was introduced to people I'd never heard of: William Langland, a medieval acolyte who wrote the dream-vision *Piers Plowman*; the sixteenth-century poet Sir Thomas Wyatt; Elizabethan lyricists with peculiar names like Orlando Gibbons and Tobias Hume (the author of the wondrous suggestion that tobacco "maketh lean the fat men's tumour"); the physician Sir Thomas Browne; the essayist Joseph Addison; the biographer James Boswell; the political philosopher Edmund Burke, whose prose I could not decipher; and poets Romantic and Victorian (Shelley and Rossetti and Algernon Charles Swinburne). Some of the stuff was invitingly strange ("Pallid and pink as the palm of the flag-flower . . ."), some was awfully hard to read, and some was just awful. But Dr. Carothers laid it all out with his reserved passion, drew for us a giant conceptual blueprint onto which we could place other courses, other books. He was precise, thorough, and rigorous. And he started his best work once class was over.

Being a professor was, for Frank Carothers, a profoundly social calling: He enjoyed the classroom, and he seemed to love the more informal contacts with those he taught, those he once taught, and those who stopped by just to get a look at this guy. He stayed in his office until about four each afternoon, leaning back in his old swivel chair, hands clasped behind his head, his bow tie tight against his collar. He had strong opinions, and he'd get irritated if you missed class, and he sometimes gave quirky advice—but there he'd be shaking his head sympathetically as students poured out their troubles. It was pure and primary for Frank Carothers: Teaching allowed him daily to fuse the joy he got from reading literature—poetry especially—with his deep pleasure in human community. What I saw when I was around him—and I hung out in his office from my sophomore year on—was very different from the world I had been creating for myself, a far cry from my withdrawal into an old house trailer with a silent book.

One of Dr. Carothers's achievements was the English Society. The English Society had seventy-eight members, and that made it just about the biggest organization on campus: jocks, literati, C-plus students, frat boys, engineers, mystics, scholars, profligates, bullies, geeks, Republicans—all stood side by side for group pictures. The English Society sponsored poetry readings, lectures, and card games, and best of all, barbecues in the Carotherses' backyard. We would caravan out to Manhattan Beach to be greeted by Betsy, the youngest of the seven Carothers children, and she'd walk us back to her father who, wrapped now in an apron, was poking coals or unscrewing the tops from jugs of red wine.

Vivian Carothers, a delicate, soft-spoken woman, would look after us and serve up trays of cheese and chips and little baked things. Students would knock on the redwood gate all through the late afternoon, more and more finding places for themselves among flowers and elephant ears, patio furniture, and a wizened pine. We would go on way past sunset, talking to Dr. Carothers and to each other about books and sports and currently despised professors, sometimes letting off steam and sometimes learning something new. And Frank Carothers would keep us fed, returning to the big, domed barbecue through the evening to lift the lid and add hamburgers, the smoke rising off the grill and up through the telephone lines stretching like the strings of Shelley's harp over the suburbs of the South Bay.

When I was learning my craft at Jack MacFarland's knee, I continually misused words and wrote fragments and run-on sentences and had trouble making my pronouns agree with whatever it was that preceded them. I also produced sentences like these:

Some of these modern-day Ramses are inherent of their wealth, others are self-made.

An exhibition of will on the part of the protagonist enables him to accomplish a subjective good (which is an element of tragedy, namely: the protagonist does not fully realize the objective wrong that he is doing. He feels objectively justified if not completely right.)

I was struggling to express increasingly complex ideas, and I couldn't get the language straight: Words, as in my second sentence on tragedy, piled up like cars in a serial wreck. I was encountering a new language—the language of the academy—and was trying to find my way around in it. I have some more examples, written during my first year and a half at Loyola. There was inflated vocabulary:

> I conjectured that he was the same individual who had arrested my attention earlier.

> In his famed speech, "The American Scholar," Ralph Waldo Emerson posed several problems that are particularly germane to the position of the young author.

There were cliches and mixed and awkward metaphors:

> In 1517, when Luther nailed his 95 theses to the door of Wittenburg Cathedral, he unknowingly started a snowball rolling that was to grow to tremendous reprocussions.

And there was academic melodrama:

> The vast realm of the cosmos or the depths of a man's soul hold questions that reason flounders upon, but which can be probed by the peculiar private insight of the seer.

Pop grammarians and unhappy English teachers get a little strange around sentences like these. But such sentences can be seen as marking a stage in linguistic growth. Appropriating a style and making it your own is difficult, and you'll miss the mark a thousand times along the way. The botched performances, though, are part of it all, and developing writers will grow through them if they are able to write for people who care about language, people who are willing to sit with them and help them as they struggle to write about difficult things. That is what Ted Erlandson did for me.

Dr. Erlandson was one of the people who agreed to teach me and my Mercy High companions a seminar—a close, intensive course that would substitute for a larger, standard offering like

Introduction to Prose Literature. He was tall and lanky and had a long reddish brown beard and lectured in a voice that was basso and happy. He was a strong lecturer and possessed the best memory for fictional detail I'd ever witnessed. And he cared about prose. The teachers I had during my last three years at Loyola assigned a tremendous amount of writing. But it was Ted Erlandson who got in there with his pencil and worked on my style. He would sit me down next to him at his big desk, sweep books and pencils across the scratched veneer, and go back over the sentences he wanted me to revise.

He always began by reading the sentence out loud: "Camus ascented to a richer vision of life that was to characterize the entirety of his work." Then he would fiddle with the sentence, talking and looking up at me intermittently to comment or ask questions: "'Ascent'. That sounds like 'assent', I know, but look it up, Mike." He'd wait while I fluttered the dictionary. "Now, 'the entirety of his work' . . . try this instead: 'his entire work.' Let's read it. 'Camus assented to a richer vision of life that would characterize his entire work.' Sounds better, doesn't it?"

And another sentence. "'Irregardless of the disastrous ending of *Bread and Wine*, it must be seen as an affirmative work.' 'Irregardless' . . . people use it all the time, but 'regardless' will do just fine. Now, I think this next part sounds a little awkward; listen: 'Regardless of the disastrous ending of *Bread and Wine*, it . . . 'Hear that? Let's try removing the 'of' and the 'it': 'Regardless of the disastrous ending, *Bread and Wine* must be seen as an affirmative work.' Hmmm. Better, I think."

And so it would go. He rarely used grammatical terms, and he never got technical. He dealt with specific bits of language: "Try this here" or "Here's another way to say it." He worked as a craftsman works, with particulars, and he shuttled back and forth continually between print and voice, making me breathe my prose, making me hear the language I'd generated in silence. Perhaps he was more directive than some would like, but, to be truthful, direction was what I needed. I was easily frustrated, and it didn't take a lot to make me doubt myself. When teachers would write "no" or "awkward" or "rewrite" alongside the sentences I had worked so hard to produce, I would be peeved and disappointed. "Well, what the hell *do* they want?" I'd grumble to no one in particular. So Ted Erlandson's linguistic parenting felt just right: a modeling of grace until it all slowly, slowly began to work itself into the way I shaped language.

When Father Albertson lectured, he would stand pretty much in one spot slightly to the left or right of center in front of us. He tended to hold his notes or a play or a critical study in both hands, releasing one to emphasize a point with a simple gesture. He was tall and thin, and his voice was soft and tended toward mono-tone. When he spoke, he looked very serious, but when one of us responded with any kind of intelligence, a little smile would come over his face. Jack MacFarland had told me that it was Clint Albertson's Shakespeare course that would knock my socks off.

For each play we covered, Father Albertson distributed a five-to ten-page list of questions to ask ourselves as we read. These study questions were of three general types.

The first type was broad and speculative and was meant to spark reflection on major characters and key events. Here's a teaser on *Hamlet*:

> Would you look among the portrait-paintings by Raphael, or Rembrandt, or Van Gogh, or El Greco, or Rouault for an ideal representation of Hamlet? Which painting by which of these men do you think most closely resembles your idea of what Hamlet should look like?

The second type focused on the details of the play itself and were very specific. Here are two of the thirty-eight he wrote for *As You Like It*:

ACT I, SCENE 2

> How is Rosalind distinguished from Celia in this scene? How do you explain the discrepancy between the Folio version of lines 284-287 and Act I, scene 3, line 117?

ACT II, SCENES 4-6:

> It has been said these scenes take us definitely out of the world of reality into a world of dream. What would you say are the steps of the process by which Shakespeare brings about this illusion?

The third kind of question required us to work with some historical or critical study. This is an example from the worksheet on *Romeo and Juliet*:

> Read the first chapter of C. S. Lewis's *Allegory of Love*, "Courtly Love." What would you say about Shakespeare's concept of love in relation to what Lewis presents as the traditional contradictory concepts in medieval literature of "romantic love" vs. "marriage."

Father Albertson had placed over 150 books on the reserve shelf in the library, and they ranged from intellectual history to literary criticism to handbooks on theater production. I had used a few such "secondary sources" to quote in my own writing since my days with Jack MacFarland, but this was the first time a teacher had so thoroughly woven them into a course. Father Albertson would cite them during lectures as naturally as though he were recalling a discussion he had overheard. He would add his own opinions and, since he expected us to form opinions, would ask us for ours.

I realize that this kind of thing—the close, line-by-line examination, the citing of critical opinion—has given rise to endless parodies of the academy: repressed schoolmen clucking along in the land of lost language. It certainly can be that way. But with Clint Albertson, all the learning furthered my comprehension of the play. His questions forced me to think carefully about Shakespeare's choice of words, about the crafting of a scene, about the connections between language and performance. I had to read very, very closely, leaning over the thin Formica desk in the trailer, my head cupped in my hands with my two index fingers in my ears to blot out the noise from the alley behind me. There were times when no matter how hard I tried, I wouldn't get it. I'd close the book, feeling stupid to my bones, and go find John. Over then to the liquor store, out into the night. The next day I would visit Father Albertson and tell him I was lost, ask him why this stuff was so damned hard. He'd listen and ask me to tell him why it made me so angry. I'd sputter some more, and then he'd draw me to the difficult passage, slowly opening the language up, helping me comprehend a distant, stylized literature, taking it apart, touching it.

I would then return to a classroom where a historically rich conversation was in progress. Other readers of Shakespeare—from Samuel Johnson to the contemporary literary critic Wylie Sypher—were given voice by Father Albertson, and we were encouraged to enter the dialogue, to consider, to take issue, to be seated amid all that potentially intimidating shoptalk. We were shown how to summarize an opinion, argue with it, weave it into our own interpretations. Nothing is more exclusive than the academic club: its language is highbrow, it has fancy badges, and it worships tradition. It limits itself to a few participants who prefer to talk to each other. What Father Albertson did was bring us inside the circle, nudging us out into the chatter, always just behind us, whispering to try this step, then this one, encouraging us to feel the moves for ourselves.

◆

Those four men collectively gave me the best sort of liberal education, the kind longed for in the stream of blue-ribbon reports on the humanities that now cross my desk. I developed the ability to read closely, to persevere in the face of uncertainty and ask questions of what I was reading—not with downcast eyes, but freely, aloud, realizing there is no such thing as an open book. My teachers modeled critical inquiry and linguistic precision and grace, and they provided various cognitive maps for philosophy and history and literature. They encouraged me to make connections and to enter into conversations—present and past—to see what talking a particular kind of talk would enable me to do with a thorny philosophical problem or a difficult literary text. And it was all alive. It transpired in backyards and on doorsteps and inside offices as well as in the classroom. I could smell their tobacco and see the nicks left by their razors. They liked books and ideas, and they liked to talk about them in ways that fostered growth rather than established dominance. They lived their knowledge. And maybe because of that their knowledge grew in me in ways that led back out to the world. I was developing a set of tools with which to shape a life.

I continued to take courses from my four mentors, and as I moved through my last two years, I found other teachers who kept the fire going as well: the progressive theologian Paul Hilsdale, the psychologist Carlo Weber, Father Trame—a historian who had us writing papers and exams every other week—the philosophers Gary Schouborg and Norbert Rigali. It was an exciting time for me, full of hope and promise. But I would not be telling the whole story if I didn't admit that with the deep satisfaction of growth came a mix of disturbance and fear.

I began noticing dates of birth and of death. Keats wrote "Ode to a Nightingale" when he was twenty-four. F. Scott Fitzgerald had two novels under his belt by his thirtieth year. A writer's best work, Fitzgerald once said, was produced by the time he was thirty. I became obsessed with impossible comparisons. Jacques Barzun started writing the 375-page *Darwin, Marx, Wagner* in his late twenties. Maslow published his first articles when he was twenty-four. And on. And on. As long as I stayed half-awake intellectually, there was no tension, no failed attempts at mastery, no confrontation with my limits. But now I was trying hard, and I could see how limited I was. It would be quite a while before I could relax into the gifts I did possess, but in the meantime, birthdates, printings, and copyrights all ticked off like some ruthless gauge of my own dim ability.

I lived a life of choice and possibility during the weekdays and then returned every evening to South Vermont. One day in the middle of my junior year, I lay down on the couch in the living room and could not get up. The TV and the table, John and my mother seemed distant, and I was cold and afraid, as if there were some indeterminate sickness all through me. I pulled my knees to my chest. My mother didn't know what to do, so she brought me blankets and a pillow. I stayed there for two days, getting up only to eat, returning quickly to keep the fear at bay, curling up again, bringing the blankets close again. Finally, I asked John to drive me out to see Dr. Metzger, the young Kaiser physician who had ministered to my father during his last year.

Dr. Metzger sat across from me and listened, ten or so years older than me, round faced, a goatee, serious. I couldn't express what it was that was making me feel cold and shaky, just that I was scared and didn't know what to do about it. He encouraged me to talk, and I did—talked about the last few years and Lou Minton and my own imagined infirmity. He leaned forward and told me that I had to move, that my mother would be okay, that she was strong and could manage. It was simple: Move. I would have to move away from South Vermont.

By the time John and I got home, I was feeling better, and within a few days I was back to normal. Dr. Metzger had released something, and eventually I would move. . . . I knew that I had to. I thought maybe I could move once I finished up at Loyola.

Those last years saw a gradual shift from the somnambulance and uncertain awakenings of my earlier time in college. I was involved, and I was meeting with success. And success carried with it its own challenges and threats, its own fears and its own further promises. Perhaps the best way to give you a sense of the texture of these years is to offer a few vignettes, a few clips from the footage that runs through my mind as I sit at my typewriter. I'll begin with one that occurred a month or so after I returned from Dr. Metzger's office.

The third course I took from Mr. Johnson was General Ethics. I was a junior and the class was a mix of juniors and seniors. One of the seniors was Brian Kelly. Brian was Loyola's pride—he was handsome, reflective, and gifted, and, by the time he graduated, he would win the triple crown of graduate fellowships: the Woodrow Wilson, the Danforth, and the Rhodes. A remarkable feat.

A course like General Ethics turns on the question of the existence of universal needs and values, and Mr. Johnson's bent was to look to anthropologists rather than theologians to provide the base for the course. He thought it might be a good idea to introduce the class to the issues by setting up a mock debate, one in which the first speaker would argue for the presence of ethical universals (like incest taboos) and the other speaker would support a strict cultural relativism. He asked me and Brian to conduct this piece of pedagogical theater, each of us collaborating beforehand and presenting the two sides of the argument.

Brian and I worked for two or three weeks, sharing materials and agreeing on methods of presentation. The debate came, and I went first, setting out the various anthropological evidence I could find in favor of ethical universals. Then I turned the podium over to Brian and sat down. He rose to the podium and knocked me flat. He couldn't check his combative instincts and discharged a formidable debater's arsenal: He spoke condescendingly. He questioned my sources and the way I reasoned with them. He brought in material I hadn't seen before. I was dumb-struck. This was big-time, no-holds-barred academic debate, and I was going down for the count. When it came my turn to re-spond to Brian, I repeated mechanically some of the things I had said earlier, but I couldn't reason with any flair. I was flushed with anger and humiliation, and my mouth dried up and my tongue felt as if it belonged to someone else.

More than a year after the debate with Brian, I won the Blenk-iron Award for excellence in English—a plaque and a hundred dollars from one of Loyola's benefactors. Ted Erlandson was by then the chairman of English, and he presided over the cere-mony. My name was called, and I walked to the podium. He shook my hand and offered me the plaque. As I was walking back and reading the inscription, I saw that the engraver had made a mistake: *Rose* was spelled *Ruse*. Ruse. A wily subterfuge. A trick. The plaque was returned and made right, of course, but the joke still went down. A peek from behind the curtain. A wink in the hall of mirrors. Was I the real thing or not?

One of the many people I met at the crossroads of Frank Carothers's office was Mike Casey. Casey was usually clad in strong opinion and a thin corduroy jacket. He edited *El Playano*, the campus literary magazine John and I used to lampoon in the old Plymouth. But I started liking Casey, and when he asked me to join the magazine, I put sarcasm behind me and signed on. I worked as an assistant for a semester, and that was fun. Casey promoted me to associate editor, and, at the end of my junior year, he and Dr. Carothers—the magazine's faculty advisor—chose me to be editor. They took a chance. Unlike the other two candidates, I had no experience with high school newspapers or annuals, and all I had done at Loyola was publish, at Casey's suggestion, a stuffy essay on Samuel Beckett and an intellectual exercise that passed for a poem.

El Playano had a small office on the second floor of the student center and was published three times a year. I learned about edit-ing, and, because the magazine had a staff of six, I learned some-thing about management. Students submitted stories and poems, and my editors and I would sit around an old wooden desk and make our decisions. I would then meet with the writers, trying to articulate things about style or plot that I was just coming to understand myself. Then came preparation of manuscripts, pasteup, design, printing, and proofreading, and the exciting day when my assistant editors and I drove to the printers to pick up boxloads of magazines.

We distributed *El Playano* across the campus: walking into the student union, the bookstore, the library, into departments and offices, into solemn places, given entrance with our magazines, probably too loud, like miners back from a long dig slapping bundles onto the assayer's counter. I had responsibilities: timetables, deadlines. I instituted subscriptions for alumni. I made pronouncements, this from my first issue: "Good writing is essential to good learning." I got us an interview with Ray Bradbury. I scouted and found some talented freshman writers. I was on the inside oiling a few gears:

> Now I'm a man
> I made 21

Every year Loyola sponsored a lecture for the faculty and the alumni. Students were not invited. The speaker for 1965–66 was the distinguished French philosopher and playwright, Gabriel Marcel. Mr. Johnson had told me about Marcel's *Homo Viator*, man the traveler, and I wanted to hear him speak. I sneaked into the auditorium through the exit at the north corridor and nestled in about halfway down the aisle. Mr. Johnson was just finishing his introduction. He turned to the left wing and announced Gabriel Marcel. The applause began, and a tiny, bent man scuttled out across the stage. He used a cane and tried to walk fast and his hips bobbed like pistons gone awry. He was white haired and looked to be seventy. Several times from wing to a desk at center stage he glanced out at the audience to acknowledge the applause. He was smiling—a happy smile, a smile that counterposed his body, all missteps and wild angles.

The auditorium was fairly small, so I could see Marcel's face clearly. I understood only bits and pieces of his speech—which was an attempt to distinguish his philosophy from existentialism—but it was not the text of the speech that pulled me in, it was the delivery. Once this old and crippled man settled into the safe confines of chair and desk, age and infirmity receded. His voice was strong and steady and his eyes were bright. He spoke with conviction and wit, and, for those moments anyway, it seemed that I was witnessing the pure mind that Yeats longed for. When Marcel hobbled out, he was ''a tattered coat upon a stick,'' but when he spoke I saw a body transformed, a promise that an aged person need not be ''a paltry thing''—that a life of the mind can bring with it at least momentary deliverance, an athletics of the spirit.

After my poor freshman year, my grades started their ascent. I did increasingly well through my sophomore year and managed to get all A's as a junior. That sort of rise, combined with my work on the campus literary magazine, made me a contender for a fellowship to graduate school. Loyola had a faculty committee charged with preparing promising seniors for fellowship applications, and they contacted me.

I could get strong letters from my teachers, but the committee believed that a further letter from an influential nonacademic—an industrialist or a judge or a legislator—would help my case, particularly with the more prestigious awards. I didn't know any such person, so they set out to have me meet a few people who were part of the wealthy Catholic network.

The first man who interviewed me was the president of an oil company with a branch in Los Angeles. His office was on Wilshire Boulevard near downtown, and when the secretary escorted me in, I entered a world of dark wood and leather and brass. I sat in a chair that took me deep into it. Across a wide expanse of mahogany sat a man in his fifties. He was pale and his white hair was perfectly trimmed and he wore a navy blue suit. He began asking me about my studies, speaking slowly and seemingly from someplace very far away. There was an ornate rifle mounted on the wall behind him. I talked about literature and philosophy and about the literary magazine, and he watched me. He asked several other questions and then shifted in his chair to ask me what I thought of the currently volatile Free Speech Movement. I said a few things in favor of the movement—academic bureaucracy, relevance, the kind of thing you'd expect—and something very quick happened to his face. The next question—one about a priest he knew at Loyola—was asked while he looked into his hands, which were lying, palms up and crossed, on his desk top. Then he thanked me, and the secretary—as if by magic—came through the door, smiled, and walked me out.

A week or so later, I was invited to join the dean and several faculty members at their lunch with a visiting speaker, a former member of the State Department under Jack Kennedy. I was seated across from the man just as the salads were arriving. I introduced myself, and he acknowledged the introduction and began to eat. He leaned over his plate, looking up when spoken to. I asked a few things about the Kennedys—superficial questions, for at that time in my life I had a *Reader's Digest* knowledge of the particulars of working politics. He answered briefly—not rude but not engaged—and returned to his food. Separate body parts were energized—an arm moving up and out from his side, fingers working away like a typist's on chicken amandine—but his face remained jowly and passive. His eyes were flat. When the watermelon arrived, he cut wedges with the knife in his right hand and spit the seeds into the fist of his left. Then he slowly opened his fist to run the palm over the edge of his plate, depositing the seeds.

I have no idea if either man wrote me a letter.

But this is a story with a happy ending. Not all my encounters with the world of academic gamesmanship were so chilly. Father Albertson encouraged me to play a long shot and apply for the big three—the Wilson, Danforth, and Rhodes—and I was lucky enough to get an interview for the Danforth. The Danforth Foundation, a philanthropic organization based in Saint Louis, leaned toward candidates who were planning a career in college teaching. The fellowships were prestigious: Your college had to nominate you, and 120 winners would be chosen from the 2,000 or so nominees.

My interview was set for nine o'clock in the Statler Hilton near downtown L.A. The buses were running late, and I had to transfer twice and sprint through the faded opulence of the Hilton's broad lobby. David Tyack was a historian from Reed College, and he greeted me at the door of his room and we sat by a window in the sun. Just the two of us. Tyack was a young man, academic, tweedy, but humane and engaging. We talked for over an hour about the philosophy I had been reading for Mr. Johnson, about the literary magazine, about my difficult first year at Loyola. I remember one moment particularly: me leaning forward into a stream of sunlight, my elbows on my knees, hands out, describing Gabriel Marcel's walk across the stage.

One year of good grades could never stack up against the best of the Danforth applicants, but Tyack wrote a strong report, and I received an honorable mention from the Danforth Foundation. A month or so later I got word from UCLA that I was awarded full support for three years of graduate study. Like those red A-minuses on Jack MacFarland's papers, the Danforth honorable mention read like a certification of ability. And I'd be going to UCLA. Good Lord. Four years before, I couldn't have shaken out their doormat.

I had promised to meet some friends at Mr. Pockets, a pool hall and pizzeria on Lincoln Boulevard close to Loyola. It was late in the evening, and I was finishing up the layout on the last issue of the magazine. I locked up the office and walked out of the student center into a thick fog. The lights from St. Robert's were out, and the lamps on Loyola Boulevard looked like big tufts of cotton stuck high up on invisible poles. I walked along the boulevard past the library; with its foyer lights left on, it seemed a glowing, fuzzy block floating back in the trees.

I was thinking about the magazine. About particular stories and how much I liked it, felt part of it, how hard it was going to be to leave it. A song lyric started drifting in and out of my thoughts:

> Me and my cat named dog.
> We're walking high against the fog . . .

I couldn't see more than a few feet in front of me, but the air was moist and it felt good to breathe it. The magazine. I started singing the lyric aloud, its silliness blending with the bittersweetness of parting. I was well past the library when my foot caught something. A white cloth on the ground. I bent over and picked a large pair of men's undershorts off the tip of my shoe. What story is this? I wondered, and kept walking, thinking, finally, about the bar and the friends waiting for me there, finding the song again, singing it louder now and twirling the underwear in rhythmic snaps over my head.

4

◆

The Poem Is a
Substitute for Love

Points of transition. The passage from South Vermont to Loyola began with me feeling angry and isolated—not knowing quite where to turn—and led toward a secure engagement with language and ideas, an engagement I wanted to shape into a career. The passage from Loyola to graduate school was one of great excitement, the major move that, I thought, would begin with deep study and lead progressively outward to work in the world. I had watched from the sidelines people whose lives seemed laden with meaningful pursuits, and I longed for such involvement. If you live long enough on South Vermont, you begin to feel not just excluded but out of the picture entirely. Ralph Ellison captured it perfectly for the black man with the metaphor of invisibility. Jack MacFarland, Frank Carothers, and the others created the conditions for me to use my mind to engage the world. What I wanted so strongly now was a program that would further develop my intellectual tools and equip me to . . . to teach? . . . to use books to change the lives of others? I was unsure about the specifics and naive about the realities of graduate study in America. Though twenty-two and sporting a baccalaureate, I sometimes felt like I was eighteen, fresh off the farm, a Dreiser character, entering an institution so large that Clark Kerr called it a multiversity. This was a vibrant life, filled with challenge. Years later I would work with freshmen who were just like this: wide-eyed, full of desire, simultaneously fretful and joyous. My attitudes about university life were destined to change dramatically,

but I could still understand—remember vividly—this transition to
UCLA from places where the clock seemed to tick more slowly.

Like those dazzled freshmen, I was taken, as well, by the surroundings of the campus, all the incidental enjoyments of living
in a place away from home. John Connor, my compatriot from
South L.A., and I and two of his friends rented a two-bedroom
apartment at the Sherry Terrace on Glenrock Avenue. The Sherry
Terrace has since been leveled; it was a nondescript old place with
eight units, a laundry room, and a pale blue front wall pitted at
bumper level with irregular holes. John and I would wend our
way into Westwood Village to window-shop or see a movie or
buy groceries. At the center of Westwood was Mom's, the con-
summate college bar. Mom's was on the second floor of a defunct
bowling alley, and you entered from a dingy stairwell into a click
clack of sawdusted rooms, each dark and malarial in its sanita-
tion. Across from the bar was the jukebox, glowing blue and orange, and you could lay your arm across its warm dome and
watch as the cockroaches outbopped the buzzard and the oriole.
Back, then, up Glenrock on beery wings to the Sherry Terrace
where, as luck would have it, only two apartments were rented
by males. We lived in Apartment Number Eight, upstairs in the
rear, so we thought of all sorts of reasons to walk by the other
units to get to our door: "Hi, got a schedule of classes? A cup
of sugar? Change for the dryer? A blue Corvair? A pocketful of
miracles?" We got to know everyone within a few weeks and
soon we were finding plates of cookies at our doorstep. Do I have
to tell you how wonderful that was?

Come morning and John and I would walk back down Glenrock to Strathmore Drive, slipping into a tan and brightly accou-
tred flow of young humanity making its way up Circle Drive and
onto the campus. UCLA was massive. At Loyola I could throw a
baseball from English to Math-Sciences. Now it took ten minutes—at a fast clip—to walk from the Research Library to John's
cubicle in Geology. Loyola had one library; UCLA had nineteen:
one for physics, one for architecture, one for medicine, one for
art. . . . There were vending machines and bike racks and giant
drooping eucalyptuses and fern pines everywhere, and traffic
crisscrossed the campus. When the hour hit and classes were dismissed, you would have thought you were jostling through the
L.A. Airport on a Friday afternoon. We would take Janss Steps

two at a time and ascend to the main quadrangle in front of Josiah Royce Hall, then John would go south and I would go north to English, where a mind-boggling world was opening up to me.

Professor Ralph Cohen spoke with a Brooklyn accent, and when he spoke he did so with the severity of an Old Testament prophet, pounding the podium with his fist, cocking his head and leaning forward to glare at us and level his charge against rival literary theorists. "Aristotle," he said during the first week of class, "is in serious difficulty." Aristotle—in difficulty?! That knocked me out. Don Johnson and Father Albertson certainly took issue with the philosophers and critics we were studying, but Professor Cohen seemed to be taking it all personally—he looked like my uncles when someone crossed them. Aristotle and Kant and Eliot pissed Cohen off. How could they think so sloppily? How could they not see the issue as he was now setting it before us? He jerked them back from the grave, woke them up just to slap them around. "Aristotle," he repeated, "is really in trouble."

Charles Gullans always wore some sort of tweed jacket and a huge pair of saddle oxfords. The course was Bibliography, ten weeks devoted to library research methods: the reference books and periodicals, the tricks and techniques of doing literary scholarship. Professor Gullans had a nice if distant way about him, sitting on the edge of the desk, one foot dangling, his forearm resting on his thigh. His voice was sonorous, and long, flourished sentences came from his mouth perfectly formed. He introduced us to *The Keats-Shelley Journal*, the *Nineteenth Century Reader's Guide*, *The International Index*, *Victorian Studies*, *Literature of the Renaissance*, *The Index of Middle English Verse*, and books whose titles I couldn't pronounce, much less read: the *Bibliographie de la littérature française du moyen-âge à nos jour*, and the *Bibliographie der Deutschen Zeitschriften-Literatur*. He discussed at length the procedures of advanced research: tales of meticulous quests for elusive sources. He described the precursors of the modern book—folios, quartos, and octavos—and summarized for us several famous manuscript studies. He taught us the reference librarian's terms of art. All this involved a number of small assignments and led to our major project: the compiling of an original bibliography on some literary figure. An original bibliography. That would mean finding, verifying, and recording hundreds and hundreds of books and articles and books and articles about the books and articles. I would be concentrating, as I never had before, on the very tools and texts of the scholarly enterprise.

During that first year, I took courses in bibliographic methods, the Romantic poets, American literature to the twentieth century, modern American literature, literary criticism, the Renaissance, and a seminar on Herman Melville. I also took a course to prepare me for one of the language requirements; we would have to know two, and I chose French as my first. The reading list for Modern American Literature had 164 items on it, and 33 were required for the ten-week course: three novels or plays or collections of poems or critical studies per week. The Renaissance list had 177 items on it, and 53 were required. This was deep reading at full tilt, a sprint with lead survival gear strapped to your back. It made sense to me when I later found out that, in the academy, a résumé was called a curriculum vita, or a biobibliography. Nobody made any bones about the fact that your biography, your vita, your life became the record of all you had to say about the particular booklists you had made your own.

My pre-twentieth-century American literature course covered the major works by the major figures, but it also surveyed a long list of writers wrapped in the shroud of history: Michael Wigglesworth, Hugh Henry Brackenridge, Royall Tyler, Augustus Baldwin Longstreet, Lafcadio Hearn. We looked at the minor works of the major authors as well: I discovered Melville's novel of the South Pacific, *Omoo*; his long, strange, rambling poem, *Clarel*; and his neglected stories, "Cock-a-Doodle-Doo," "The Tartarus of Maids," and "Jimmy Rose" ("God guard us all—poor Jimmy Rose!"). But it wasn't just a time to accumulate facts, though we certainly did that. It was also a time for widening the frame of reference within which to consider a work of art. My notebook for Modern American Literature, for example, had twenty dense pages on Theodore Dreiser that included information about his life and the historical context in which he wrote, dates of publication and discussions of the successive drafts of several of his novels, and surveys of the major critical works on him. We were being shown how to consider a novel or poem—how it's written, what it says, how it was received—in terms of the social and historical context out of which it came.

We also learned to refocus the lens to the micro level, looking very closely at a single work, poetry especially. I had learned to read poems carefully from Frank Carothers and Father Albertson. But this was different—I almost said more exacting, though that's not quite it. It was different because the unstated agenda was that we should come up with an original interpretation, argue that what seems fairly simple is really complex, that traditional readings miss the point, that yet another reading is possible. We would examine a poem, then, with great care and cleverness—scrutinizing sentence patterns, meter, images, and alternate meanings of words to support our argument. One of my papers from this time was a ten-pager on the way the subordination of clauses in Shelley's "Hymn to Intellectual Beauty" supports and illustrates the epistemology he proposes in *A Defense of Poetry*. This was hardball.

In some ways, I was prepared. I had received good training at Loyola in the areas I cared about: the twentieth-century American novel, modern poetry, and Shakespeare. And I had learned to read closely. But there were whole stretches of English literary history that I knew little about: eighteenth-century poetry, Victorian prose, Chaucer, Milton, the seventeenth century. Most of my fellow graduate students could read another language; I could not. My writing, by now, was pretty good, but it contained the telltale signs of its origins: sociolinguistic gaffes (using *different than* rather than *different from*, *lie* for *lay*, *drug* for *dragged*) and run-of-the-mill misspellings (*Isreal, aquaint, prestiege*) as well as confusions that elicited from my professors witty jabs in the margins: writing *emersing* for *immersing* or *chaplin* for *chaplain*—a blunder that, in this context, was like having your fly open at a cotillion. I started keeping vocabulary lists, for I daily heard and read words that were foreign to me: *beguile, nib, dapple, reify, kismet, culpable, damask, crimp, evanescent, denizen, piquant, lassitude, skein, diffident.*

Most of the first-year graduate students were friendly—the pressure of the program brought us together in manic goodwill—but what soon emerged among them, and certainly was present in older students, was a fierce competitiveness. It became clear to me that the production of knowledge in graduate programs like this was more than a calling, it was a contentious enterprise. It was in this arena that I was most ill equipped. My father was a quiet man laid low by illness, and my mother was silenced by hard work. And for all their classroom challenges, Jack MacFarland and Frank Carothers and the rest didn't really encourage competition. My ill-fated debate with Brian Kelly—in Mr. Johnson's General Ethics course—was my one previous encounter with high-powered disputation, and I got hammered. Around my third month at UCLA, I had to prepare a discussion of a short poem for Twentieth-Century American Literature. I chose one by Robert Frost. My presentation went smoothly, and it was followed by a brief period for questions. A fellow in the back, bespectacled and severe, said it was clear that I was misreading the last four lines and forcefully wondered if I had considered the interpretation he then put forth. I felt that old bite in my chest. Brian Kelly. I repeated a few things I had said earlier but was going blank fast. Fortunately, the professor was annoyed and slipped in and nailed the guy. I wondered for weeks if my explication was adequate or an embarrassment. Did I need protection, or was the professor miffed for his own reasons? Whatever the case, it didn't take much for the podium to crack and send all my insecurities flooding back over me.

I would get up early and read at the kitchen table in our apartment and then join up with friends and walk to class. After class I would go to the library, supping on Hormel chili and candy bars and Cokes and corn chips from the vending machines in nearby Bunche Hall. The library lights would flick on and off at a quarter to ten, and I would pack up my books and sidle through turnstiles out into the night air stiff and logy—my cortex bloated with print—and walk fast across the campus and back to the comforts of Sherry Terrace. One of my roommates was an Iowa farm boy named Norm who kept things tidy and could cook "American style." I would round the corner of Glenrock and run up the stairs at Sherry Terrace to hear someone warbling that love disappears overnight and inhale the vapors of a ham or a meat loaf or a tray of cookies. I still have a note from Norm that says: "Mike, there's two pork chops in the oven."

And so it went. A great deal of isolated time in the library, some postadolescent joy at Mom's, and some wonderful conversations with my neighbors. I would lean against the banister in the hallway or sit on the front steps talking to them: a wealthy dancer from New York, a graphics designer who taught me something about Judaism, an apartmentful of Chicanos who were the pride

of their bordertown high school and who later became my roommates, a black kid who slighted every course but chemistry, a
sweet and caring girl named Maria, a very bright med student
named Hendrickson who would go on to be a professor at Stanford, and a towheaded Motown enthusiast who—even in notes
to the mailman—called himself Capt. Soul. It's no surprise that
the faces and the hallways and all the emotional bric-a-brac from
that apartment building have developed a musical quality in my
memory—a joyous synesthesia in which touch and sound play
off each other like a light and airy melody.

I was on a fellowship, but I had to do something for spending
money. I started working for the guy who managed our building
and a number of the other buildings around us. I kept the
grounds and did minor repairs: clogged drains, cracked windows, toilets that kept running, that sort of thing. Most of the
work was between-quarter preparation of apartments as one
stream of students rushed out and another rushed in: scrubbing
resolute stains off toilets and sinks and floors, patching holes left
by pictures and shelves, slapping the landlord's cheap white
paint on the walls.

As I was stacking mattresses or cleaning out closets or yanking
a couch out to the middle of the floor, I would find a sock or an
earring or a page from a diary or a scarf with flowers and crescent
moons. Some of this was junk—left for someone else to throw
away—but some had been lost, hidden in the crevices that trap
the bits and pieces of our affairs. I'd lean the broom against the
wall and hold them—like a nightclub seer divining a life from car
keys—and wonder about the owner. Who passed through here?
What fragment of life did a diary page reveal? ''. . . we drove
straight through to S.F. and Jim kept wanting to stop and I kept
saying no, no, no Sweetie, I wanna get to the Fillmore. And we
did.'' It is impossible to determine exactly how our abilities
develop, but I suspect that my desire to write poetry shaped itself in these apartments. The quiet, empty rooms and the cast-
away pieces of other people's lives were soon evoking other
rooms in earlier houses, feelings and events that somehow
blended with the music that had caught my ear since childhood.

When I was introduced to poetry by Jack MacFarland and Dr.
Carothers, I was drawn to T. S. Eliot's sharp images, the lyrical

play in e. e. cummings ("who knows if the moon's / a balloon coming out of a keen city / in the sky . . ."), and the tight shapes of William Carlos Williams:

> the back wings
> of the
> hospital where
> nothing
> will grow lie
> cinders
> in which shine
> the broken
> pieces of a green
> bottle

But way before the printed poem was the radio dial, the only lyrical index I had on South Vermont. The lamentations of Hank Williams and Kitty Wells, the phrasing of the blues, the rhymes and rhythms and sent-from-God saxophone breaks of rock 'n' roll—this was the score on which T. S. Eliot and Dr. Williams played: honky-tonk angels and hot-rod Fords and trucks on a lost highway; rivers of whiskey and ducks that would dive to the bottom and never, never, ever come up; lips as sweet as "petals falling apart"; a hotel on Lonely Street where "the desk clerk's dressed in black"; a beleaguered soul who feels like "a one-eyed cat peeping in the seafood store." This, I think, is where it started. And a room, quiet but for the running water, and a lost object wedged between the cushions of a couch would shuttle me back inside some ruminative core. I would hold the earring or the scarf or the page of someone's diary, and familiar longings and distant lyrics and musical cadences would reify into an image at the center of a poem.

I did very well that first year. I got one B; the rest were A's, and I got to know several professors. Leon Howard was an old-style Southern academician—simultaneously homey and sophisticated—who had written a number of books and articles, a graceful biography of Herman Melville among them. Frank Lentriccia was brand-new, a very young Ph.D. who would go on to become a major literary theorist, and he taught me some valuable things about close, close reading. Professor Gullans thought that the bibliography I did for his class could be made publishable, and that I should continue working on it. And Howard and Lentriccia told me that a paper I had written on Melville's story "Bartleby the Scrivener" was just about ready for print. The fact that I didn't follow up on their suggestions, I realize now, was a sign that something was wrong. At first, the disillusionment was probably at trace level: a daydream during a lecture, a fleeting sadness in the library. But as the year slipped along toward summer, other things happened that were harder to ignore.

One of the books I had to read for Twentieth-Century American Literature was Sherwood Anderson's *Winesburg, Ohio*, a series of sketches about dreamy and dislocated people in a small Midwestern town. I thought the stories were wonderful; they reminded me of some of the men I had known on South Vermont. I went to see the professor to talk about the stories. He was nice but reserved and told me a little bit about a critical study of Anderson I should read. He also recommended one of Anderson's novels, *Poor White*. He told me that he thought Anderson's sentimentality limited him, and he wondered aloud if there might be a dissertation topic for me in some of the novels that the critics had neglected.

After my first quarter, I was invited to see the chairman of the department. He explained that he liked to keep tabs on the department's fellowship students, and he wanted to see how I was doing. I had started making my first real passes at writing poetry and had simultaneously been studying modern American poetry. I told him that I thought my own writing was making me understand something that I hadn't quite understood before about the poems I was studying in class. He smiled and continued, explaining about the departmental exams and what courses I should be taking to prepare myself for them. He was cordial and helpful, but by not addressing it, he made clear to me the department's attitude toward my own direct involvement with the writing of poetry versus the analysis of it.

Two of the graduate students I made friends with were Rich McBriar and Steve Drinkard. McBriar was corduroy and shuffly and balding; Drinkard was curly and given to sprees of wiry enthusiasm. Language washed over them. McBriar never met a poem he didn't like; he always found something—an image, a turn of phrase—to excite him. We'd be reading, say, the colonial

American religious poet Edward Taylor, and I'd be grumbling about the arcania and the piety. McBriar would lightly touch my shoulder and say: "Yeah. Yeah, I know. But look at these two lines here: '. . . dye the same in heavenly colors choice, / All pinkt with vanisht flowers of paradise.' Now, that's nice, isn't it?" By the third quarter, both McBriar and Drinkard were making plans to leave the program. "It's deadly, man," McBriar said, hunched over a beer at Mom's. "They could give a shit if you like this stuff. They could GIVE A SHIT."

When you walked out of the Research Library at closing time, you were hit with the fragrance of jasmine and the light greens and dark yellows of shrubs and ferns, wet from the sprinklers, bright from ground-level spotlights. Angle right and across the broad patio that led from the library and you would see jacarandas heavy with purple flowers rising above the benches where students ate their lunches. You would also pass the English Building. I passed it a hundred times and started to notice that some of the lights were on. The illuminated panes were sharp among the jacarandas. One of the poems I read that year was Wallace Stevens's "Arrival at the Waldorf." Stevens was consumed by the tension between the vital but uncontrollable natural world versus the crafted and orderly but artificial world of art. And this poem was quintessentially Stevens; he represented the wildness of nature with lush Guatemalan jungles and opposed them dynamically to the architecture of New York's Waldorf Hotel. My professors spent endless hours with their books. Some were in their offices as I was going home, reading *Macbeth* or *Moby Dick* again, but more often a book you would find only in the card catalog of a research library. They pursued the little-known fact, the lost letter, the lucky fissure in language that invites one more special reading. It was not uncommon for me to spend eight hours a day in the library—and for a while that was fine, for I was learning so much—but when I began to think of a career of those eight-hour days, to think of the unending drive to find one more piece of intellectual property, something went cold within me.

"The wild poem is a substitute / for the woman one loves or ought to love," says Stevens. And the poem's suitors—or, more exactly, the suitors to the anthology in which the poem rests amid its critical gloss—will spend decades at her hem, and she will take from them and take from them, and though she promises much, she is, contra Stevens, not particularly wild. The scholar will write and write and only a few will know, for the world of this romance is very narrow, solipsistic. It is focused back forever on itself, an endless regress, like an Escher print, of readings and readings about readings read by a few suitors in a few other private rooms behind purple jacarandas. I began to feel more and more a desire to open the door, to go out and read the world: "alien, point-blank, green and actual."

I didn't know what to do. I talked with Leon Howard about the possibility of stopping at the master's-degree level and teaching in a junior college. He was understanding in his gentlemanly way, and he said he'd be glad to write me a letter of recommendation. But, all in all, he thought I was making a mistake. I drove out to see Dr. Carothers. He recognized the disillusionment but assured me it would pass. "It's just that you've got such a good fellowship, Mike. Please think it over." "I have been, really, and I'm stuck," I said. "I don't know what the hell to do." There was more I should have told him, but I didn't know how to go about it. It seemed so strange and personal. The tight partitioning of the library carrels, the vacant hallways of the English Department, the solitary meals—leaning against a vending machine rehearsing to myself the names of the Italian Neoplatonists or Van Wyck Brooks's line of argument in *The Ordeal of Mark Twain*: All this was becoming a variant of hiding away in a house-trailer on South Vermont, reaching into a dusty breach of "The Drunken Boat" to underline the isolated cries of Arthur Rimbaud.

I began wondering about psychology. Three years before, Mr. Johnson had introduced me to Maslow's *Toward a Psychology of Being*, and since that time psychology had tugged on my thoughts. One of the things that drew me to Maslow was his ability to marshal evidence from fields as diverse as anthropology, cybernetics, theology, and biology to support his optimistic vision. Would coursework in psychology enable me also to turn scholarship out onto human affairs? I thought about this through spring and finally decided that I had to take a chance, that I had to find out. I could take a leave of absence from graduate study for one year and still have my fellowship held for me. I could pick up where I had left off. How else would I know? So I signed up for courses in the Psychology Department. My only previous coursework was a flimsy introduction during my first year at Loyola, so I had to take a series of upper-division surveys before I could apply for graduate study. Over the course of a year, I took Abnormal Psychology, Learning, Developmental Psychology, Perception, and Social Psychology. I also took a seminar on theories of alienation in the Sociology Department. It felt a little strange to be an undergraduate again, sitting in large lecture halls, sunk down deep in the seat. But it wasn't the end of the world. And it certainly was less pressured than graduate study in English.

My hope was that these courses would give me access to the work that Maslow had opened up to me: the study of human growth; the fusion of religion, psychology, and philosophy into a science of values; the contemplation "of the basic human predicament, that we are simultaneously worms and gods." What I got instead was a bit more of the worm's-eye view. Learning took me on a strange tour through behaviorism: cats in puzzle boxes, rats in complex mazes, John Watson scaring the bejesus out of Baby Albert with white rats and loud noises, Clark Hull creating theories of human behavior with the language of classical mechanics. Social Psychology was built on studies of voter behavior, social power, and attitude change. Abnormal Psychology looked systematically at mental illness and offered a set of classification schemes and a variety of psychotherapies for deviant behavior. Perception was pretty much neurophysiology: sensory inhibition, Mach band phenomena, iconic storage, and the like. I was being introduced to the world of academic social science, and it was not what I had expected.

I would read my textbooks and then, on my own, hunt down books that were more directly concerned with the study of health and human possibility. I read all of Maslow. I found other theoretical psychologists and psychotherapists who were also trying to advance an affirmative study of mind: Carl Rogers's *On Becoming a Person*, Rollo May's *Existential Psychology*, Viktor Frankl's *Man's Search for Meaning*. And they, in turn, led me to thinkers in other fields. A Maslow footnote sent me to the library to browse through books on the creative processes of mathematicians and scientists. Another reference had me reading Kurt Goldstein's studies of the cognitive consequences of brain injury. One of my great finds was the Jewish theologian Martin Buber, who seemed to be speaking right to me in his epigrammatic prose:

> . . . if there were a devil it would not be one who decided against God, but one who, in eternity, came to no decision.

> He who truly goes out to meet the world goes out also to God.

All this was going on in the late sixties, so, of course, I dabbled as well in the Westernized Zen of Alan Watts, heard Timothy Leary's psychedelic prayers, read, openmouthed, Carlos Castaneda's apprenticeship to a Yaqui medicine man, put my fingers in the crack between worlds. There were fatuous moments. I borrowed some money, went to Esalen, a "growth center," and heard people seduce each other with breathy catchphrases; in a mineral pool under a Big Sur sky, I waded gingerly out of the clutches of a hairy psychiatrist from Oregon. I learned something about the difference between a serious and quiet pursuit and a popular movement. Humanistic psychology—and particularly the so-called human potential movement that mutated from it—has come under a good deal of legitimate criticism, and I have to agree, but with a reservation. For though I too would eventually tire of the superficial offshoots, my reading of Maslow and Rogers and the others enabled me to counter the profound enviromental messages I had received on South Vermont. I was surrounding myself with a discourse of possibility rather than succumbing to images of defeat.

It was a year of casting about. And, despite my grumbling, hindsight allows me to add that Learning and Social Psychology and the rest of it turned out to be beneficial in unexpected ways. In the mid-1960s, many academic psychologists were doing their work with the aid of experimental designs: ways to test hypotheses that were adopted from the sciences, agronomy particularly. In the most typical design, the experimenter separates a group of subjects into two or more groups. One group is exposed to some sort of treatment (ranging from electric shock to a teaching method) that is withheld from the other, control, group. A statistical test is then run to determine what the odds are that the results obtained came about because of the treatment. And it is crucial to identify and account for all other possible causes of the results, for if the experimenter doesn't, another researcher will.

My reading in humanistic psychology was sensitizing me to the problems with such a mechanical approach to human thought and feeling, but I developed some valuable habits of mind by reading about these attempts to separate out aspects of human behavior and control them experimentally. Too much of literary study involves the unique reading, the clever association, the felicitous turn of phrase, the witty leap from one premise to another. Certainly experimental psychologists covet ingenuity as well, but training forces them to achieve it within a system that makes them slog along, ticking off each variable, each possible explanation for a result. It was good tonic for me to watch this. I learned to be cautious and methodical. And I began to appreciate the remarkable complexity of human action and the difficulty of attributing causality to any one condition or event. This would prove to be most valuable when I later entered the world of education. As with so many reductive pursuits, the academic psychology I studied taught me a great deal by what it could not do.

There is another element to my education during these years. I received a steady stream of letters from a half dozen or so people I had gotten close to at Loyola and met on arriving in Westwood: Mike Casey, my mentor on Loyola's literary magazine; Art Mitz, whom I'd known since high school; Pete Boland and Jack Hailey and Jeff Thornton, three friends from Loyola's brain trust; and Linda Peinhardt, a long-legged, athletic beauty who lived down the street on Glenrock Avenue. They were curious and disquieted, and they traveled across the country and through Europe and North Africa, alone or with lovers, consumed with a desire to study under a famous teacher, or to live in an exotic place, or simply, in Linda's words, "to be gone." They were young and, despite the postures of cynicism they sometimes adopted, they were painfully idealistic. When I met these people, I was the least adept of the lot. But we were drawn to each other—I had a South L.A. rambunctiousness, I suppose, and, to be sure, a passion for this mental thing—and I am blessed that we connected, for I learned a great deal from them, in person and in letters. They conducted a postgraduate correspondence school in politics, social theory, and the literature that was just then hitting the book-racks. And they helped me with my writing. The letters, I realize now, were each a looking glass, and the image they reflected confirmed my membership in an intellectual world. Here's Casey, writing in a blue aerogram that tells me, in Gaelic, how to peel it apart: "Rose, baby, I gave you your start, so I expect you to float a few bucks my way when you get your first Guggenheim." It would be a long time before I knew what a Guggenheim was, but it didn't matter, for I caught in Casey's minor jocularity a major declaration of faith.

The letters contained book lists. Linda telling me to go out and buy what I could find of the black experimental novelist, Ishmael Reed. Art Mitz, studying intellectual history at Stanford while driving a cab in Oakland, "revising our literary agenda: scratch *The Magus,* add Borges." (Sending me, as well, a Xerox of the cover of Richard Brautigan's *Trout Fishing in America*.) Pete Boland clipping to his letter a copy of a poem by Don L. Lee: "ultra cool was bop-cool / ice-box cool so cool. . . ." Jeff Thornton writing from a fourteenth-century abbey to tell me about William Burroughs's *The Soft Machine.* And Jack Hailey taking a year abroad at the Centre for Cultural Studies at Birmingham, writing me aerograms crammed with type and crabbed handwriting along all four margins. He told me he was reading Wittgenstein, Durkheim, and Levi-Strauss, names I hadn't heard of but that I suddenly started to see, picking up *Philosophical Investigations* or *The Savage Mind* in the old College Book Company on Westwood Boulevard, leaning against a rack and losing myself in print, the smell of pine and new books in the air.

By now I was typing up the poems I had been writing over the past year or two and slipping a few into my letters. The poems had an interesting moment here and there: Jesus buying a six-pack, and a line like "your hands succumb to velvet," and a few tangible objects: toothbrushes and potatoes, a rearview mirror and a jade earring. But essentially these were verse melodramas about love and loneliness—sappy and imagistic, Tammy Wynette singing haiku. My epistolary friends became my first real audience, and through their encouragement and their criticism, they also became my first editors. "Get a jolt into the rhythm here if you can," writes Jack Hailey alongside a flat line. "Don't preach; you've got the answer before the poem begins," he scribbles on the bottom of another poem. Sometimes what I did worked for him: "This image is nice here." "I like this pun." "These lines have a real good rhythm to them." "Write more poems like this one." His criticism wasn't easy to swallow, and there were times when I jammed his letter back in its envelope and put it out of sight in a desk drawer. But his comments were precise, and, I soon had to admit, they were accurate. He was treating me like a serious writer. I started incorporating his suggestions into my poems. Art Mitz relied on a different tactic. He'd single out the poem that showed the most promise and sidestep the rest:

> Michael, I really liked the one about the Mexican girl. It made me jealous with its wit and irony. . . . I think your work will get overripe unless more poems like this one begin to emerge.

I would then look closely at Art's choice and compare it with the others I sent him. And gradually the goo started to drain out of my poetry.

And when the book lists and the literary critiques and the wordplay receded, the heart emerged. Linda writes from North Carolina, describing an old farmhouse she and her boyfriend are refurbishing: a garden, a potbellied stove, a sunporch. She is putting up peaches for the winter and fighting that ache to be gone again. Jack Hailey's letter comes from England. He has refused induction into the army. He is sitting at his desk trying to sound lighthearted, though he is "surrounded by stacks of letters to draft boards, lawyers, and General Hershey." Casey describes peace marches in Paris and Amsterdam. Boland details a Black Panther rally in Ann Arbor. And then a letter comes describing the painful breaks with family that all this yielded: "You don't know how much you've disappointed me," a father yells at his son. "I could never bring you around my friends." Finally, the message was loneliness. "Rose, you old metaphor you," writes Jack Hailey, inquiring about his truelove here in the states, "call up Sally and see how she is, would you? . . . Cheer her up. And tell her this—tell her that I'm a good guy, and that I think about her all the time. . . ."

I filled in the remaining blanks on my final examination for Perception, gathered up my books and pencils, and left the lecture hall. I was coming to realize over the last few months that I had been skirting around a harsh truth: Though my introduction to social science was not without its moments, graduate work in academic psychology wouldn't satisfy whatever vague thing it was that was fluttering within me. It would be a specialized and distant pursuit, no different, really, from studying the collected letters of a not-so-famous American author.

I walked out of Franz Hall and over to the Graduate Division, where I would sign the forms to resign from my fellowship and exit me from UCLA. There was a light drizzle in the works and the clouds were full, light and dark masses shifting in the late morning sky. I had read a newspaper article on the National Teacher Corps and had sent away for information. The Teacher Corps, a Great Society program, placed teacher interns in poverty-area schools. Maybe that would be the way to go. I turned into the administration building and down the main hallway to the Graduate Division. It didn't take long to complete the forms—they were brief, and the questions were simple. Ten minutes, maybe. I thanked the clerk and started home, down Janss Steps and toward the student apartments of Westwood.

The winds were starting up and splattering rain across the sidewalk. I walked along Strathmore and up Glenrock as though I were lost in thought, though nothing particular was at the center of concentration. The trees were shaking in the wind. By the time I reached the steps of Sherry Terrace, I was crying and the rain was falling hard. I couldn't make sense of this. I seemed distant to myself. It was midday and no one was around; I was the only one in the building. I walked up the stairs to my apartment, sobbing now and not believing it. A fellowship. A goddamned fellowship is doing this to me. Big deal. I unlocked the door and went in and lay face down on the bed. The rain was streaming off the roof drain and down along the window. I could see my father. His face was quiet, comatose, his cheeks soft and stubbled. His lips were open slightly. Dad? I slid my arms under his arms—he was hot and damp—and tried to sit him up in bed. Dad, sit up. Please. "Come on, Dad," I heard myself cry. "God dammit, Dad. Dad. Dad. Oh, Dad, I'm so sorry."

5

◆

Literate Stirrings

The sign announced that we could get our passport photos *and* our children's first communion pictures here—quickly. Next to it, above another storefront, hand-lettering invited us to visit—*visítenos*—for this was a wholesaler open to the public: *precios de mayoreo al público.* A little shop selling *artículos religiosos*—pictures, medals, and statues of Jesus and the Blessed Virgin Mary—was next to a dark, dark bar with a blond speaking Spanish on a Budweiser poster, and that bar was cheek-by-jowl to a *zapatería* with unclaimed, dusty shoes in the window below a promotional sign that read, in English, "invisible half-soling." It was all part of a walking tour of Brooklyn Avenue with Lillian, a compatriot in the Teacher Corps, who translated the Spanish along this busy East Los Angeles street with its mix of merchants and shoppers. The buildings were off-white and decorated in once-bright yellows, reds, oranges, and blues. Print was everywhere, neon, ornate lettering, and crude, hand-painted signs: *carnicería, farmacia, frutas tropicales, panadería, chorizos, camisas, tortillería.* There were many smells in the air, and they were strong and varied—mesquite, grilled pork, baking bread, leather, honeydew, wet wood, mothballs—and Norteña, the music of the north of Mexico—played loud from a record shop, its upbeat, choppy accordion counterposing lyrics of great sadness:

> *O tierra del sol*
> *suspiro por verte*
> *ahora que lejos*
> *yo vivo sin luz; sin amor*

"He's terribly homesick," explained Lillian. "He's saying he's living without light and without love. Pretty serious, huh?" *Quisiera llorar*, wailed the singers, *quisiera morir de sentimiento*.

The Teacher Corps separated its volunteers into teams, and each team was attached to school districts in depressed areas of the county. Lillian and I were part of a team of five: Joe Palacios and Monica de la Torre were the other two interns, and Benigno Campos, a seasoned teacher, was our supervisor. Lillian's father was Edward Roybal, a member of Congress and a longtime advocate of progressive social policy, so her involvement in Mexican American affairs started in her childhood. Lillian and I and the others had been together for two months now, and we would soon be going into the elementary schools of Ben's district in El Monte, a community eight or so miles to the southeast of Brooklyn Avenue. Concurrent with our internship, we would be taking courses at USC, the home base for the Los Angeles Urban Teacher Corps. We were in two of them then, Social Stratification and Sociology of Education, and we would continue taking courses for the next two years that, in various ways, were oriented to the work we would be doing in the schools.

Half a block down from the record store was a market that opened out onto the street. Crates of lemons and oranges and banana squash were shoved together along the sidewalk; the squashes were cut open, and webbed clusters of their yellow seeds spilled out onto the wood and concrete. Lillian stopped by a crate of *nopales*, the cactus that women strip and put up in bottles to marinate. "It was a special treat," she said, "to go to our grandmother's house for breakfast. She'd scramble little bits of nopales in with our eggs." Above the market was a row of small apartments. Some of the windows were cracked and held in place with masking tape that crisscrossed the glass. Others were smooth. And still others were decorated with lace curtains, tied carefully back. The window above the place where Lillian had parked her car had orchids on the sill and a cactus with bright red flowers.

Lillian walked over to the driver's side of her car while I waited at the curb, absentmindedly finishing off a bag of potato chips. A little boy and, I guess, his younger sister were trying to get a kitten out of an empty shopping cart. The kitten stayed fixed in a far corner out of their reach. The boy heard me saying something to Lillian as she was reaching across the driver's seat to unlock my door. He left his sister and ran up to me with his hand out: "Papitas, papitas." He grabbed the leg of my jeans and gave it a tug: "Papitas!" I gave him some chips just as his mother was walking out of a store. She stopped cold and stared at me. Lillian was watching this, opened her door, and rose half out of the car, smiling. She spoke to the boy's mother in Spanish, and the woman smiled back and called her son. I got in the car and asked Lillian what she said. "I told her that you were okay—for a gringo," and gave me a poke in the shoulder. "Let's go. There's one more place I want to show you."

We drove further down Brooklyn, passing more shops and cafés, and soon business started mixing with housing: faded bungalows and two-story Los Angeles houses, white and tan and gray. I was reminded of the quiet, old houses along the side streets of South Vermont. One place had a nice porch, and two old women were sitting on wood chairs cutting some sort of vegetable into pans set between their feet. Another house was built back from the street, thirty feet or so. Cars were parked at angles in the yard, and two men, bare-chested, were upholstering the front seat of one of them. Less than a mile from the heart of Brooklyn, we crossed Mednik. To the left of the intersection was a broad stretch of housing projects: rows and rows of run-down cottages that looked like old military barracks.

Lillian explained that these houses had been built in the early 1940s and had since become the bloodiest place in East L.A. It was generally believed that the police wouldn't go in there unless they had heavy support. If they went in at all. Kids were playing baseball and tag and war on the dirt and brown grass. Women were talking to each other from the front steps of their homes. Shirts and sheets were fluttering from makeshift clotheslines. Two cars were up on blocks. An old Ford pulled around our car and into the projects, and a man in grease-covered overalls got out and limped around back of the hut closest to us. "This project is called Maravilla," said Lillian. "And do you know what that means? It means 'the marvelous place.' Can you beat that?"

Many of the people in Maravilla hold onto the hope of moving into communities to the east: Monterey Park, San Gabriel, Montebello, Rosemead, El Monte. El Monte, my assignment, was

named in the 1860s and means "wooded land." From its chris-
tening down through the 1940s, El Monte had generated its income primarily through farming—walnuts and, later, cauliflower
and onions. Ben, my team leader, was born in one of the city's
agricultural settlements, a shantytown for migrant workers
named for the owner of the land on which it sat: Hicks Camp. A
few people still lived in Hicks, a blighted cluster of one-room
shacks, but El Monte had grown beyond its camps. It was a city
trying to do its best. The brochure from the historical society announced that El Monte's airport was among the seventy busiest
airports in the country and that Crawford's Country Store was
the biggest country store in the world.

Northern El Monte ranged from middle to upper middle class,
but the rest of the city had a high percentage of working-class
whites and poor Mexican Americans and Mexican nationals who
were laboring in warehouses and foundries and orange groves to
support families here and across the border. The Teacher Corps
required its interns to familiarize themselves with the neighborhoods in which they would work, to get to know the people out
of whose homes their students would come. This, I would discover, was a very special kind of teacher training. We visited social agencies and community groups. We talked with school
board members and principals, teachers and parents, conserv-
ative priests and militant Brown Berets. And we drove by and
drove by again the small white house with the chain-link fence
that was the headquarters for the American Nazi Party, a reminder of what poor whites were willing to do to explain away
their misery. Ben had made it out of Hicks, so he knew all the
local historians and all the nooks of their history. And he still
walked with a trace of the *cholo*: a hint of a slouch to the stride,
the right arm swaying slightly behind the butt. Ben and Joe, Monica and Lillian were all Mexican American, so I had the benefit of
linguistic and cultural guides.

In some ways, though, I wasn't a greenhorn. There were South
L.A. experiences that transferred to the East Side and to the
streets and back alleys of El Monte. But one poor slice of a county
is not another. All have different political histories, different cultural clashes, dreams shaped in different ways, different languages. When I was growing up, my mother worked on Broad-
way in downtown Los Angeles, about three miles from Brooklyn

Avenue. Six days a week, she took buses from South Vermont into the heart of the city and then, enervated and mechanical, she took buses back out of it. Her life did not radiate outward, and, for a long time, neither did mine. We were webbed in close, a four- or five-block stretch: the pet store at Ninety-second street, Palazolla's Market at Ninetieth, a long and venturous walk four blocks north to the Bank of America. There would be new landscapes for me to get to know. But as I walked along, watching the children or reading the signs with Lillian or, later on, as I drove with Ben down Santa Anita or through Medina Court, it seemed as if moments of personal history were being projected out onto the streets, reshaped and out of phase but familiar: the faces and buildings of an unsettling childhood dream.

One of the households I visited was that of Rosa Ramirez. Mrs. Ramirez had four children. The youngest was Lucy—Luz de Maria: Light of Mary. She was five years old, and Carlos, the oldest, was sixteen. Mrs. Ramirez's husband worked in a dairy, and on the weekends he laid tile, installed lawn sprinklers, cleared weeds, and did whatever else contractors would pay him under-scale to do. Mrs. Ramirez's kitchen table was adjacent to a small pantry, and as we sat at the table drinking a soda and talking about her children, I watched the wind move strings of garlic and oregano and dried red peppers hanging by the back door. Small bags of pinto beans and flour and lentils and jars of marinating vegetables were lined up on shelves around the stove. Above a large metal sink was a picture-calendar of Saint Martin de Porres, the mulatto Dominican who cared for the poor in the small towns of Peru. I hadn't seen my grandmother's house since I was a child, but this was it, one little view of it—garlic and peppers swaying in the breeze.

Mrs. Ramirez and I walked outside. The yard was fairly long, forty feet maybe. There was a garden: peppers, lettuce, chayotes, tomatoes, jalapeños, mint, a few cornstalks. To the side of the garden was a toolshed and a small garage. Behind the cornstalks was Carlos and his Saab. I had met Carlos during my first visit the week before; he looked up and said "hi" and turned back to the engine. He had a smudged and dog-eared repair manual propped open against the dirty windshield. The grass around the Saab was cut low, but right at the tires it was hubcap-high.

"How long has he been working on this thing?," I asked Mrs. Ramirez.

"Months," she said, smiling and shaking her head.

Along the left side of the car was a rectangular piece of gray tarp. On it were a distributor cap and its leads, a package of new sparkplugs, four or five screwdrivers, a set of wrenches, and a notebook opened to some sketches and scribbled writing. I asked Carlos about the notebook.

"It's really hard to get parts, so I make drawings and copy down stuff from the manual and go around to junkyards. Sometimes I find what I'm looking for. . . ." His voice rose quickly, "Oh, hey, listen," he said, straightening up and reaching for the manual on the windshield, "I can't figure this part out. What are these words?" He handed me the manual and pointed to "canister" and "detrimental" and "sector," the stilted English of translated technical writing. I explained them. He nodded, satisfied, and scribbled some notes in the margins of the manual. "Thanks a lot," he said and returned to the alternator.

Mrs. Ramirez and I walked back to the house. "Wouldn't it be a lot easier," I asked her, "for him to get an American car? Something that he could get parts for, quick—and cheap?" "Yes, I guess so," she said. "But don't you see? The Saab is very special to him. There are no Saabs in El Monte."

We four interns would be splitting our time between two elementary schools in the center of El Monte. Shops and small industries had built up around the schools, causing poor neighborhoods to slide even further. Right along the west side of one of the schools was a large appliance store, its parking lot extending to the fence of the schoolyard. Across the street was a run-down trailer court: One house-trailer was boarded up and weeds were growing high around cracked concrete slabs, foundations for trailers that had long since rolled away. Facing the entire north side of the school was a factory that manufactured metal fittings. Both the south and east boundaries were residential: Small one- and two-bedroom houses with cracked fences, weeds, wild roses, and nasturtiums. Several windows displayed handwritten signs advertising a room for rent. The school itself was a connection of one-story rectangles and prefab huts, a cross between light brown and dirty gold, built in the fifties and kept up, with a wide stretch of grass for baseball and football. In the mornings or at noon, you could always find children in the center of the yard playing tetherball and dodgeball and twisting themselves through various jungle gyms. Kindergarteners had their own little spread of grass where they rejoiced in a circular sandpit and coaxed teacher's aides to push their swings toward the sky.

Lillian, Joe, Monica, and I worked three days a week in El Monte; the other two were spent in the education classes at USC. Joe lived very close to the schools, so we would go to his apartment in the late afternoon to help his wife make extra dinner and to talk about teaching. Joe had a storeroom with a cot in it, so I sometimes slept there and drove into SC with him in the morning. We couldn't have full responsibility for instruction as we weren't yet credentialed, but we observed classes, aided teachers, and assisted with special projects. Patti Masters, an old friend from Westwood, made me three long ties, so I fit in visually with the professional staff. And, before very long at all, the teachers and the aides, the secretaries and the cooks and the custodians were treating us like part of their community. We ended up spending a lot of time around children, and that was particularly good for me. I grew up in a neighborhood of storefronts and retirees and wasn't all that familiar with the way kids learn and do. I joined the Teacher Corps for a variety of reasons: frustrations with graduate study, a desire to work with people, my draft board, which, once I left UCLA, was after me. But essentially I was moving away from dead ends more than being drawn toward children. I had a lot to learn.

There were many pleasant moments, and some disturbing ones. Glimpses into the realities of schooling. I was shooting baskets with a fourth-grade boy. He had a nice touch, a good sense of how to execute his shots. I was asking him questions about his schoolwork while we played, and he told me, matter-of-factly and without guile: "I used to be in the dumb math group, but then, um, my teacher found out it was too easy for me. So now I'm in with the smart kids." The groups, of course, had various nondescript names to hide from the children the truth that they divined immediately. I was beginning to understand scholastic folkways.

I got to watch a lot of teachers. The worst was Mr. Wilson. He was a young, frumpy-looking guy who was full of himself, and he treated his fifth-grade students like a cohort of mechanical clerks. He would have one of his best students read aloud a passage from a science or language arts textbook, then have all the students fill in the blanks on various mimeographed sheets supplied by the textbook publishers. Mr. Wilson explained to me that this method was supported by psychological theory: By having children fill in the blanks, he was ''reinforcing'' the material they heard read aloud. Poor Skinner, I thought, even his pigeons would shudder at this. While the good reader was reading, most of the other children were looking off into space—and many spaces on the sheets were left blank while children doodled in the margins. Fortunately, Mr. Wilson's methods were an exception. Most of the teachers I saw thought more carefully about learning and seemed to care about their children. And they certainly worked hard. It was not unusual to have a classroom of thirty children, many of whom needed a lot of attention. From what I could tell, the teachers spent a good deal of time considering their students' needs and abilities. I would later come to question the way they were trained to determine these needs, but even when that time came, I could not deny their commitment.

Several of the teachers were extraordinary. I first met Rosalie Naumann one afternoon in the teachers' lounge. Monica and I were sitting around with four or five teachers, and one began talking about a child in her class: "When we're doing social studies, she wants to draw, and when we're in the middle of an art lesson, she'll go over to the bookshelf. . . ." The teacher continued for a bit longer, expressing her frustration, when a somber-looking woman—short, tennis shoes, a close crop of gray hair—looked up and asked her why that bothered her so much. She didn't ask the question in a nasty way; in fact, it seemed an invitation to think the problem through. And the way the others responded made it clear that she held status in this lounge. I later found out that this was the school's reading specialist. I was also told that her kids loved her. I actually saw one of her students, a fifth-grade boy, slug a sixth grader who was not one of her students, for mocking the way she walked. I asked Ben to make sure that she was my master teacher. And Ben arranged it so that she was.

Two trailers had been rolled in onto the grass by the prefab huts, and Mrs. Naumann worked out of one of them. They were creaky and thin and close, and hers was filled to the point of clutter with maps and posters and children's drawings, art paper and crayons, hand puppets and vases and bowls. There were long shelves of books and a rangy philodendron had grown over the top row. The serious demeanor I saw in the lounge was also present in the trailer, and the kids took it just right: They would talk to her, for I suppose they sensed she cared. She looked at them when they spoke and always had her hand on their shoulders. They drew and wrote and read around the table. And I moved quickly from observing to helping her work with small groups. Soon after my arrival she was saying, "Mike, would you please get me that book?" or "Mike, listen to this story of Loretta's" or "Mike, would you mind working on Manuel's story with him?"

Somewhere toward the end of October of that first year, Rosalie suggested that I alter my routine of observing and assisting and start working directly with some kids who could use the extra help. I suppose she thought I'd be excited by the idea, but I automatically said no: "Isn't it too soon?" I asked, a little surprised at my reluctance. What if the kids didn't listen to me? I thought. What if, after all, I couldn't help them? I'd been protected up till now by Ben, by the safety of the team, by my observer status. I sounded like an echo in the teachers' lounge. Rosalie pooh-poohed my apprehension and said she'd take responsibility for me and work something out with the principal. She did. When she saw me the following week, she explained that she had selected fifteen of the school's poorest readers—fourth and fifth graders—and had arranged for me to meet with them in the cafeteria every Thursday after lunch.

I asked Rosalie for some guidance. She simply said, "Do something nice with them. Their lives are pretty dreary." And when I pressed her further, she said that the schools try things that don't seem to work, and she might speak too much with the voice of the schools. "You're closer to them than I am. Use music; use your poems. Do what you think is best." I went home, wanting to do something very special, but came up short. I sat at the desk I shared with my roommate, Matias, and sketched out, then crumpled up, ideas for lessons. I watched a cat pawing at butterflies in the courtyard. I looked absentmindedly around the room:

macramé, grape ivy, Huelga stickers, John and Yoko naked, Jimi Hendrix. All sorts of fantasies about my first solo teaching came and went, my anticipations ranging from Hellenic pastorals to feral colloquia danced around my severed head. "Do what you think is best," Rosalie had said, and after all that fretting, I quit trying to create the golden lesson and went with something simple I had seen her do: I'd have them write about pictures. I took a poster of John Kennedy from Matt's bulletin board. I clipped an advertisement from *Life* showing a little girl looking out of a single apartment window set in red brick. And, for spice, I peeled off my wall a particularly grungy photograph of Ron McKernan, aka Pig Pen, the hirsute keyboardist for the Grateful Dead.

The next day, as the lunch crowd was clearing out, I went to the far west corner of the cafeteria and pulled two tables together. Pots and tin trays were clanging over the whirr of dishwashers; the tables smelled sweet and oily. I leaned against the wall and thought back to a graduation party at my old grammar school. Crepe paper was twisted overhead, and there were dull metal bowls of Kool-Aid on folding tables. The smell was just the same.

The one o'clock bell rang. My students started walking in: scuffed pumps and knee socks, print dresses, sneakers and pants stained with grass, the odors of milk and exercise. They were quiet. Some looked apprehensive. I asked them to sit around the table, then I sat down on a stool that brought my knees up to belly level. I was a little nervous. I introduced myself, and they looked on. Some sat up straight, others slumped down in their chairs. No one was smiling. I explained that we would meet once a week, that we would tell stories and write stories, and that there would be no grades.

I then asked them to tell me a little bit about themselves: their hobbies, their friends, their pets. Things started to loosen up. A few smiles. Some relaxed postures. And that helped me relax. I got up slowly and took my three pictures out of their folder. "Do you ever watch people?" I asked them. "You know, really look at them and wonder about them? Well, here's three I want you to look at." I taped each picture to the wall. Kennedy first—and some of the children said his name to themselves. Then Pig Pen: oohs and ahs and giggles here. Then the little girl at her window. "She looks lonely," someone said. I asked them to take turns talking about the pictures. What did they see? What did they think each person was thinking? What would these people have to say to each other? To them? Some kids stayed silent. Others talked. A few got animated. I then asked them to pick a picture and write. Rosalie had warned me that some of the children were such poor writers that they'd get stuck right away on spelling, so I had better cool them out. I did. I repeated that their papers wouldn't be graded, that I wanted them to just write what came to mind and not worry if they couldn't spell a word. We'd fix that up later. Two kids still refused to write unless I helped them right then and there. So I spelled troublesome words for them. By the time we did all we had to do, they had about twenty-five minutes to compose.

Here's a sampling of what they wrote. First, on Pig Pen, who proved to be a big hit:

I think the hippy on the chair looks weird.

—JOEY

He needs a shower. The way he is sitting, he needs a haircut. He's too much.

—CASEY

He makes me lonely and he is creepy and ugly. And he has long hair and funny eye-glasses. He makes me feel lonely because he is in a big room.

—DORA

Anthony wrote about the little girl in the window and formatted his writing so that it looked like a poem:

> Very lonely in the world.
> No one will talk to you.
> Think about it.

And Juan chose to write on the picture of JFK:

John Kennedy is more important than any other person I know because he was going to make a good world. By stopping the war, that's why.

When the bell rang, the children scrambled out, and I walked around the table collecting their papers. Everything had gone well. They wrote for me. No disasters. I typed up the essays, correcting aberrant spelling and punctuation when necessary, and glued them onto individual pieces of art paper. Then I borrowed some masking tape from the office and hung them on the cafeteria wall.

All of these students had been judged poor readers and writers; at the least, they were reading one year below grade level. But within the group, there was quite a range. For two of the students, writing seemed a torture. They bent over their papers, holding their pencils tightly, chipping out one word, then another. Most of the other children weren't so badly off: there were misspellings and problems with commas (too many or too few) and some difficulty determining where one sentence should start and another should end, though this seemed to me to result from confusion about the rules of capitalization. Only in one case was a student's writing composed of one streaming, boundless sentence and words spelled in unusual ways—for example, a vaguely phonetic *woun* for *when*. I'm not sure exactly what I expected, but most of what I read was better than I thought it would be.

The days after this first lesson had a nice feel to them. I was still a little unsure, but could tell that our one brief hour made me a part of things in a way I hadn't been before. The kids would come up to me in the playground and ask what we were going to do next week—as though I knew!—or toss me a basketball and invite a free shot at a netless hoop. The real kick came when I walked through the cafeteria a few days after our lesson and saw two of my students showing their posted essays to a third child who was not in our group.

The posters and pictures worked well, so I asked Rosalie if she thought that it would be a good idea to supply magazines and let the children find pictures of their own. She said that sounded fine. On the next Thursday I met the class with a box of scissors and a pile of old magazines: *Sports Illustrated*, *Life*, and a *National Geographic*. I told them what I wanted them to do and turned them loose: "Do what you did last week, but this time you find a picture that you like."

Hilda cut out a photo of a longhaired flutist sitting under a tree, but could write no more than a single associative sentence:

I saw a hippy in the park.

Joey found a picture of *Apollo 9*:

The Apollo 8 went around the world, and Apollo 9 went around the moon. If you were in there, it would make you feel dizzy.

Lupe was taken with a wispy advertisement of two women in wedding gowns walking through a forest:

The picture is of a summer when the colors were beautiful and clothes were hot for girls because they were long. But no more! Now dresses are short and summers are cool.

Eduvina wrote about a photograph of a doctor talking with a patient:

Doctors help you when you are sick. You help your friends and your friends help you. Your friends help you get out of jail.

And Jesus, a migrant worker's son who was struggling with English, found a photograph in *National Geographic* of a forest in winter:

The snow is very pretty and I wish I could live there.

The most interesting piece of writing was Mark's, a response to a color photograph of a doctor delivering a baby:

The doctor is helping a baby to get out from the mother because it is in danger from the blood. If the baby came out, he will look red. It will be so funny that the mother will sell her baby to the Indians. The baby will grow up and hunt animals like deer, bear, and birds.

Mark's black hair was thick and rich, and he had a small, precise crescent scar on his right cheek. He spoke up readily, and the other children seemed to like him. This was his second year at our school. After the session, Rosalie told me his story. At his previous school, his entrance IQ tests had yielded a score of 62. Retarded. He had a slight lisp that used to be more pronounced. The kids in the other school used to tease him about it, so he stopped talking. Rosalie speculated that his silence probably confirmed the low assessment of his intelligence.

That evening I had dinner at Joe's house. Joe and Lillian were sitting in the front room working on a social studies lesson, and Monica was arranging folding chairs around the card tables that she would soon be covering with white cloth. Sheilah, Joe's wife, was stirring the sauce for our pasta, and I was peeling carrots and cucumbers for a salad. Monica was telling a story about one of the girls in her school, a precocious fifth grader who showed up that morning in nylons and high heels.

"She could barely walk in those things. She just wobbled along with a big smile on her face. And the—the *nylons*. The nylons were *way* too big. They were probably her sister's, and they sagged all over."

"Did anybody say anything to her?," Lillian asked from the other room.

"Well, yeah, sure. The vice-principal came over and took her aside. But, God, what a sad sight. There must have been ten runs in those stockings. She's trying to grow up, and she doesn't have a clue."

"The pasta's done," announced Sheilah, pouring it into a colander. I opened a can of sliced olives and spread them over the salad, and we sat down to eat.

During the week, the children had been taking one of the many standardized tests that are a part of life in elementary school, and Joe, whose keen eye didn't miss much, had been helping the teachers administer it.

"What got me was that a lot of the kids were just kind of fiddling around. I mean here is this test, and it's gonna go into your file, and it's gonna follow you around, and—it just didn't mean anything to them."

"Well, why should it?" asked Lillian. "I mean, what's it got to do with anything in their lives?"

"Yeah, yeah, I know. But I just kept thinking about how I used to get all cranked up about these things, and, well, I mean the point is that these tests will be cited when people talk about the low IQ of minority kids and all that bullshit. From what I saw, it only measures how well they want to play the game."

I had been thinking about Mark all day, so I started retelling Rosalie's story. For whatever reason—bad day, bad English, bad test—Mark had scored in the range of the mildly retarded. "And what gets me," I said, "was that the kid had clammed up to protect himself from the other kids, and all the while his silence was confirming what the *test* said!" It was lucky for him, Lillian pointed out, that his parents moved. Files precede kids, but at least he got a second chance with new classmates. Lillian knew who Mark was, and she thought he looked happy and alert. "If Mark's IQ is 62," she said into the steam rising off her pasta, "then I'm Baboo the Chimp."

Because of the Thanksgiving holidays, I wouldn't be meeting with my students for several weeks. I was surprised by the response I had gotten to some pretty simple assignments, and it seemed time to try something a little more ambitious. I began to wonder what would happen if I asked the children to write about pictures of themselves. There was an audiovisual specialist at USC who kept urging the Teacher Corps interns to use his equipment, so I checked out a camera and picked up some Ektachrome. For two days I roamed around the school looking for interesting shots: I caught Joey on the monkey bars and Casey spiking the tetherball; Esther posed for me, hand on hip, by the cafeteria door; Anthony and Jesus never even looked up from their game of marbles; Rosalie Naumann contributed her wistful smile. By the time we met again, I had put together a low-budget slide show. I used one of the school's old record players and, while playground images flicked across the cafeteria wall, I played "Everyday People," Sly Stone's funkish plea for tolerance and racial harmony:

> There is a blue one
> who can't accept the green one
> for living with the fat one
> trying to be the skinny one.

There were lots of squeals, and pointing and poking; however, when it came time to write, some children simply described what they saw:

I liked the music and the pictures. I liked when Keith and I were in the picture, when Joe was playing baseball, and when Esther did that pose that was boss.

—DAVID

But a few of the writers picked up on the lyrics and wrote about brotherhood:

> Everyday people are black, red, yellow, and white—and we have to live together. No matter where you go, you will find people, for God put all kinds of people around. So you can hate them, or like them, or love them. But you have to live with them, no matter what kind of people they are.
>
> —LUPE

And two of the boys let loose with the joy of seeing themselves on a screen. In one slide, Danny is making a muscle and Mark is looking on. Danny adapted a Three Stooges tableau and wrote a comic dialogue to go with it:

DANNY: "Do you think I am great? I think so."
MARK: "Why?"
DANNY: "Because I have muscles, and I am a hero."
MARK: "No! Because each time you put your muscles up, they go down."
DANNY: "Mark, don't say that!"
MARK: "It's true, Danny!"

Most of the children seemed to enjoy being one of the "everyday people," but I was caught off guard by the reaction of one girl. While I was walking around the schoolyard with my camera, I came upon Hilda bouncing a ball. Hilda was a bubbly kid with a quick, high laugh, so when she let go of the ball and put her thin hands over her face, I missed the signals completely. I joked with her, saying something I no longer remember, and she raised her head and looked at me, teary-eyed: "Go away. Would you just go *away!*"

A week before, I had brushed against another child's tender side. Dora was the girl who, during our first meeting, had written that Pig Pen was "creepy and ugly." At thirteen, Dora was only in the fifth grade. She missed one year when her parents emigrated from Mexico, and she was later held back another grade so that her low test scores would match her grade level. She was embarking on adolescence with children at her side. Dora and the others had finished writing, so I did something I had seen Rosalie do:

"Dora, why don't you read your story to us?"

"No. I don't want to read."

"Oh, Dora," I pushed, "that's a good story. Let's hear it."

"I don't like it. I don't want to read it."

At that point, Casey looked over her shoulder and started reading her paper. She slapped it down on the table and grabbed his essay and read it quickly. "See," she said with anger, "I can read if I want to!"

I felt terrible. I had been paying a lot of attention to the children's writing and had been avoiding the full meaning of the rest. Suddenly I felt like some weary psychoanalyst, seeing sorrow and damage wherever I looked. There was Mark, of course, with the cruel and secret quotient of his intelligence. And Lupe, the girl who wrote that "God put all kinds of people around," had also been labeled retarded, but by a person rather than an instrument. She was an obese girl who had been plagued by a series of thyroid and tonsil problems, and a second-grade teacher mistook her lethargy and reserve as a sign of intellectual defect. Eduvina's brother had been shot to death in a street fight, and Joey had a long jagged scar along his forearm whose cause I had been reluctant to pursue. And there was David, the little boy who wrote that Esther's pose was boss. He was an absolute nonreader until Rosalie got her hands on him the year before. He was so withdrawn that his fourth-grade teacher had feared him and had speculated that his silence might indicate childhood schizophrenia.

The churches these children attended told them they were made in the image of God. But I began to wonder what images they were creating for themselves as they came to know that their physical being was so vulnerable, that whatever beauty they bore could be dismissed by the culture or destroyed on the street. The schools could have intervened but instead seemed to misperceive them and place them on the margin. Here's the essay Dora wouldn't read, a response to a picture of a tenement she had torn out of *Life*:

Crazy people are going around with guns killing others
without asking their names or who or what they are and
without looking to see if it is a woman or a man or a child.

What were my students coming to believe about their faces and their bodies and their spoken and written gestures?

The hopeful thing was that not one child gave in. Most of the children were adding a little more detail, trying to elaborate their writing as best they could. Even the poorest writers were spending more time on their work and were moving beyond tentative, one-line productions. I kept encouraging them to let their imaginations go, and some did, catching themselves in linguistic mousetraps, but pushing ahead, involved in what they were doing—if only because they knew it mattered to me. Jesus, the migrant worker's son, started drawing a line about a quarter of the way down his writing pad. He would then bend over the paper, his face close to his pencil, and work until he had written beyond his mark. As soon as he passed it, but not before, he would look up smiling and call me over.

Teaching, I was coming to understand, was a kind of romance. You didn't just work with words or a chronicle of dates or facts about the suspension of protein in milk. You wooed kids with these things, invited a relationship of sorts, the terms of connection being the narrative, the historical event, the balance of casein and water. Maybe nothing was "intrinsically interesting." Knowledge gained its meaning, at least initially, through a touch on the shoulder, through a conversation of the kind Jack MacFarland and Frank Carothers and the others used to have with their students. My first enthusiasm about writing came because I wanted a teacher to like me.

After the "Everyday People" exercise, I spent some time looking back over the work the students had produced since their first day with me. One thing that was evident was that many of the children used pictures as stimuli to create stories, so, for our fourth lesson, I decided to go with some old-fashioned storytelling. As soon as they were settled around our cafeteria work station, I placed the needle on "Rocky Raccoon," Paul McCartney's comic rendering of a frontier romance and shootout. The story goes like this: Rocky's girlfriend, Nancy, had run away with someone named Danny, and Rocky, having tracked them down, burst into their room, announcing a showdown. Just as Rocky was kicking down the door, I lifted the needle from the wobbly turntable. "Okay class," I shrugged, "looks like you have to write the ending." Snickers, swaggers, *ka-pow*s, and they settled in. A few children wrote brief conclusions:

> He shot Danny.
> Then he danced
> with his girlfriend Nancy!
>
> —EDUVINA

But most, the boys particularly, played out the story more fully:

> Rocky broke in, got his gun, sat down and watched. Dan went for his gun. Rocky fell down laughing. Rocky got up and shot him. Then Rocky went home and Nancy walked in. Rocky shot her too. The fuzz came for him. He died for killing Nancy.
>
> —DAVID

And several children asked to come back after school to finish their long, detailed endings, fuller and richer than anything I or their teachers had yet seen them write. I had to help Hank with spelling and with the complexities of punctuating dialogue, but, otherwise, this was his:

> Dan said, "Step outside, I'll be ready."
> Then he went out. Rocky Raccoon kissed the girl and went out. The girl went out too. All the people went into the saloon and watched through the windows and doors. The sheriff went out.
> Rocky said, "Get away, Sheriff."
> "No," said the sheriff.
> So Rocky Raccoon shot the Sheriff and Dan shot Rocky. The girl ran outside and laid on Rocky. The people went out too. The Deputy came and got Dan.
> The people said, "The Sheriff, the Sheriff is dead."
> The girl was sad and went away. The people were sad and went in their houses. The Deputy was sad. Everyone was sad! The girl got on a stagecoach and was sad all the way.

Rocky's tale mirrored a thousand awful Westerns, and Hank and some of the others knew exactly what to do once the macho raccoon kicked in that door. I didn't tap the most noble of humanity's pursuits, but I had to admit there was something just in Hank, a Navajo, taking the plot line that had served to degrade his people and appropriating it to produce a testament to his literacy. He had been tagged a "slow learner" in the second grade and had been doing poorly in school for a long time.

The next day Ben and I had lunch away from the schoolgrounds. I wanted to tell him about Hank and the others and get some advice on what to do when I met with the children next week. Ben took a route through Medina Court, a poor section of El Monte, and as we drove along he told me that I should collect the writing my students had done so far and make little books for them: "Kids like them. It gives them something of their own. Ask Rosalie about it." Ben was starting to say something else when he slowed down by an empty lot. He gave a little wave to a man sitting on the bumper of an old Ford truck. The man appeared to be in his forties. By him was a younger man squatting in the dirt in *cholo* fashion: feet splayed outward, hand dangling—cupping a cigarette—shirt buttoned at the collar but open from there down. He was smiling and looking at the ground in front of him. Back in South L.A. we used to talk about a guy "standing behind a fix." It seemed that these two had just positioned themselves. The man on the bumper looked lazily up at Ben and raised his hand off his leg in a slow wave.

"Who are those guys?" I asked Ben.

"The one on the truck is Ernie. He's my second cousin."

"Ben, umm, is he high?"

"Yeah, looks like it, huh? He used to just sell it. He was a—a businessman, you see. But now, well, now he's a heavy user."

Ben and I found our restaurant and continued to talk about my work, but I couldn't shake the image of his cousin waving listlessly from the truck. Months before, while Lillian and I were walking down Brooklyn Avenue, I had a powerful realization that South L.A. hadn't trapped me, that I could come back to neighborhoods like mine and do things. The streets seemed full of life and promise. What I felt as I sat with Ben, and realized I'd been feeling on and off since arriving in El Monte, was something quite different: It was the powerlessness of South Vermont, an impotence as warm and safe as a narcotic. It wasn't clear despair—it wasn't that articulate—it was more a soft regress to childhood, to hot and quiet afternoons in an empty lot. Little things could trigger it—a smell in the cafeteria, a ramshackle house—and whatever

I was doing—creating a lesson, working with the children, shaping an observation for Joe or Lillian—would begin to feel unworthy, lifeless from the inside. I did my work in spite of all this, but with an inner labor the I was just now appreciating, holding a hazy and familiar ineptitude at bay with one hand while framing a lesson with the other. This, I thought, was how South Vermont kept hold of its errant children. You can leave those streets, but the flat time and the diminished sense of what you can be continues to shape your identity. You live with decayed images of the possible.

When I met with the children again, I had them, as Ben suggested, make books out of the four assignments they had written. I came rattling into the cafeteria with a dining cart piled high with red and yellow construction paper and pieces of poster board, trays of pens and colored pencils, boxes of scissors and staplers and glue. I told the children a little about books and bookmaking—simple things I had learned in Dr. Gullans's bibliography course at UCLA—and showed them a sample I had mocked up of the kind of book they could make from their own pieces of writing. I then outlined a procedure for them to follow and turned them loose: they had their stories (typewritten because they had been on display) and piles of magazine photographs and the mimeographed lyrics to "Everyday People" and "Rocky Raccoon." Some of the children drew pictures to accompany the stories while others pasted pictures alongside them. Dora and Eduvina combined their stories into one big book. Lupe took the ribbon out of her hair and made a bow and glued it onto her cover. Danny added a sentence to one of his stories, carefully printing it below the typescript.

I had asked Monica to come by near the end of the hour. She could letter with precision and flair, and I wanted her to print the children's names on their books. When she showed up, she sat at the end of the table, and as the children finished, they came forward and Monica, with her careful script, wrote: "Lupe's Book," "Danny's Book," "Casey's Book," "Anthony's Book" on their poster board covers.

My students knew they were considered poor readers. We were approaching the last session I would have with them, and I wanted to leave them with something snappy that would allow them, if just for an hour, to gain entry to the sophisticated vocabulary that would probably serve to intimidate them for some time to come. Here's the lesson I came up with, pretty contrived, I admit, but it was fun to play out. I printed on strips of art paper words that had unusual spellings or that would sound funny if exaggerated slightly:

Macabre
Eulogy
Misanthrope
Lampoon
Paranoid

And so on. I also clipped out pictures that could accompany each word: For example, for *eulogy* I used a picture of a priest reading from a Bible at a funeral. I spread out the words on the table— saving the pictures for later—and told the children these were big, important, snazzy words, and they were to pick one that looked weird or was spelled funny or that hit them in any way. They then had to explain why they chose their words. Finally, I gave the meanings of the words and spread out the pictures before them, asking them to find a picture they thought went with their words. After all this rigmarole, they were to write a story to fit the words and pictures they had chosen.

Rodrigo picked out a picture of a man, eyes wide, with his hand over his mouth. Rodrigo's word was *macabre*:

> This man used to like girls very much. One night he was driving a truck when he saw a girl and stopped. He went over to see the girl. When he saw her face, it looked like a horse! He ran as fast as he could! He jumped into the truck really scared, and he never liked girls again.

We labeled this "Rodrigo's Macabre Story," and it, like all the essays before, went up on the cafeteria wall. Danny wrote the word *misanthrope* over the two pictures he chose: one of a boxer posed for a punch and another of a TV private eye elbowing a man across the face.

These dudes think that they are smart, but they aren't. These dudes hate everybody! They look mean. They kill. And most of all, they are dumb.

And Delores chose *lampoon*. Delores was tall and overweight and wore glasses that were a little too large for her face. In a moment of sweet revenge, she turned her own catalog of insult toward the boy who sat next to her in her regular class, displaying one of the motives that has perennially impelled writers to write:

Hi everybody. Guess what I am writing about? I am writing a lampoon of Tommy! He looks so funny. Let me tell you how he looks, O.K.? He has four eyes, and long hair, and is so fat that he has to wear a size 60! In town he can't even fit through the door. They have to push him out! And you should see his hands. They are so big that they could cover your face. And he is only nine years old! And boy, I tell you, he is so big that we hate him. You know what we call him? Fat-head Fatty!

That afternoon Casey came running up to me in the schoolyard: "Hey, I wrote something for you all on my own!" and held out a piece of paper, folded in four. Casey was one of my favorites. He was an affable boy with sandy hair, a perennially scraped elbow, and an awful home. His father was long gone, and his mother cocktailed and sometimes didn't come home for two- and three-day stretches. Casey was rambunctious and was always getting in trouble—not serious, nasty trouble, but fooling around, talking-in-class trouble, little bruises on the shins of Conduct. I would look at him during our class and think of Dave Snyder, the guy I tip-tapped through biology at Mercy High. I listened to the defensive wit he had developed about his mother and simultaneously wanted to laugh with him and hold him close to me: "Last year, my mother gave us turkey dinners," he told Ben and me just before Thanksgiving holiday. "*TV* turkey dinners! But she gave us two apiece." Here he paused for a beat, "After all, it *was* Thanksgiving."

So here was Casey with a story for his teacher. "I'll be damned," I thought, "I've flicked the switch." I unfolded the note as Casey looked on:

Mike

How are you. Do you want to tripout today. I have a lid of
wead. I will meet you in the park. You are a kool guy. I am
going to take a crap.

> so long
>
> your buddy
>
> Casey

Jesus! What in the hell—what am I gonna say? Was he really
carrying marijuana? Worry flipped quickly to anger. Casey was
pushing—pushing. . . . And as I stood there, I saw . . . as though
rising out of confusion, I saw that Casey was doing what so many
of my high school friends loved to do: freak the teacher. And he'd
succeeded. I pretended to read the note a moment longer, giving
myself a chance to come up with something. I pointed to the end
of the last sentence and looked solemnly down at him: "You
know, Casey, you spelled 'crap' perfectly. Congratulations."
"Awwww," he said, "you're no fun," and started laughing. I
tapped my fingers on his head and grunted, and then he and I
walked out onto the wide, grassy field to talk, man to man, about
the risky methods people devise to show their need and their
affection.

I used versions of this curriculum again with other groups of students, tinkering with it, being more cautious with the "Everyday
People" slide show, streamlining the exercise with the big words.
Still, whatever adjustments I made, there were lots of ways, I
can see now, that the curriculum fell short, even considering the
general limitations of time. While there was some continuity between the exercises, each didn't build carefully on the ones preceding it, didn't take full advantage of what was developing in
prior lessons. The "Rocky Raccoon" exercise, for example,
tapped knowledge of plot line and story structure, and there were
some students who should have had a further chance to use what
they knew.

Another problem was that the curriculum was somewhat self-
enclosed. While it did not prohibit children from drawing on their
interests and the events in their own lives, it failed to elicit creatively the tales and folklore and genres that were part of their

various families and cultures. Finally, I could have done much more than I did to get the children to reflect on this mutual venture into literacy. How would they explain the work they were now doing? What did it mean to create stories? Were they noticing any changes in the way they wrote? Could I get them to reconsider the attitudes they must have developed about themselves as readers and writers?

But for all the limitations of my fledgling curriculum—its shortsightedness, its fragmentation—something unusual was going on. The essays many of the children were producing, flawed as they were, were not jibing with the various assessments of their ability that I had heard and read. A series of achievement tests and the grades and comments of assorted teachers had designated these students as having significant problems with written language. By the fourth or fifth grade, they had been pretty thoroughly defined as limited. The question, then, was what was the nature of the curriculum and the assessments that provided the base for this definition?

The English curricula that I saw, and the English textbooks particularly, were almost entirely oriented toward grammatical analysis. Subskills. Every year the children faced about two hundred pages that required them to circle or underline subjects or verbs or pronouns; that directed them to fill in the correct noun or pronoun or verb form; that asked them to read lists of sentences and indicate if they were simple or compound or if their purpose was to tell, raise a question, or exclaim; that told them to indicate whether a noun was singular or plural, simple or compound, common or proper; that told them to indicate the tense of verbs, to label action verbs and linking verbs, and to decline irregular verbs. And the tests they took measured how well they had learned to do these tasks.

There ended up being little room in such a curriculum—unless the inventive teacher created it—to explore the real stuff of literacy: conveying something meaningful, communicating information, creating narratives, shaping what we see and feel and believe into written language, listening to and reading stories, playing with the sounds of words. Writing and reading are such private acts that we forget how fundamentally social they are: We hear stories read by others and we like to tell others about the stories we read; we learn to write from others and we write for

others to read us. The curriculum I saw drained the life out of all
this, reduced literacy to the dry dismembering of language—not
alive, not communicative at all. The children's textbooks were
colorful, and little boys and girls and dogs and cats cavorted
around the exercises, but the exercises themselves were not all
that distant from the ancient descriptive grammar books I had
learned about in graduate school—grammars that analyzed language down to its smallest parts and invented a meticulous, even
finicky, classification system to contain them. This was a science
of language that was "not . . . intended to help with teaching,"
as the historian H. I. Marrou once observed. It was an exercise
that was "all analysis and no synthesis," pursued for its own
pedantic ends.

It seemed to me that such a curriculum was especially troublesome for children like the ones in my class: children who had not
been prepped in their homes to look at language in this dissected,
unnatural way; children for whom English was a foreign language; children of particularly mobile families who fell out of the
curricular lockstep demanded by this approach to language; children who might have some problems with their vision or with
the way they process written language; children who, like me
long ago, just didn't see the sense in such analysis, and, before
long, were missing it, not getting it and falling behind. And so
these children would fail at the kind of literacy activities the
school system had woven throughout its curriculum and turn off
to writing and reading in general. But that did not mean that they
were illiterate.

Given that cognitive growth does not proceed in miraculous
leaps, my curriculum was clearly not kicking these children's development into fast-forward. It had to be eliciting and shaping
something that was already there. Hank could write his sequel to
"Rocky Raccoon" because he knew something about Westerns.
Mark deployed his vivid imagination in a wild-child narrative to
create a boy who hunts deer, bears, and birds. Danny relied on a
dopey and familiar joke to produce a comic dialogue about deflat-
ing muscles. And Delores—Delores rambled, but she wrote the
most elaborate essay her teacher had yet seen her produce. She
appropriated slapstick and hyperbole to the delicious purpose of
lampooning the fathead who made her life miserable. There were
times, then, when emotions and desires and all sorts of child

knowledge about movies and sitcoms and slapstick and family stories blended in complex ways to yield a piece of writing that belied the schools' assessments of these students' literacy.

———◆———

I was in Mexico for the weekend. I went there to visit my mother. When I came back home, the whole town was burned! I went through all the houses and hotels, but no one was there.

I walked to Los Angeles because the cars were all burned, and even L.A. was burned. I saw something. It was in the street. It looked like a girl. It was. She was still alive! I took her to a hotel. She was lucky, there was some medicine, I was the medicine! With me everybody lives. She lived too. She was pretty and we went upstairs. There was only one bed, so we both slept on it, and that is it!

—WILLIAM

He is going to the world of rotted people. He is rotting already. He is getting scared. He is seeing rotted people. He don't know he is rotting. Already they are getting uglier.

—KENNY

Once while I was walking,
I saw a man swaying in the shadows.
I saw his face under the light,
And there stood a picture of sadness.

—ANGIE

The children in El Monte certainly produced for us their fair share of dog and pony stories, and good guy–bad guy cop and Western tales, and gooey romantic fables, but it was striking how often the testaments to their literacy were formed from the dark side of their dreams and from the harsh events and troubling protective fantasies of their day-to-day lives. The impressive nature of the children's achievement would mask the full import of the visions of violence and delapidation, the sexualized apocalyptic landscapes, the textures of peeling walls and pitted floors. If I looked at the world through these stories, held them to the light like a prismatic lens, the courage and hope of working-class El Monte grew dim, and anger and quiet despair came into focus.

Violence and abandonment, the guns and pregnancies, the paralyzing fatigue. Men waiting in their trucks in the heat, smoking,
gone to fat, looking through the windshield at nothing, so deeply
tired that only a gunshot could jolt them. A father screaming at
an older boy, pushing him out the door, slapping him hard on
the back of the head. The boy turning to face the father, silent,
big as the father now. At Bob's Big Boy, a pouty blond sits in the
corner booth. Bleached, teased, wearing an anklet, she's gazing
off, a cigarette in her right hand, inattentively smoking while her
husband looks into his plate. She was the queen of the local prom
perhaps—she's pretty enough—or, more likely, the bad girl, the
defiant rock 'n' roller, married now, long red nails, kids, holding
down a counter job that betrayed the promises of her adolescence.

It was across these emotional landscapes that some of our children were condemned to wander, and, at times, they recoiled,
flailing out by the classroom door. Ray had vandalized the
school—broken windows, splattered eggs and mud over the
walls—and then claimed to not know why. Rosemary was frequently absent or tardy and alternated between verbally abusing
her teachers and flat-out ignoring them. When she did come to
school, she simply went through the motions, mechanical, detached—all the earmarks of a dropout while still a sixth grader.
Terry had broken another boy's jaw, and was generally viewed
by his peers as wild and explosive: they still talked about the time
he chased off a gang of boys with a tire chain. When I was growing up, I saw this kind of rebellion and assault as potency. Terry
was the kind of kid I sidestepped on South Vermont. Now I came
to understand something about the misery that sparks such combative defiance, the desperation it reveals: The children's rebellion was all the more troubling because of its ultimate loneliness.
The vandal, Ray, lived with battling alcoholic parents, and it was
not uncommon to find him sitting on the curb outside the school
an hour or so before the gates were opened. Rosemary was one
of ten children. When she skipped school, she would sit alone in
her barren and usually crowded house and watch other worlds
evolve on the daytime soaps.

Terry's home was worse. Garbage and auto parts were strewn
across the front yard, and the house was as dilapidated as any
city house I'd seen. He lived alone with his mother, who be-

longed to a white supremacist motorcycle gang and who, from what Terry told me, was most likely a prostitute. This was where Terry had to establish who he was, find guidelines where few existed, explain to himself the things he had seen done to his mother. By his tenth or eleventh year, he had developed a tough, detached public self—isolated, distant, minimacho—a future angel from hell in frayed sneakers. He would let nothing, *nothing* affect him. His guard was up, constantly—his seething motto: "I don't like to be pushed around"—on the defensive, constantly, for the affront that taps the confusion and anger that churns beneath the surface, that began with the first vision from some violated crib. He kept to himself, and there didn't seem to be any way to reach him. It was revealing, I thought, that the path to Terry's heart was found by someone more vulnerable than he was. This is what I saw one late afternoon from the office window: Terry was shooting baskets alone when a young girl, noticeably hydrocephalic and retarded, wandered onto the playground. She saw Terry and walked over. Terry said something to her I couldn't hear, and she responded, and he handed her the basketball. She tried to bounce it, and it hit the tip of her shoe and shot off. Terry ran after it, and for about ten minutes he tried to show her how to shoot a basket. Then he took her by the hand and led her back out of the schoolyard.

A week or so later I was driving back to El Monte from an errand in East L.A. It was getting dark and I was late for a dinner meeting with my teammates at Joe's and I had to bring the wine. I spotted a seedy little store, pulled over when I could, and quickly hopped out. When I was walking back to my car, which was a good twenty yards away, I saw three boys—fifteen or sixteen maybe—coming toward me. They were tough-looking kids, and their gaze was fixed. Suddenly two of them split off to the left and one to the right and I felt before I knew—something fast and helpless and strangely clear—that I was about to get jumped. By reflex, I grabbed the wine bottle by the neck and brought it across my waist. Just then, a car pulled up, and an old woman began struggling to get out of the passenger side. The boys looked at each other and kept on walking, one saying as he passed me, "Hey, man, you're a lucky motherfucker." I got in my car, my heart pounding, and relived the moment again—and again. Later at Joe's I found myself, in the middle of yet another replay, telling my teammates about Terry. How long before he'd end up on those streets? Was he there already? I kept shuttling back and forth in my mind between the scene with the retarded girl and the feeling I had when I saw those boys split up to flank me.

When the principal first told me about Terry, he showed me a drawing. A boy is sitting at a desk, his hands cover part of his face, and he is terrified. He screams, "I will kill you!" Terry's fear had been expressing itself in violence. But it was not inconceivable that such fear could evolve into the protective sympathy I saw revealed with the girl on the playground. The fear was too raw, however, and, in a strange way, played too readily into a dark American mythology. The other children shrank from Terry, but they told stories about him with relish, the breathless rendering of the wildly swung tire chain. The fledgling outlaw, the man outside society. Terry's public identity was shaping already, and it most likely would prove to be too powerful an identity to avoid, a way to live with and through his volatile pain. On the deserted playground, though, the place where threat was momentarily suspended, he could be the helping child, could guide the powerless. But I know that what I saw was probably fading already, receding with each passing assault to his spirit and with each of his public acts of defiance.

Looking back on my notes and reports from this time, I see a continuing and uncomfortable waver between a celebration of individual potential and a despair over the crushing power of the environment: the children's literate affirmations versus the economic assault and psychological injury of Hicks Camp and Medina Court and "the marvelous place," Maravilla; the narrative testaments I weekly taped to the cafeteria wall versus the squalor of Terry's home. My notebooks reflect a kind of conceptual manic depression: quotations from progressive educators extolling the creative spirit alternate side by side with passages from Martin Deutsch's *The Disadvantaged Child*, with grim discussions of "the culture of poverty" and "deprivation" and "environmental deficiencies and handicaps." And, more than I was then able to admit, this was not simply an intellectual tension.

I was living through the very conflict I was cutting and pasting into my notebooks—the conflict between two visions: one of individual possibility and one of environmental limits and determiners; the vibrant power of meaningful work versus the absorbing threat of South Vermont. One day I saw the emerging human spirit, the next day the naturalist's dreary landscape. Both were true. And, I guess, this was a tension the children felt, in their way—something they couldn't articulate, perhaps, as I couldn't when I was a child, but they were living it, absorbing it into marrow. The school itself became the stage for playing out this drama, creating—at the hands of teachers like Rosalie Naumann—a place that fostered growth and celebrated possibility, but creating, as well, the social conditions for intensifying the child's marginality. It was around this time, well into my second year in the Teacher Corps, when I began working with Harold Morton, and he came to represent for me both the basic human conflict—that we are simultaneously heroes and prisoners—and the fact that our schools can respond to a child's misery as well as institutionally define him by it.

Harold Morton was in the fifth grade, and he was small for his age. His straight brown hair fell half-combed across his forehead, and his clothes were clean but rumpled. He stood by Mrs. Naumann looking straight ahead—not at me particularly—his eyes twitching, his mouth open a little. Occasionally he would grimace and swallow hard, his lips going tight. Rosalie introduced us, and Harold looked up and said hello. She explained to him that he and some other children would be meeting with me to tell stories and write. Would that be okay? He said that it would—a soft yes—and Mrs. Naumann put her hand on his shoulder and said that she thought he would enjoy spending time with me. She moved her hand down across his back, smiled at me, and led him out to the playground. What a strange kid, I thought. I wonder what's wrong with his eyes.

Harold's group, like the first one I worked with, met once a week in the cafeteria. I used some of the same assignments; for the first week, the children wrote about pictures of John Kennedy, Pig Pen, and the little girl at her window. Harold didn't put pencil to paper for quite a while, then, slowly and with deliberation, wrote about Pig Pen:

The middle one makes me feel funny.

While he was writing this disturbing, solitary sentence, his eyes were twitching and he moved about and grimaced, not talking to other children, sometimes just looking at the paper for long stretches, his gaze blank except for the flicking of his eyelids. I watched him and felt uneasy, worried that I was about to open up more than I could handle.

When the bell rang, I collected the children's essays and, on a whim, asked Harold to help me gather the pencils. I didn't know what to say to him, but I knew I didn't want to let go of him just yet. He went to each messy station at the table and put the pencils neatly in their box, all points together. We took everything back to the teachers' lounge—Harold walking a step or two behind me—and I asked him for one more favor. Would he mind helping me carry some art paper out to my car? I handed him a packet, and we walked to the parking lot. When I opened my trunk he saw a football and said, "I like to play football." I reached in and handed him the ball. He held it and turned the threads upward and said: "What I like to do best is kick." "I'm not very good at that," I said. "Someday you'll have to show me how you do it." He looked up and gave me a half smile. And that was how we started.

During the next two weeks, I looked for Harold on the playground, dreaming up any lame excuse to have him give me a hand. I'd ask him to set up chairs with me around the cafeteria table or carry in scissors and pencils and glue for the rest of the class. We talked about football, and about things he saw on the way to school: squirrels fighting in a tree, trucks unloading materials at the factory across the street. I found out that he had a job retrieving shopping carts for a local market, so we talked about that as well. He was soon talking more readily and his facial tics began subsiding. And his writing took a dramatic upswing. He found a picture of children carrying presents through the snow and wrote a night-before-Christmas story:

> It is Christmas Eve. We have to go to bed early tonight. It is 12 o'clock. I heard something on the roof. It was coming down the chimney. It woke me up. I opened the door. I saw Saint Nick.

His teacher, Mrs. Berry, had been giving a nice series of lessons on the haiku, and though the poem Harold wrote for her didn't match the form, he had clearly appropriated the *idea* of haiku, the compressed language, the imagistic focus:

The eagle dives after the fish
The fish swims away from the eagle.

I wasn't too concerned about spelling, but I couldn't help but notice that Harold's spelling was relatively error-free. I took a quick look through his file—a thick and depressing catalog of failure—and saw that you could never have predicted the work he was doing now.

Harold began talking a bit more regularly with the other children—he still grimaced and twitched occasionally, but seemed more open, less sealed up, less distressed by whatever it was that tugged at his face from the inside. I sat in on Mrs. Berry's class and saw that although he fidgeted and looked off into space and spent an undue amount of time straightening his desk, he was also volunteering answers. Mrs. Berry noticed the difference. She had found in the past that when she could sit alone with Harold and go over lessons he would respond, but she had five other children who required a lot of private help as well, and she couldn't give them all they needed. What was going on now, however, was unusual: Harold was coming alive in the midst of others.

Over the next month, I gave my extra time to Harold—working on his reading and arithmetic in pretty traditional fashion, but occasionally trying something out of the ordinary. Once I taped an interview with him. We pretended that I was a reporter who was writing his story; when we were done with the interview, I typed it up and used it as a reader. I discovered that he had three older sisters and a younger brother, and that his father hadn't been around for quite a while. When he was much younger, Harold used to go camping and fishing with him, and those memories remained important—witness the haiku. His favorite pastime was fishing, and for several years, since third grade, he had been walking alone two miles to a lake on the south side of El Monte. We talked a little about fishing, and then I asked him what he did while his line was in the water:

"Think."

"Do you think a lot, Harold?"

"Yes."

"About what?"

A long pause. Then: "Mountains. About going to the mountains and camping and fishing."

Harold's other favorite pastime, of course, was kicking the football. One of the attractions was that he could do it alone: "I practiced kicking at home until I could do it like the real ones."

"You mean until you could kick a spiral?"

"Yes. I kept doing it. Then one day, I did it right. So I do it like that all the time now."

We talked about school and, no big surprise, he didn't like it: He had failed so often and could sense the way the school perceived him. When I asked Harold what he'd prefer to do if he had his way—spend tomorrow at school or at home—he opted for home, dreary as he made it sound:

"What would you do at home?" I asked.

"Nothing. If I'd be at home, I'd probably have to stay in."

The small patch of lawn at Harold's house was overgrown with foxtails, and scraps of old newspaper were fused like mâché grafts onto the dead bushes by the door. A broken hinge had set the screendoor ajar. After our mock interview, I realized that I had to find out more about Harold's life at home. I knocked on the door's flapping edge, and Harold walked out of the darkness of the parlor and let me in. He was quiet, and his eyes were twitching. He left me with his mother, who was sitting on a couch alongside the door. The television to my left was on; newspapers and tabloids were stacked beside it. A bookcase filled with knick-knacks was on my right. There were some photographs on the walls—school pictures of children, mostly—and a tinted drawing of Christ with a trimmed beard and a luminescent heart. Mrs. Morton asked me to sit down; I took a chair by the bookcase. The couch on which Mrs. Morton sat had an old bedspread thrown across it: the spread was tangled, and part of it was jammed into the crevices between the cushions. She was sitting in the middle of the couch, sunk in partially, for the springs were gone. She told me that this was the first time anyone from the school had visited the home. "They're always calling me to go there, but I can't always. I have to work. And I've been sick for a while."

One of the temples of Mrs. Morton's glasses was taped to its rim. She was wearing a loose print dress and stockings that were rolled down below the knee. Her hair was brown and gray and wispy. Harold's father walked out when the boy was five; he had been in jail for the last two years. "They used to go fishing at the lake. Harold really liked that, and I know he misses it. He looks through these books a lot." She pointed to a pile of books on the bottom shelf of the bookcase. I didn't see them at first, so I got up and paged through them. There were magazines like *Field and Stream*, some children's books on whales and dolphins, and two simple books on freshwater fishing.

"Does he have anybody to take him fishing now?" I asked.

"No, not really. My son-in-law works all the time. There's nobody that can do that."

I remembered, then, that Harold had said that he walks to the lake alone.

Mrs. Morton and I talked for about an hour. "Harold is doing better in school this year," she said, "because people are finally leaving him alone." The people, in this case, were the specialists, and Mrs. Morton was angry about the way they had bothered her son. Harold, of course, was doing as poorly as ever, except for the last month, but I was interested in her perception of things, though even here her emotion was flat. She spoke slowly with little rise and fall to her voice. She sat with her arms out to her sides, palms up, fingers curled in. "Junior is just like me. He'll sit in the background, like I do, until someone gets him out."

Mrs. Morton worked in the laundry room of a local hospital and had to alternate shifts. She received no money from her husband and sometimes had to miss work because of an arthritic knee. "We have a hard time of it." Then a long pause. "It got so bad last summer that Junior had to go and stay with his sister and her husband." That didn't work out very well—Harold had to sleep on the couch and got in the way—and almost led to a rift between Mrs. Morton and her daughter. I asked again about the books that Mrs. Morton had shown me. Some remained from the days when her husband was with her; others came from the Sav On down the way. When Harold was younger, he would ask her the names of the fish he was looking at. He could remember the names she told him, and she took this as a sign that he was, in her words, "normal." Harold's little brother came running in asking about supper, so I started making moves to go. I thanked

Mrs. Morton for having me to her house and stood up, extending my hand. We shook hands, and as she looked up from the couch, her eyes were small and cloudy behind the thick lenses of her glasses. "Thank you," she said. "Thank you for coming by."

The week before my visit, my students had turned the topic of discussion to loneliness. We talked a little about the times we'd felt lonely, and then I captured the opportunity and had them write a story about loneliness. Here's what Harold wrote:

> I am lost in the woods. I cannot find my way out. I yell and yell. No one answered me. I climbed a tree then I fell out of the tree and broke my arm.

As I was walking out of Mrs. Morton's yard toward my car, I saw Harold halfway down the street setting a football on a kicker's tee. I waved to him and he waved back and then executed his kick. The ball flew off the tee into a pretty good arc, and when it hit the street, it took a weird bounce and rolled under an old panel truck. I pulled up alongside him and told him I thought he was a good kicker. He gave me a confused smile: a tentative grin with eyes averted. I smiled back, said good-bye, and, once past the corner, leaned over to roll down the passenger window to let the wind blow across me. I felt as if I had descended into something dark and warm and couldn't keep my breath.

I drove back to the school to find Ben, but by the time I got there his car was gone. The principal's car was still in the lot, though, so I went in. I had decided to have another look at Harold's file. The principal handed me the thick folder, and I took it to the teachers' lounge and closed the door. As I went through the pile of smudged and dog-eared pages, slowly this time and with my weeks with Harold and a visit to his house behind me, I saw how his teachers had increasingly misread his tics and twitches and detachment as signs of organic damage, how they had gradually despaired of helping him, how he was progressively defined by the school as the outsider his mother felt him—and herself—to be. The folder displayed the sad and elaborate chronicle of what happens to a child who is too distressed to fit neatly into our classrooms.

The first document in the file was a copy of a reading readiness test given to all entering first graders. His score placed him in the "high average" category; that predicted a good chance of success in learning to read. Surprising, given the trouble with reading he would experience.

After the readiness test came a whole set of forms on which teachers had written comments about student progress. The first of many entries was recorded several months after the start of first grade:

Harold has trouble keeping his eyes on the page or "tracking": the eyes seem to jump away from their visual patterns. He has trouble orienting himself to any written work. He also has to work very hard on his written work.

The second entry comes four months later:

Harold is unpredictable, is easily distracted, lacks continuity of effort, has a short attention span. . . .

Three weeks later, the teacher added these observations:

Harold needs *medical* help as well as much careful teaching. He appears neither to have ability nor to care—is immature, but this child has real ability.

With the second entry, the teacher's frustration sneaks into her commentary: Words like *unpredictable* suggest a growing mismatch between her expectations and Harold's behavior. But it was the third entry that caught my eye, for it contained both a final outcry of hope ("this child has real ability") and a final abdication of potency: The teacher looks for help to the medical expert outside her domain.

When Harold was in the second grade, he was tested again. The first series was given right after Christmas. His reading score was below grade level: It placed him at 1.3, first grade, three months. (A further test taken four months later registered 1.7; he was still behind but was growing apace.) His math was close to grade level: 2.3. His IQ was 96, a little below average. One month after the tests, his teacher wrote the following entry:

Harold has become quite verbal but otherwise progressed little. He enjoys sharing and telling about things he sees. He attempts to do arithmetic but rarely gets any written work correct. He is able to give some answers verbally.

She requested that Harold have a diagnostic workup. The form teachers had to fill out to initiate this further testing listed a number of items and provided room for the teacher to write in brief comments. Among other things, Harold's teacher noted the following:

Reason for Filing Report: Progress very slow. Very short attention span. Dreamy.

Social Maturity and Adjustment: Seems immature. Has few friends.

Emotional Stability: Placid most of the time.

Special Interests and Abilities: None that are noticeable.

Reading Level: Preprimer.

Language Ability: Poor. Speech problem.

Arithmetic Ability: Poor

Home-School Relationship: No one came to the conference. I don't know the parents.

Place, with me, the teacher's written comment about Harold's classwork alongside the formal request for further testing. Her prose may damn with faint praise, but it gives some hint of life ("has become quite verbal," "enjoys sharing and telling"); the standard form, however, offers a gloomier picture of detachment and ineptitude. Perhaps the language and format of assessment combined with the sluggishness of school bureaucracy led her to emphasize the negative. This sort of report might have been necessary to get action, but it also pretty convincingly defined Harold as a marginal child.

Harold's third-grade teacher entered this comment:

Harold brings many books and encyclopedias to school with pictures that relate to our area of study. However, he has difficulty in reading and written expression. Needs individual attention and supervision.

The books, I suppose, were those I saw at his house, and there was promise in his attempt to connect the literacy of home and school. By now, though, Harold had been placed in a special class; he spent one period a day with a remedial reading teacher. Here is her observation:

Harold's problem is neurological. Perhaps aphasia. I think
that the problem is even too great for remediation. He needs
a clinician to work with him.

Harold had been defined as slow, as being in need of remedy,
but the person designated by the school to provide remedy saw
the problem as beyond her, as "too great for remediation." She
appealed to the clinical setting and applied the neurological designation, aphasia, the impairment of the power to use words.
Harold's first-grade teacher had invoked general medicine. Now
the appeal was to neurology: a designation seemingly more precise—and more weighted with status. With this assessment, Harold was, in a sense, excluded from the school, pushed further
away from the healing possibilities of the teacher-student relationship and further toward the cold instrumentation of the
clinic.

Harold's fourth-grade teacher filed an Observation Report, a
form with a series of characteristics for the teacher to check off.
She put marks by the following:

PHYSICAL CHARACTERISTICS   PERSONALITY TRAITS

Poor coordination   Unpredictable
Pale   Inactive
Facial grimaces   Restless
Speech difficulties   Demands much attention
Frequent bathroom   Inability to follow direction
requests

By an entry labeled "Language Ability," she wrote "oral only."
On a reading scale that ran "Good, Average, Poor" she wrote in
"None." After "Progress in School" she wrote "None. Is being
considered for other placement."

"Other placement" meant that Harold was being considered
for a slot in an EMR class, a setting for mentally retarded children
who were "educable" and who had the potential to profit from
certain kinds of highly structured schooling. What interested me
was the way the teacher's assessment reduced Harold to a child
without any ability to read or write. Although he was behind grade
level almost from the beginning, Harold's earlier teachers gave
testimony to some degree of literacy, and my work with him certainly revealed a literate capacity. Had he completely closed him-

self off in the fourth grade? Or did this particular teacher so despair of helping Harold that she wrote him off? I wondered if a highly structured curriculum would best serve a child who was already failing in the considerably structured curriculum of the regular classroom? Harold's minor successes with me were not the result of any structure I provided, for I provided relatively little. It seemed that Harold was responding to human connection and to an encouragement to express himself in a setting where some of the strictures of the standard curriculum had been momentarily suspended.

Harold had been increasingly defined as a child who was limited organically, who had some sort of medical or neurological impairment, who had problems that were "too great for remediation." I turned, then, to his medical records, also a thick bundle, for many of the assessments he had accumulated brought with them visits to physicians, neurologists, speech therapists, and opthalmologists. I went through these records carefully, but could find no indication that Harold's problems were primarily physiological.

All eye examinations registered Harold's vision at 20 / 20 and made no mention of the kind of muscular or neural problems that would result in irregular eye movements. Medical examinations listed purely physical problems—enlarged tonsils, caries—with one exception: "missed many on finger to nose." That warranted a neurological workup at the local hospital. The results were negative. Harold's developmental history was normal; except for "a severe attack of bronchial pneumonia" at age three, there was no record of serious illness, head injury, or convulsions. During his stay in the first and second grade, he saw the district's speech therapist. After a good deal of work, the therapist finally registered the problem as being primarily orthodontal:

> Harold is still having difficulty making an "s". His bite is poor and he is unable to close his teeth in order to make a good "s". Has made as much progress as possible. Dismiss from speech class.

By the vagaries of shuffling, one of the last sheets in the medical file was a report from an opthalmologist. He had scribbled a note on the bottom of his diagnostic report that brought Harold's journey full circle:

The problem is psychological.

I read that sentence and thought of Harold pushing shopping carts along Peck Road, alone, absorbed, perhaps, with thoughts of fishing, hunting, and his father.

When I finally closed the file, it was dark outside. I was to have supper at Joe's, and I was over an hour late. I went to the secretary's desk and called, apologizing and explaining that I'd be along shortly. Then I went back to the teachers' lounge and sat down. The thing that was most affecting me was the sheer weight of the file: the endless assessments, the multiple referrals, the accumulation of voices saying, "No, no, not us." There was no denying that Harold *was* a strange kid: He was very far behind, he drifted off, his face registered the irregular beat of some inner pulse. But his response to personal attention was too dramatic to be ignored. The way the schools are set up, however—the loads teachers carry, the ways they're trained to deal with difference, the vast patchwork of diagnostics and specialists—make it very hard for someone like Harold to get what he needs: a guide sitting down on the steps by him and building a relationship through the words on a printed page.

One day, several weeks before, Harold came running up to me as I was getting out of my car. He was carrying an album by the Angels, one of the "girl groups" of the early sixties, that had belonged to his oldest sister. The Angels' big hit was "My Boyfriend's Back," and it was one of Harold's favorite songs. He wanted me to play it for him and help him write out the words:

> My boyfriend's back
> And you're gonna be in trouble
> Hey la de la, my boyfriend's back. . . .

What fluff, I had thought at the time. But I saw now what I had entirely missed then. At the heart of the la de la was the promise of return and protection. A boyfriend—or a father. How sweet that must have sounded.

I thought a lot about Harold over the next few weeks. There were things in the books I had been reading before entering the Teacher Corps that made a lot of sense here: Maslow's cautions about psychological labeling: "What is stressed . . . is the category in which the person belongs . . . *not* the person as such";

R. D. Laing's objection to the diagnostic language used to describe malady: "The words one has to use are specifically designated to isolate and circumscribe the meaning of the patient's life." Harold's file gave testament to an extensive network of assessment, to a sophisticated diagnostic technology, but there was little in it that illuminated the core of his loneliness or that could be used to guide him toward competence.

Still, one of the assessments continued to nag at me. Was Harold, as the reading specialist suggested, aphasic? The neurologist's report was negative, but the word carried such ominous and final implications that I felt I had to find out more for myself. I went to the psychology library at USC and checked out a stack of books; one thing I could certainly do after graduate work in English was conduct research. I went through the *Aphasia Handbook for Adults and Children*; *Aphasia, A Clinical and Psychological Study*; *Differential Diagnosis of Aphasia with the Minnesota Test*; and three or four more. What I found was increasing diagnostic and clinical disagreement.

Aphasia was broadly defined as an impairment in the ability to use symbols, the ability to speak, read, and write. As the authors got more specific, they generated lists of characteristics, but some of the lists were so long and sweeping that they seemed to lose their diagnostic value. One book, for example, detailed twenty-nine characteristics of aphasia, ranging from short attention span to epilepsy to withdrawal to hypoactivity to hyperactivity to poor hand-eye coordination to poor judgment. What value was a list like that? Furthermore, some authors even questioned the usefulness of the diagnosis, particularly with children who did not have clear supporting evidence of neurological damage. Several books included samples of aphasic handwriting, and I compared those with Harold's script. I double-checked the spelling in the writing he had done for me. I thought back to the "high-average" score on his reading readiness test. I thought about our conversations. I thought about his home. The diagnosis revealed more about a teacher's need to reduce the complexity of troubling behavior than it did about the nature of Harold's difficulty with written language.

There were times with Harold when it was no more than a flicker, indistinguishable, almost, amid the tics and grimaces. But there was no doubt that it was light, like the headlamp of a miner trapped deep in the wood and vapor of a collapsed tunnel. And, sometimes, the light did shine: "The eagle dives after the fish/ The fish swims away from the eagle." Harold had been on a shuttlecock odyssey: his intelligence was calibrated, his eyes checked, the rhythms of his brain monitored. The journey yielded snapshots, but they were cropped of his history: camping with his father, his solitary walks to the lake. His past was being replaced by a sterile chronicle of assessments that couldn't get to the living center of the problem: the lost father, the mother receding slowly into a dim parlor, the growing weight of the assumption of his feeblemindedness. Harold was made stupid by his longing, and his folder full of tests could never reveal that.

"Most of them have been terribly hurt about their intelligence," Lillian said, and paused, seeming to reach inside, trying to catch the right word. "We think that if . . . if we can only give these kids more study skills, that'll solve their problems." Again a pause, then focus—and eloquence. "But poor reading is not at the core of the paralysis they feel. They continually relive all the old hurt." The American educational system is an extraordinary achievement. Secondary and higher education is not systematically regulated—as in many other countries—by examination or quota, and even if you're poor, there are schools you can afford. We have provided elementary education for virtually all American children for some time now, and we fret more than many societies do about meeting the diverse needs of these young people. We test them and assess them—even kindergartners are given an array of readiness measures—in order to determine what they know and don't know, can and can't do. The supreme irony, though, is that the very means we use to determine those needs— and the various remedial procedures that derive from them—can wreak profound harm on our children, usually, but by no means only, those who are already behind the economic and political eight ball.

Kids *do* come to school with all sorts of linguistic differences, and some kids, like Harold, arrive on our doorstep with big problems. But what happens at school can then further define the child as unusual, as marginal. Our approaches to language and literacy as often as not keep us from deep understanding of differences and problems—and possibilities. As Mark, Danny, Hank, Delores, and many of the others I worked with demonstrated, kids labeled as marginal have a literate capacity far richer than the numbers in their folders reveal. We set out to determine what a child knows in order to tailor instruction, but we frequently slot rather than shape, categorize rather than foster. And the poorer the kids are—the less power their parents have—the more likely are their chances of being, as Lillian put it, hurt about their intelligence.

American meritocracy is validated and sustained by the deep-rooted belief in equal opportunity. But can we really say that kids like those I taught have equal access to America's educational resources? Consider not only the economic and political barriers they face, but the fact, too, that judgments about their ability are made at a very young age, and those judgments, accurate or not, affect the curriculum they receive, their place in the school, the way they're defined institutionally. The insidious part of this drama is that, in the observance or the breach, students unwittingly play right into the assessments. Even as they rebel, they confirm the school's decision. They turn off or distance themselves or clam up or daydream, they deny or lash out, acquiesce or subvert, for, finally, they are powerless to stand outside the definition and challenge it head-on. Teachers like Rosalie see through this behavioral smokescreen to the pain and fear underneath, but class load, bureaucratic protocol, the sheer weight of the child's record, the difficulty of reversing established institutional perceptions, and a dozen other factors make it very hard to act fully on their teacherly instincts. Meanwhile the children gradually internalize the definition the school delivers to them, incorporate a stratifying regulator as powerful as the overt institutional gatekeepers that, in other societies, determine who goes where in the educational system. There is no need for the elitist protection of quotas and exclusionary exams when a kid announces that he just wants to be average. If you want to insist that the children Joe and Monica and the rest of us taught had an equal opportunity in American schools, then you'll have to say that they had their equal chance and forfeited it before leaving the fourth grade.

———◆———

The dance floor is dim, and colored lights give the bland cafeteria walls and the sagging crepe the snap of fiesta. On a makeshift stage, an older man is playing the *bajo sexto*—a bass guitar with six double strings—and the accordionist pushes and pulls on a button squeeze box: a jumpy vibrato, tremulous, happy. Your feet and shoulders move, even if you stand along the back wall, as I am, for the dances, the Norteña polka and the *corrido*, are so expressive and merry. The *corrido*, a quick dance with rapid turns, the woman pressed in close, the man's right hand firm in the small of her back, their feet moving in swift shuffle steps, their shoulders bouncing—a dance simultaneously abrupt and delicate. We celebrate the end of English classes, a night school for adults. We are having a graduation of sorts, one of those moments when time is stopped with colored lights to honor achievement, the achievement here of people working to make English a full second language.

Our stay in the Teacher Corps would soon be over. Almost from the beginning of our work in El Monte, Ben Campos got us involved in things you'd never find in the traditional ed school bill of fare. Ben possessed the kind of binocular vision I needed so badly. He was able to see head-on the community's poverty and despair, yet saw as well the many points of desire and possibility. He knew where to tap. He'd identify a need and figure out a way for us to help. Of all our special projects, one of the most tentative but most enjoyable was an English program we set up for Spanish-speaking adults. It was probably Ben's most instructive move.

We met two evenings a week in the empty cafeteria, arranging those long Formica tables into stations at each corner of the room. The participants came from the houses and crammed apartments that surrounded the school; many of their children were in the classes we taught and observed. Some of these people were in the United States on temporary visas and others were here illegally: migrant workers and ditchdiggers and other day laborers trying to keep a Mexican family in shoes and clothes with American wages. Every so often, the INS, *la migra*, would raid the apartment buildings in which they lived, and we'd lose a tableful of students, to be replaced, eventually, by new workers who started coming to our program with relatives and neighbors. Ben

counted it all up one day and announced to us that we must have
seen a hundred people. We got to know some of them quite well,
and, I think, had decent success with them. Others, though, would
show up for two or three or four weeks, and then voluntarily or
otherwise go back to their families in Baja or Jalisco or Michoacan.

Our lessons were practical. Mostly, we focused on spoken English, though we did work on reading with those who were already gaining fluency in their new language. What curriculum
we had, we tried to build from the situations most immediate to
them: role-playing and modeling how you'd hire a lawyer, determine price, and express your satisfaction or displeasure; how to
converse with your child's teacher, a physician, an Immigration
official. We'd ask them what current problems they were having
in their communities or on their jobs and try to structure the conversation accordingly. This work was exciting for us; we had
never taught adults. Ben, who knew about second-language instruction and who took the least skilled students himself, laid out
some general guidelines about relevance and role-playing and
language acquisition and then eavesdropped on our lessons.
After the first few sessions, the people we worked with began
shaping the encounters themselves. They'd start showing up at
six-thirty and stay until nine—sometimes later—to talk over concerns about jobs or kids. Occasionally, Ben and I would then go
with a few of the men to the local bar, where Spanish and English
fused on the jukebox and on the shifting channels of a dusty TV.

Most of the participants had grown up poor, so their Mexican
education was limited—that, combined with uncertain English,
made it unlikely that they would have many official contacts with
American schools. A number of them told us that they were concerned about how their children were doing, but felt funny about
seeing the teacher, for their English was so bad and . . . well . . .
who were they to presume to talk to the teacher about what she
does? Our night school was different for them, though, and they
showed us that in a variety of ways. After working all day, they'd
arrive with a bowl of *pollo con mole* or a tray of *chiles rellenos* or a
bag of pastries: *pan de huevo, elotes,* and *empanadas,* little turnovers
stuffed with pumpkin or pineapple. Occasionally Lillian and I
and the other interns would grieve to Ben that we didn't know
enough to really help, that we weren't advancing our students'
English quickly enough. Ben would pause—the thoughtful pause

was characteristic of him—and then point out that the sessions, by all signs, were valued by these folks, that just using English in the company of native speakers was a good thing. Most important, he'd say, tapping his spoon on the rim of his coffee cup, the classes were bringing them comfortably into the schools, breaking down some of the intimidating barriers that traditionally keep them far away, distant from the places where their kids were learning how to read and write. We were too focused on specific outcomes, said Ben, slipping into educationese for our benefit; there's more to look for here than just an increase in vocabulary. I believe him now more than I believed him then, though interesting illustrations of his point surrounded us. Take, for example, my student Tranquilino.

When we completed our classes at the end of the school term, we got various cards and notes of thanks from the participants. Tranquilino sent me a card with a long note written inside it. He thanked me for the lessons and worried that I might not understand his letter, which was in Spanish. He wished me well and hoped that I found myself "enchanted with life"—a beautiful way to say that he wanted things to go well for me. He wrote further about several classmates we both liked and then closed with *disculpeme por los borrones y lo mal espresado*—"pardon my erasures and the poor way in which I express myself," a respectful gesture to the language teacher and a reminder of how intimidating the use of written language can be. But the part of this that was most linguistically revealing—and certainly touching in a complicated way—was the fact that the card Tranquilino had sent was a sympathy card: It had a tableau of praying hands on the front; "praying God will comfort you," it said on the inside. A gaffe of a different order from those for which he apologized. I knew that Tranquilino was capable of deciphering most of the individual words, yet the message of the Hallmark text went by him, a sign that he was still a beginning reader of a new language. He heard the individual sounds but missed the song. He probably thought the card was appropriate for his teacher because it looked and sounded elevated, respectful. I thought a lot about the card, was alternately flattered and moved—for the error in choice was so engaging—yet I fretted too, for I felt I should have done a better job with Tranquilino's reading.

I had finished with Tranquilino in April, and as June approached, so did my time to leave El Monte. Lillian and Monica and Joe were applying for jobs in the school district. I wasn't as focused. During these last few months, I found myself thinking more and more about my exit from graduate study at UCLA. I left too many fragments behind. I had taken enough courses to be close to a master's degree; all I had to do was pass an oral comprehensive and a French exam. A friend of mine heard about a job he thought I'd like and recommended me. An educational program for returning veterans needed someone to tutor English. It sounded just right. I could tutor twenty or thirty hours a week and study the rest of the time. After that . . . well, I'd see. Lillian, Joe, Monica, Ben—we'd be splitting up soon, though we would write and visit. An awful lot still seemed loose and uncertain to me, but something very good came from my two years with them, something basic and sustaining.

I was long gone when Ben saw Tranquilino again. He bumped into him walking out of the market. Tranquilino's English was much improved. He told Ben he'd taken another course in adult school and that he was feeling better about it, a little more confident. Tranquilino asked about me, so Ben relayed the greeting with a telephone call. "Who knows," he said, "we probably got him on the road. It all helps." Tranquilino might have done just as well without us, gone to adult school on his own and become proficient just as quickly. But the more I come to understand about education, the more I've come to believe in the power of invitation. Programs like the Teacher Corps—and many others that developed through those years—generated possibilities for all kinds of people who had traditionally been excluded from the schools. My expectations for Tranquilino had been, in a sense, too narrow. I didn't appreciate the effect we might be having not just on "decoding skills" and "ability to comprehend the gist" but on his attitudes toward schooling and toward the use of English itself, on the way he felt sitting in an American classroom. Much, much later I found out that some of the children of the people we taught—youngsters when we knew them—had gone on to careers in education themselves: they're now teachers in the schools in those East Los Angeles communities. Whether or not we had any small and indirect influence on these lives, I'll never know. But I can't help but wonder what nascent desires for education blossomed as the parents of those children came to feel part of the schools.

6

◆

Reclaiming
the Classroom

There was not much space in Room 316, the third-floor office of the Veteran's Program, but the staff managed to fit a desk and two chairs into a storeroom, just inside the door. That was where I tutored. There were stacks of mimeograph paper and old files and textbooks behind me. A portable blackboard rocked noisily on wobbly casters. The Veteran's Program had been fashioned by an educational psychologist named Chip Anderson and was, in effect, a masterful crash course in the three Rs of higher education. It was housed in the old UCLA Extension Building in downtown Los Angeles. Students were enrolled right out of the service—the Marine Corps particularly—or through veteran's centers in Southern California. Virtually all who signed up were men. They took classes in English, speech, and mathematics, and participated in workshops to improve their reading and study skills. They were also enrolled in The Psychology of Human Relations. This introduced them to the mysteries of the college lecture course and had the additional benefit of dealing with communication and social interaction for a group returning to a culture that must have seemed pretty strange. All students received tutoring and academic and personal counseling. The curriculum was comprehensive and sensible; it provided an opportunity to develop the speaking, reading, writing, and mathematical abilities needed for college. The men I worked with called it academic boot camp.

I tutored three afternoons a week, and saw about five or six students a day. Our discussions ranged from subject-verb agreement to the taking of timed essay exams, and, fairly often, ranged outward to the NFL draft, music, wives, lovers, anger about the past, and confusion about the future. On the average the men were in their mid-twenties, some were younger, a few were lifers: gunnery sergeants or petty officers who, in their forties, were trying to change radically the direction of their next twenty years. Most of the students had been in the military from four to six years and had been, to use their term, the grunts—the privates and corporals who, in the years just after the prom, found themselves in marshland and firestorms. Some of these men started the program during their last few months of service, and others had been out for anywhere from weeks to years. Hair length became the dating gauge. If a student hadn't been to Vietnam, he came to the program with a legacy of boredom and a handful of firm resolves; some of those who were in Vietnam brought other things. They came directly from hospitals or drug and alcohol rehabilitation centers and, in a few cases, from prison. And some of them were continuing treatment as outpatients for particularly destructive physical injuries or for flitting horrors that could not be stitched or trussed.

I got to talk pretty intimately with men who saw the world very differently from the way I did and who had been through things I could barely imagine. The politics of the group ranged from reactionary to radical, white supremacist to black nationalist, with most mixing hawkish foreign policy with fairly liberal social mores. Some had dropped out of high school, were functionally literate, and were coming to the Veteran's Program to gain their high school equivalency; others were readers and theory builders and street poets. From what they told me, it was clear that most of them had academic histories like the kids in El Monte and the guys in Voc. Ed. Their school memories were dreary; I was seeing people at the other end of a frustrated educational journey. They were mustering their resources, though, for one last go at it. About a third of our students were wild boys with few responsibilities, while others were somber men with families and debts. Some had been shot while others spent their time in a sleepy town. I started noticing the scars. David had lost most of his right thumb—he held his pen in place with a nub—and had a scar that ran up beyond his wrist. Richard was missing the tops of two fingers, and the nails on Clayton's hands were replaced by fungus. The underside of Bill's arm, the place where the radial muscles flex to a rounded fullness, was gouged—a layer of slick, brownish skin stretched into place like wet and wrinkled paper.

The ethnic and geographic mix was rich: whites, Chicanos, blacks, a few Asians, fewer American Indians; New Yorkers and Oregonians, men from the Motor City and men from Southern farms. They drove in from El Toro or Camp Pendleton seventy miles to the south, from apartments scattered from Orange County to the far end of the San Fernando Valley, or from homes in East L.A., Lynwood, or Compton. A few lived in awful places close to the program, like the Morrison, a musty hotel that gained a flicker of notoriety when it was photographed for the cover of a mediocre Doors album. And some bused in from the Veteran's Hospital in West Los Angeles. Their needs were profound and, at times, overwhelming to someone as young as I was. They came for education, for counseling, for friendship, for decompression. They came to get themselves back into the stream of things.

The Extension Building is on South Grand Avenue, five or six blocks this side of the rich hub of downtown Los Angeles: Citi-Corp, the Bonaventure, the Arco Towers. It is one block east of Hope. It is a dirty beige stone building, four stories high. A fire escape crisscrosses all but the first floor of the south side. The windows are opaque, and the curtains you can see on the second floor are light gray. One is torn from its rung and tied back. Next door is a sandstone-colored hotel with bars on the ground-floor windows and 1120 crudely painted on a stucco post by the front stairs. It has no name. In the immediate vicinity are two parking lots and some small, depressed industries: sewing machines, garment hangers, baby furniture, Boston Shoe, ADM Button and Belt. Jo's Liquor and the Morris Cafe are a few blocks to the south. Beer and wine and pool.

Every quarter, fifteen or so teachers and tutors and a couple of hundred students moved in and out of the hallways of the Extension Building, moving through the elevators, the lobby, the lunchroom in the basement. And during breaks between classes, Grand Avenue would intermittently feel the tingling scrape of peripatetic chatter and the heat of a quick smoke. The main meeting place was the lunchroom, presided over by Al Petrillo, a vendor of sandwiches, a player of ponies, and an indefatigable dispenser of jokes with punchlines like "Jeez, Doc, I hope they don't amputate around here, 'cause I'm only in for prickly heat!" Al was a short man with sleepy eyes who would cradle his forehead in his left hand and slowly look up at you as he made change and insulted your choice of sandwiches or your looks. And behind him, a hundred people lamented and laughed and made bets and dreamed.

I had been tutoring for about two months when Dr. Anderson called me into his office and offered me a full-time job. He said he had been talking to the men and decided he wanted me to teach English and reading and maybe do a little counseling. I would be taking my master's orals at UCLA in December, so I'd be set to go by January, the start of a new quarter. How about it? I liked working with the veterans very much, felt at ease, for so many of them had grown up in neighborhoods like mine. I accepted on the spot. It was after I left Anderson's office that I started having second thoughts.

In the Teacher Corps I worked informally with small groups of children and had ongoing connection with a team. And tutoring in the Veteran's Program seemed a lot safer than teaching. Someone else created the curriculum, set the assignments, and gave the grades. I was a coach, a compatriot, helping the men as they struggled with their test taking and their writing. If they thought an assignment was stupid or a grade unfair, I could just nod sympathetically and get on with the paper before us. Now I would have to fashion my own curriculum, give the grades, and take the heat for it.

I worried most about the curriculum. One of the English teachers in the Veteran's Program had fashioned a wildly inventive set of assignments that had the students comparing two apples one week and writing a poem the next. It was a maverick curriculum, and I admired its ambition, but a lot of the men I tutored were simply perplexed by it. The other teachers relied on more traditional curricula: a handbook of rules of grammar, lectures on subordination and parallelism, papers requiring students to narrate and describe. I went to the UCLA bookstore and browsed through the various texts in use on the campus: more grammar handbooks. This all seemed cheerless. And the old standby, the writing of essays on unforgettable grandparents and My First Job, seemed as appropriate for the veterans as a hymn at a crapshoot.

I had a month, so I started looking around for a base on which to build my course.

The first possibility that offered itself was, of course, Vietnam. It would seem natural to draw on the veterans' experience, present and vibrant as it was. Such a curriculum would be relevant at a time when relevance was dearly sought. But when I imagined teaching a course on the war, it didn't feel right—felt presumptuous, intrusive. After spending two months with the veterans, I could see that each man was on his own psychic timetable: Some were fairly comfortable talking about Vietnam; others couldn't bear to do it, at least not publicly. And in either case, they were looking forward to an education that would create a future, not one that would force them back through a past of shrapnel and deadly surprise.

It was when I started thinking about why the men had come to the program that I found an answer, one that lay at the intersection of the veterans' lives and mine. The men wanted to change their lives, and for all their earlier failures, they still held onto an American dream: Education held the power to equalize things. After Vietnam, they had little doubt about what their next step had to be: up and out of the pool of men society could call on so easily to shoot and be shot at. From what they told me, it was clear that a number of the veterans were a high school teacher's bad dream: detached or lippy or assaultive. They were my Voc. Ed. comrades reincarnated. But here they were now: "I'm givin' it a hundred percent this time." There's probably little any teacher can do with some kids in some high schools: the poverty and violence of the neighborhoods, the dynamics of particular families, the ways children develop identities in the midst of economic blight. You rely on goodwill and an occasional silent prayer to keep your class from exploding, hope that some wild boy doesn't slug another, pray that your authority isn't embarrassed. But here those students were, five or ten years down the line: different life experiences, different perspectives on learning. It makes you think about those sullen high schoolers in a different light, see their lives along a time line. Maybe no one could have gotten to some of the veterans when they were sixteen, but they were ready now. They were bringing with them an almost magical vision of what learning could do for them, and regardless of what I had come to know about the realities of higher education, I could sure understand the desire to be transfigured by books.

The veterans' encounter with college led me to reflect on my education in a way I hadn't done before. More than I realized, I had learned a lot in El Monte about developing a curriculum: I approached learning carefully, step by step, systematically. I found that I knew what questions to ask. What had I really learned from studying history and psychology and philosophy and literature? I thought a lot about my best teachers, about Jack MacFarland at Mercy High, about Dr. Carothers and Ted Erlandson and the others at Loyola. I browsed through the books that had mattered and thought about those courses that had opened up ways of considering the world. What intellectual orientations persisted? I went back to UCLA and sat in on a few lectures in the humanities and the social sciences, listening, this time, with a different ear. I talked with other teachers. And this is how I started to think about the curriculum I would fashion.

Given the nature of these men's needs and given the limited time I would have with them, could I perhaps orient them to some of the kinds of reading and writing and ways of thinking that seem essential to a liberal course of study, some of the habits of mind that Jack MacFarland and the many that followed him had helped me develop? If I could do this in some systematic and manageable way, then I would be enhancing the veterans' chances of participating in the institutions they would soon be entering. And while I wanted to be pragmatic—college preparation was the name of this game—I also wanted to go beyond utility. I was looking for a methodical way to get my students to think about thinking. Thinking. Not a fussbudget course, but a course about thought. I finally decided to build a writing curriculum on four of the intellectual strategies my education had helped me develop—some of which, I would later discover, were as old as Aristotle—strategies that kept emerging as I reflected on the life of the undergraduate: summarizing, classifying, comparing, and analyzing.

Liberal studies had really sharpened my ability to find the central notion in an argument or the core of a piece of fiction. Thinking back on it, I couldn't imagine a more crucial skill than summarizing; we can't manage information, make crisp connections, or rebut arguments without it. The great syntheses and refutations are built on it. The veterans would have to have practice summarizing various kinds of academic materials. It would give them a nice sense of mastery if they could determine and express the gist of readings that might, at first glance, seem opaque as medieval texts.

Classifying. You could almost define the undergraduate's life as the acquisition of the ways Western scholars have classified their knowledge. The very departments in which I took my classes represented one way to classify inquiry, and I encountered classification schemes in every course I took: taxonomies in biology, genres and periods in literature and the arts, the catalogs of motive and behavior in psychology and sociology. I wanted the veterans to become familiar with academic classification schemes, to sharpen their own abilities to systematize what they study, and to develop a critical awareness of the limitations of the classification schemes that will surround them. I thought up some simple exercises: Bring to class twenty copies of paintings of the human body. Have the paintings represent a wide range of styles, from Florentine humanism to cubist geometrics, but have all information on artist and period removed. It would be the students' job to classify this collection of paintings by any system they could develop. They would probably begin with a simple binary scheme: some of the paintings look like people and some don't. But through my questions as well as through the observations rising from their interaction, they would be encouraged to elaborate and revise until they'd agreed that they could go no further. I would then ask them to discuss what they felt was gained and what was lost as they classified paintings and moved from one scheme to another.

Another thing that became clear to me was how much knowledge in the arts and sciences is gained by methodically examining one object or event or theory in relation to another. What comes into focus when a student places *A Farewell to Arms* alongside a piece of journalism? What understanding is gained by listing the features of French schooling next to a description of American education? Entire disciplines—comparative politics to comparative anatomy—are built on this intellectual strategy. Simply by virtue of their humanity, the men in the Veteran's Program continually made comparisons, but I wanted to give them the chance to develop confidence and facility in comparing points of view and explanations and works of art.

The further along I got in college, the more I was asked to "analyze" an artistic product, a physical phenomenon, a social event, *to analyze* meaning to break something down to its constituent elements so as to better understand its nature. But that wasn't the whole story. There was a kind of implied directive to the request to analyze, and it took me quite a while before I realized it. Students are not usually told that such analytic investigation is always carried out with a set of assumptions, and these assumptions are crucial determinants of how you proceed in your examination, what you find, and how you explain your discovery to others. I figured that developing the ability to probe the assumptions beneath an analysis or explanation would be exciting and empowering for the veterans, a little insight into how to pick the academic lock. They would be able to read with a critical eye and thus speak and write with more authority. While I could probably develop this critical awareness by modeling it for the class and by questioning them on their reading, I thought they might also benefit by engaging in a kind of intellectual role-playing that would highlight the assumptive base of analysis. I could, for example, present them with a newspaper story about a man who commits an apparently senseless murder. Next would come an account of how Freud would explain violent behavior. It would be the student's job to slip into that perspective and discuss the story as though they were psychoanalysts. This passage would be followed by one written by a more existentially oriented social critic. The class would then discuss the crime with that perspective, discussing as well what happens to their analysis as they shift assumptions about human nature. How did the frameworks they used affect what they saw?

Most of the veterans were considered to be "remedial level" students. Even those who came to the program as pretty capable writers were hesitant and wrote prose that displayed the signs of an inadequate education: misspellings, verbs that didn't agree with subjects, sentences that strangled in their own convolutions. As for the less capable students—the kinds of writers I saw struggling as children in El Monte—composing was a source of embarrassment, a halting, self-conscious duty that resulted in stunted, error-ridden prose. It has been customary for remedial writing programs to focus attention on the kinds of grammatical problems that were found in the pages these men wrote. The programs instruct students in principles of grammar and usage ("Use a comma between coordinate adjectives not joined by 'and'"), distribute workbook exercises that require students to select correct forms ("Write in 'who' or 'whom' in the following sentences"), and assign short, undemanding bits of writing. The assumption is that error can be eradicated by zeroing in on the particulars of language. And that assumption seems to rest on a further assumption that grammatical error signals some fundamental mental barrier to engaging in higher-level cognitive pursuits: until error is isolated and cleaned up, it will not be possible for students to read and write critically, study literature, or toy with style.

It would not be until later in my career that I could methodically challenge these assumptions; at this early stage in my development as a writing teacher I had to rely more on the feel of things. It just didn't make sense that not knowing the delicacies of usage or misplacing commas or blundering pronouns and verb forms or composing a twisted sentence indicated arrest at some cognitive-linguistic stage of development, a stage that had to be traversed before you could engage in critical reading and writing. Such thinking smacked of the reductionism I had seen while studying psychology at UCLA. Besides, I had never gotten some of this stuff straight, and I turned out okay. It seemed that, if anything, concentrating on the particulars of language—schoolbook grammar, mechanics, usage—would tremendously restrict the scope of what language use was all about. Such approaches would rob writing of its joy, and would, to boot, drag the veterans back through their dismal history of red-pencilled failure. Furthermore, we would be aiming low, would be scaling down our expectations—as so many remedial programs do—training to do the minimum, the minimum here being a simple workbook sentence free of error. The men had bigger dreams, and I wanted to tap them.

My students needed to be immersed in talking, reading, and writing, they needed to further develop their ability to think critically, and they needed to gain confidence in themselves as systematic inquirers. They had to be let into the academic club. The fact that they misspelled words or wrote fragments or dropped verb endings would not erect insurmountable barriers to the benefits they would gain from such immersion. A traveler in a foreign land best learns names of people and places, how to express ideas, ways to carry on a conversation by moving around in the culture, participating as fully as he can, making mistakes, saying things half right, blushing, then being encouraged by a friendly native speaker to try again. He'll pick up the details of grammar and usage as he goes along. What he must *not* do is hold back from the teeming flow of life, must not sit in his hotel room and drill himself on all possible gaffes before entering the streets. He'd never leave the room.

My students, too, were strangers in a strange land, and I wanted to create a safe section of the city and give them an opportunity to acquire the language. We would cover some common errors together during the first few days of class, but, for the most part, I and the tutors I now had would work with students individually through the quarter as particular problems came up on particular papers. This would be a more sensible way to deal with grammatical error and would, as well, give students the sense that grammatical correctness is only one of the concerns of a writer, not the only one, and certainly not the force that brings pen to paper.

Aiming high, however, brought with it a real risk: There was the possibility that I would overwhelm the men, defeat them once again by asking them to do things that were beyond their reach, mystify them with impenetrable language. The only article of faith I had came from a little book by Jerome Bruner called *The Process of Education*. Bruner begins one of his chapters with this remarkable dictum: ''Any subject can be taught effectively in some intellectually honest form to any child at any stage of development.'' I transposed the promise and challenge of that sentence to adults. It seemed that I could honor the challenge if I used accessible materials and if I had the students work with them in ways that built from the simple to the complex.

I paged through newspapers, magazines, and political pamphlets. I copied out song lyrics. I rifled the books I had been collecting since my days with Jack MacFarland. I excerpted, deleted, Xeroxed, cut, pasted, and rewrote. To give students a sense of how social criticism reads, I used an Erich Fromm essay from *McCall's* rather than assign a section out of *Escape from Freedom* or *Socialist Humanism*. To provide illustrations of psychological states for our analysis assignments, I relied on song lyrics like John Prine's "Donald and Lydia." To raise liberal studies themes like Appearance and Reality, I lifted a few pages from *Invisible Man*. And so on.

Each quarter, I began by having the students summarize short, simple readings, and then moved them slowly through classifying and comparing to analyzing, which became the capstone of the curriculum. I didn't do enough of this careful sequencing in El Monte, and my curriculum there suffered for it. I explained and modeled, used accessible readings, tried to incorporate what the veterans learned from one assignment into the next, slowly increased difficulty, and provided a lot of time for the men to talk and write. So, for example, I introduced them to the strategy of comparing with this pair of sentences:

> In the whole world no poor devil is lynched, no wretch is tortured, in whom I too am not degraded and murdered.
>
> —AIMÉ CÉSAIRE

> There exists among men, because they are men, a solidarity through which each shares responsibility for every injustice and every wrong committed in the world.
>
> —KARL JASPERS

I asked them to talk about the message each sentence contains and to talk, as well, about the way each is written: the academic sound of one, the emotional quality of the other. Did the sound affect the message? I would tell them a little about Césaire, the African poet and statesman, and about Jaspers, the German philosopher. Did that information about time and place affect their reading? They would go through many such pairs—finger exercises, as a friend of mine would later call them—doing them orally, writing on them in class as a tutor and I provided advice on wording and direction, and then, finally, going it alone at home. Within three or four weeks, they were working with more difficult passages, like these two cosmogonies—one an Australian Aboriginal myth, the other from an astronomy textbook:

I

In the very beginning everything was resting in perpetual darkness: night oppressed all the earth like an impenetrable thicket.

(And) Karora was lying asleep, in everlasting night, at the
very bottom of the soak of Ilbalintja: as yet there was not
water in it, but all was dry ground.

Over him the soil was red with flower & overgrown with
many grasses & a great pole was swaying above him.

. . . And Karora's head lay at the root of the great pole; he
had rested thus ever from the beginning.

And Karora was thinking, & wishes & desires flashed
through his mind. Bandicoots began to come out from his
navel & from his arm-pits. They burst through the sod above
& sprang into life.

And now dawn was beginning to break.

From all quarters men saw a new light appearing: the sun
itself began to rise at Ilbalintja, & flooded everything with its
light.

Then the gurra ancestor was minded to rise, now that the
sun was mounting higher.

He burst through the crust that had covered him: & the
gaping hole that he had left behind became the Ilbalintja
Soak, filled with the sweet dark juice of honeysuckle buds.

II

Theoreticians have calculated a "standard" model of what
the big bang may have been like. In the beginning we
imagine a great primeval fireball of matter and radiation. We
do not have to imagine any particular mass, or even a finite
mass, for the fireball. Its density was very high and it was at
a temperature of perhaps 10^{10}K.

At first the matter consisted only of protons, neutrons,
electrons, positrons, and neutrinos, all independent particles.
After about 100 seconds, however, the temperature had
dropped to 10^9K, and the particles began to combine to form
some heavier nuclei. This nucleogenesis continued, according
to the model, for a few hours until the temperature dropped
to about 10^8K. During this time, about 20 percent of the mass
of the material formed into helium. Some deuterium also
formed (deuterium is an isotope of hydrogen with a nucleus
containing one proton and one neutron) but only a small
amount—probably less than one part in a thousand. The

actual amount of deuterium formed depends critically on the density of the fireball, if it was fairly high, most of the deuterium would have been built up into helium. Scarcely any nuclei heavier than those of helium are expected to have survived. So the composition of the fireball when nuclear building ceased is thought to have been mostly hydrogen, about 20 percent helium, and a trace of deuterium.

For the next million years the fireball was like a stellar interior—hot and opaque, with radiation passing from atom to atom. During the time, the temperature gradually dropped to about 3000K, and the density to about 1000 atoms/cm^3. At this point the fireball became transparent. The radiation was no longer absorbed and was able to pass freely throughout the universe. After about 1000 million years, the model predicts that the matter should have condensed into galaxies and stars.

We emphasize again that the fireball must not be thought of as a localized explosion—like an exploding superstar. There were no boundaries and no site of the explosion. It was everywhere. The fireball is still existing in a sense. It has expanded greatly, but the original matter and radiation are still present and accounted for. The atoms of our bodies came from material in the fireball. We were and are still in the midst of it, it is all around us.

I knew from my own early struggles that students who have not had a privileged education often freeze up when they see readings like these, particularly the big bang discussion with its superscripted numbers, the vocabulary of its first two paragraphs, and the heady notions in the last. And they don't have the background knowledge or the conceptual grab bag of received phrases to make connections between scientific theorizing and mythic explanation. But give them time. Provide some context, break them into groups or work with the whole class, involving everyone. Let them see what, collectively, they do know, and students will, together, begin to generate meaning and make connections. One person once read something else about big bang, and his knowledge helps a second person understand the nuclear processes in paragraph two, and that second person then asks a question that remained ill-formed in the mind of a third. And the teacher darts in and out of the conversation, clarifying, questioning, repeating, looping back to link one student's observation to another's. And so it is that the students, labeled "remedial," read and talk and write their way toward understanding.

◆

The Teacher Corps introduced me to the risk and reward of education, but it was the Veteran's Program that really enabled me to come into my own as a teacher, to publicly define myself as someone engaged with the language of others. It was a good place to grow up. The work, successful or failed, had unusual power. The students possessed long and complex life histories, and they were trying to reclaim a place in the classroom they once lost or never really had. Here are a few of those students and a few of the pieces of their history.

It was the third or fourth day of my second quarter in the Veteran's Program, and I was, by now, very much aware of a bald man staring at me from a rear seat along the west wall of the room. His skin was dark, dark brown, his head perfectly slick, his ear pierced by a tiny gold ring. He wore a leather pilot's jacket and kept his arms folded tightly across his chest. I noticed the arms. Pilot's jackets are big, loose things, and this man's upper arms filled out the sleeves, the leather stretching firmly over his shoulders and biceps. As I moved around day after day talking about writing, and memorizing names, and tapping people on shoulders, and getting one man to address another, this man, Willie Oates, sat back and said nothing. He seemed all forearms and pectorals and husky silence.

At the end of the fourth class, he walked slowly up to the podium, waiting his turn behind the three or four men who were asking about their assignment. I kept talking, half hoping they wouldn't leave. But they did. Then Willie took a step forward and began speaking, pounding his fist on the podium in slow pace with each deliberate word: "You," he said. "You—are—" and here he looked up from his fist and into my eyes. "You—are—teaching—the—fuck—outta—me!"

Willie had just spent two years in federal penitentiary. His muscles were the muscles you get from lifting weights two and three hours a day to cleanse your respect in spasms of rushing blood.

During this time, Willie started reading. He read all the literature in the prison library, and while some of that was Hemingway, some of it was also Jane Austen. As he read, he wrote in a journal, and he began to develop a style that was ornate as a drawing room.

Willie Oates and I spent a lot of time in the lunchroom. Al Petrillo would be holding court at the cash register, and we'd be in a far corner, Willie's papers and Cokes and open bags of potato chips spread before us. Willie had all sorts of stylistic moves; it was my job to get him to weigh their merits. I would go over an essay sentence by sentence, showing him where he'd kill an effect with excess, or get himself into a hopeless tangle with his eighteenth-century syntax, or use a word that sounded pretentious to the twentieth-century ear. The assessing gaze that Willie had fixed on me was gone. Now there was a gentler look, one full of need—an unprotected intensity of mind. He slid into schooling like an athlete lowering himself into a whirlpool, feeling the heat deep in his tissue. He read Chinese poetry and stories by Pirandello. He wrote a paper using the British social historian J. H. Plumb to analyze American counterculture. He talked about Malcolm X and Eldridge Cleaver, two other black men who had transformed themselves in a prison library.

When Willie was released from the service years before, he returned to a neighborhood that was poor and burned out. He was an aching, dreamy man who couldn't dull himself and who, eventually, stole some money and a car to try to rip away from the projects and pool halls and indolent streets. He was caught within a week. And now, two or three years later, he saw his chance again. He wanted to know everything, was as hungry as anyone I'd seen. One day he showed me the journal he kept in prison—it was a thick National copybook with a cardboard cover pressed to look like leather. As I paged through it, I saw black, working-class experience fused with the language of teapots and Victorian gardens: whole pages of *Sense and Sensibility* and *The Mill on the Floss* copied down, strained and awkward imitations, beginnings of short stories, reflections on prison that seemed forced but that contained elegant moments. It was a remarkable book, the record of a clash of cultures and a testament to the power of Willie's desire.

He kept a journal now, one filled with assignments from

Speech and Psychology and Math and various rough drafts for me. He continued to write down quotations that caught his ear, these from the lectures and books that presently surrounded him. One from my class that I remember seeing there came from Niels Bohr: "Your theory is crazy—but not crazy enough to be true."

Willie was finding a way to direct his yearning. I would pass on to him books I was just discovering—*The Other America; Black Skin, White Masks*—and we would talk about the anger that used to knot him up, the hopelessness that landed him in prison. We talked about education and the use of it to direct the anger outward—dissent rather than involuted despair. Willie developed into a truly individual writer and, as well, learned to handle the academy. He received A's in psychology, English, speech, and mathematics. He went on to major in English at a local state university. He continued to write in his journal. Writing, now, in the university, writing to try out new ideas, writing to redefine himself. Writing and writing and writing.

Sergeant Gonzalez was a twenty-year man, a Marine who, at forty, was near retirement. He was tall and square-shouldered as a recruiting poster. He spoke his mind and he rarely smiled, and he was getting, at best, a C from me. He tried and tried but his writing remained too stunted, too abbreviated and superficial. He tended toward literal interpretations and preferred unambiguous answers. He had worked hard all his life, and hard work always gave him tangible results. So here he was, dropping his head and going over tackle again, and yet again, but with the same step, no little juke, no variation. I knew that he would never give up but that he was close to despair.

I set aside an hour after class and dug up something that I thought might help, a poem from Edgar Lee Masters's *Spoon River Anthology*:

BUTCH WELDY

After I got religion and steadied down
They gave me a job in the canning works,
And every morning I had to fill
The tank in the yard with gasoline,
That fed the blow-fires in the sheds
To heat the soldering irons.

And I mounted a rickety ladder to do it,
Carrying buckets full of the stuff.
One morning, as I stood there pouring,
The air grew still and seemed to heave,
And I shot up as the tank exploded,
And down I came with both legs broken,
And my eyes burned crisp as a couple of eggs.
For someone left a blow-fire going,
And something sucked the flame in the tank.
The Circuit Judge said whoever did it
Was a fellow-servant of mine, and so
Old Rhodes' son didn't have to pay me.
And I sat on the witness stand as blind
As Jack the Fiddler, saying over and over,
"I didn't know him at all."

David could follow Butch Weldy's story. The poem depicted a real-life situation and did so along a straight narrative line. It nicely fit David's own interpretive predilections.

"So why," I asked him, "does Masters have Butch say 'someone' left a fire going, and 'something' caused an explosion? 'Someone' and 'something' sound pretty vague to me. Is Butch a little slow?"

"No, he's not slow. He just don't know who did it."

"David, who is Old Rhodes' son?"

"I'm not sure."

"If he's someone who has the ability to pay money to Butch, what position would he hold?"

"The boss? No. The owner. He owns the place."

"The judge said that whoever caused the accident to happen was a worker like Butch, and so, therefore, the owner wouldn't have to pay Butch. Pay for what?"

"The accident."

"What would we call it now if someone paid for the accident?"

"Workman's comp."

"Okay, David, now here's an interesting question for you. You're the head of a motor pool, right?"

"Right."

"If one of your soldiers stumbled and released the trip on a jack, and a car fell on a mechanic and injured him, whose fault would it be? The Marine Corps'?"

"Well, no."

"Could you think of any situation where it might be the Marine Corps' fault?"

We went on like this for a little while longer, and then I asked David to list all the information we had gleaned about Butch and his situation: He was seriously injured at work, is now blind, won't receive compensation, is being shuttled through the legal system, and so on. After making our list, I picked up the questioning again, this time about Butch Weldy's past ("What does the first line—'*After* I got religion and steadied down'—tell us about Butch before he got this job?") and about the degree of control he seems to have over his life. This last issue was an interesting one to pose to David, for he was clearly a man who prided himself on being at the center of his actions.

"David, could you picture yourself in Butch's situation?"

"Well, yes and no. I mean I could imagine getting hurt, but—"

"But? But you would have been more careful?"

"Yeh. Yeh, I'd have been more careful."

"How does Masters describe the ladder Butch was climbing?"

"Rickety."

"Yep."

And so it went. Within a half hour, we had a long, rich list of detail about Butch Weldy. It was then that I started turning the key.

"Okay, David, look at the wealth of information we got from this little poem. Could we really understand the mess Butch Weldy is in without all this detail?"

"Um, no, no we couldn't, not really."

"That's right. The detail makes the whole thing come alive to us."

This continued for a few minutes, then: "Now, look, you are a powerful guy, and you take charge of things, and you like to have answers, and you can answer for yourself short and sweet . . . but, man, not everyone is like that. Butch is in a hell of a mess, and to tell somebody about it, we'd have to give a little history, and spell out what we know about the accident, and explain what kind of person Butch seems to be and how he feels. . . . Now, what sorts of things are we sure of; what can we say straight out?"

"Well, we could say what happened in the accident, I mean

the ladder . . . the gasoline . . . the explosion . . . all that stuff. And we could say he's blind now and he's going to get screwed by the law.''

"Right. Good. Now, what will we have to hedge our bets on? What will we have to say we're unsure about?''

"Hm. Well, we don't know who left the fires going, and we don't know exactly how the explosion happened.''

"Okay. And, again, what are the words Masters uses?''

"Um . . . 'someone' and 'something.'''

"Now, what about Butch's character? What kind of guy is he?''

"It's hard to say, but he don't seem to have a grip on things, and maybe he never did. He sure as hell is lost.''

"Good. And remember, you started what you just said with 'It's hard to say,' and that's a perfectly acceptable way to talk about some of the things going on in this little snapshot of a man's life.''

I won't tell you that this session made David a dramatically better writer; only in Hollywood pedagogy does such change happen overnight. But the paper he wrote on "Butch Weldy" was richer in detail than was his previous work, and it displayed attempts to deal with the uncertain. David's writing started getting a little more ambitious and a little more specific. He was learning some new moves, a few ways to take chances in his writing. That created another set of problems, of course. Saying complex things forces you away from the protected syntax of simple sentences. But error that crops up because a student is trying new things is a valuable kind of error, a sign of growth.

Jerry Williams was thin and walked with a slight sideways bend at the waist; he wore wire-rim glasses that were deeply tinted. Jerry was quiet and solitary and tended to be irritable and rude with the other veterans. No one was close to him. He was a poor writer ("I think that the state of blacks in the U.S. is a easly debated subject. I think this becaus their is evidence if you want to look at it . . ."), and he'd miss class often. The tutors and I kept trying to catch him up, but then he'd miss school again, and we'd try again, and he'd slip further and further behind. He was a Seconal junkie, "reds," and the other men called him Redhead. He was loaded most of the time I worked with him. I would guide him as he wrote a slow paragraph or talk ineffectually with him about an essay he'd forgotten to read. He'd look at me, eyes half-closed behind amber lenses, and respond to my suggestions with hip monosyllables: "dig it" and "right on" and like that. I hoped something was sinking in, though I didn't think much was. He stopped showing up at all during the last two weeks of school.

On the last day of that quarter, while the men were writing their final in-class papers, the door to my room slammed open and Jerry stumbled through. I had never seen him anywhere near that stoned. He made his way down the right aisle, steadying himself against the wall, and walked slowly to my desk. The class had stopped writing and was watching us. "I want to take the exam," he said. I told him I didn't think that was a good idea, that he was way too loaded to write anything. "Motherfucker," he yelled, "don't tell me that!" He slammed his hand on the desk and, in a quick tipsy glide, slid behind me. I wheeled around and grabbed his arms. Two or three guys in the front were out of their seats. But it was a burst of rage, and it faded quickly. Jerry put his hands back on the chalk tray and slumped into the blackboard. "Just let me take the exam," he slurred. Beneath the fuzz of the Seconal was some quavering desire to be schooled. He looked back up, not at me, but at the men in the first few rows: "I got a right to take the exam."

The veterans and I spent a lot of time talking about language. Sometimes a major part of a class would be taken up with a poem or song lyric, other times I would sneak a quick opportunity for word play into a lesson: "Try writing a sentence like this one from *Native Son*," or "Give me a phrase someone said or a song you heard that caught your ear today." That would go on the board and spark discussion. A lot of the men took to language. For some, linguistic play was part of their culture; for others, it seemed okay to fool around with words if the teacher was getting all worked up about them, was—for God's sake—walking backward into the podium because of a turned phrase.

Jack Cheney was a special kind of student. Every quarter we would get two or three men who had read a lot and were skilled writers. These were the guys who were bored to tears by high school—didn't fit in, were out of step, quit going. But unlike some gifted dropouts, they weren't from families who could afford to send them to special schools, so they were scooped up by the military with all the other uncovered eighteen-year-olds.

Jack could do the program's work easily and started asking for books to read on his own. I had a copy of *The Great Gatsby* in my desk, so I gave it to him. A week or so later, he stopped by the office to tell me about a line of Fitzgerald's: He describes the sound of a phonebook hitting the floor as a *splash*. The metaphor stirred Jack's curiosity. "So I picked up our phonebook," he said, all enthused, "and dropped it. It hit on the spine and went thud. Then I tried it again, and the pages hit, and—check it out, Mike— it splashed! How about that?"

Jon Davis wasn't as well-read as Jack, and, in fact, never saw himself as an intellectual, didn't care much for school. He entered the Veteran's Program just to gain a few months reprieve from a Marine Corps life that had become intolerable to him. But during his twelve weeks with us, his deep need to be free of military codes and restrictions fused powerfully with his growing facility with written language. Halfway through the program, he made me promise not to laugh and then told me that he thought he might want to be a writer.

Jon still wasn't sure about college. The military had seeped so thoroughly into his being that his response to any institution— church, school, state—was harsh and physical, an existential gag reflex. So when he finished the program, he headed north, away from L.A.'s industrial terrain, toward that magical, rootless garden so many young Americans were seeking. And the era met him, of course, with its Zen farmers and hippie craftsmen, with Kesey and Brautigan and Gary Snyder. Several months after he left, I received a long letter telling me he'd settled, finally, in a small town in Alaska. The stores weren't crowded, he said, and he worked in the forests, and he lived in a fine old house:

I was sitting here smoking cigarettes . . . half-listening to some A.M. discjockey . . . letting thoughts come and pass and thinking maybe one will take hold. . . . Alaska affords a fellow a good atmosphere in which to think and write: there's a lot of air and ground, trees and tundra; wide open meadows where you can spy moose if you're quiet and in a pious mood at early dawn. . . .

No one could doubt the veterans' motivation; some were nearly feverish. But over my time with them, I had come to see how desire was only part of the equation. A number of the men—like me during my early schooling—had skated along the surface of true education, had read too little, were propelling themselves forward on the jet streams of fleeting dreams. So they did all the things that learners, working class to upper crust, do when they lose focus or get scared or give up: They withdrew or faked it or cheated or got stoned or stayed home or blew up.

I and the other English teachers had three tutors to assist us— Tony, Patrick, and Kevin—and once we began to understand the fear of failure at the origin of the veterans' troubling behavior, we refused to give in to it. The more we worked together, the more we pepped each other into trying almost anything to reach the men we taught. We would flatter and plead and use the phone and yell and breathe deep and, more than once, walk down to the Morrison Hotel to pound on a door. Sometimes we pushed too far and found ourselves in situations we were too inexperienced to handle—like the time I sat in a shabby apartment with a blue-eyed addict and looked at the needles and saw open up before me a hopelessness and screaming rejection that I could not begin to address. But we also succeeded, and our successes fueled us. Kevin once said about one of our students: "If I have to, I'll kiss his ass to make him learn." If any of us could have translated that into Latin, it would have become our motto.

Morgan was a Marine scout who had been sent back to the states with two Purple Hearts and bits of shrapnel alongside his knee. He was a quiet man and his childhood couldn't have been more different from mine. He boxed, wrestled, and played up on the line and graduated to racing motorcycles and hunting wild boar with a handgun. At first glance, Morgan did not look all that imposing—five feet nine maybe—sloping shoulders, a slightly large rump. But then you think about it, about the guys you've seen with that certain angle to their trapezius muscles and with that wide beam and those thick thighs, and then you know: This man carries a tremendous centered power.

Morgan had meant grief for teachers since the day he got off his kindergarten mat. He had shined on innumerable lessons, sneered at too many ideas, turned thumbs-down on the mind. He had driven his parents nuts, wildly, almost suicidally trying to forge an identity. But he had something, and though his tolerance for diversity rivaled the Emperor Nero's, you wanted the guy to like you. I used to require students to see me after I'd returned their essays. One of the first times I was scheduled to meet with Morgan, he appeared in my doorway with his essay crumpled and proceeded, in a remarkable act of frustration, to bite off the corner of the paper. His grade wasn't so hot, and, to make matters worse, he found out that another student he couldn't stand had received a higher mark. He walked around the room and ranted and waved the paper and, finally, sat down begrudgingly and smoothed it out so we could work on it. We went at the essay point by point, and I remember how happy I was, thinking, "I got him now. I've really got him."

◆

The Veteran's Program gave me both the incentive and the courage to try new things, to lead outward and follow my curiosities, many of which were being sparked by my teaching. I realize now that I was creating for myself the kind of rich interdisciplinary course of study I couldn't find at UCLA, one that was grounded in my work, that fused mind and world. In higher education, there is a politically loaded distinction between "pure" and "applied" study. Pure study is elevated because it putatively involves the pursuit of knowledge for its own sake—mathematics and literature are good examples; applied study (engineering, medicine, education), because it is situated in human affairs, is somehow tainted, is less—well—*pure*. What a bewildering distinction, I would have thought. What a silly, bloodless dichotomy.

While I was in graduate school, I kept a list of words I didn't know—*evanescent, lassitude, diffident*—an attempt to catch up and keep up. Now I started buying notebooks again, wide-ruled Vernon-Royal composition books, but this time because language had become so vibrant. Exotic words lifted off the pages of novels like butterflies: *canescent, cadenza, Xantippe, chandelle*. I wrote out the names of plants (Bishop's Cap, Black Vesuvius, King of Blues); diagnostic terms from psychiatric manuals—*cerea flexibilitas*, the waxy flexibility of the catatonic's arms and legs; road signs—these from the route to Joshua Tree: Yucaipa, Cabazon, the Honey and the Rock Motel. I copied sentences I thought were rhythmic or clever or richly imagistic, like this one out of Ishmael Reed: "The street was a dumpheap of Brueghel faces, of Hogarth faces, of Coney Island hot-dog kissers, ugly pusses and sinking mugs, whole precincts of flat peepers and silly lookers." I clipped out and pasted poems I wished I had written: "Blackie, the Electric Rembrandt," "Corazon," "Oh Taste and See." I Xeroxed descriptions of marvelous things—here's an ecstatic flight of Saint Joseph of Cupertino: "He rose into space, and from the middle of the church, flew like a bird onto the high altar, where he embraced the tabernacle."

I found a linguistic companion in Kevin, the tutor who worked with me in the Veteran's Program, for he was writing short stories and was on the scent of his own elusive language. I would meet with him in what he came to call his office, the rear of an old wooden garage behind a Venice apartment building. The garage was narrow, and Kevin's Volkswagen took up the front half. In what remained, room for an old Chrysler maybe, he had wedged the oak desk that had been his father's, two chairs, three metal bookcases (one on top of the desk itself, steadied by the rear garage wall), a tiny electric heater, and, underneath it all, a frayed red Oriental rug. You could see through the loose wall slats to the adjacent garage: a primered Chevy raised tireless on ornamental brick. Kevin and I would lean from the two chairs toward each other, sharing a handwritten poem or my notebook or one of the heavily underlined novels we were currently using to educate ourselves. "Listen to this," he would say bending forward, each elbow on each knee, splitting the spine of *The Bushwacked Piano*:

> Payne opened his mind like the sweet dusty comic strip from
> a pink billet of Fleer's bubblegum and saw things as deep
> and appropriate as soft nudes on the noses of B29's. He saw
> longhorn cattle being driven over the Golden Gate Bridge,
> St. Teresa of Avila at the Mocambo, pale blue policemen
> nose-to-bung in an azure nimbus around the moon.

Then he would look up smiling and reach back feeling for a pen on his cluttered desk. "Jee-sus! Is this guy ever having fun!"

All this worked its way into my poems and my teaching. I was spending more time writing: Whole afternoons disappeared as I sat in my apartment's little alcove, the window open to a Pacific breeze, saying the words out loud, trying to catch their rhythms, trying to render some curious thing I had seen. I had never taken a creative writing course—I don't think they were even available at the schools I attended—so I relied for instruction on the people I was reading; and Kevin's good ear; and Dr. Carothers, my Loyola mentor, whom I'd drive out to see when I had written a folderful. I started mimeographing the poems, stapling them together into little books and giving them to my friends. They would put them on their tables or take them to work to pass around, then others would ask for copies, and, so, finally I began sending a few poems to small press magazines, many of which were mimeographed themselves. I didn't think it right to bring these things into my classroom, but working on the poetry certainly got me to thinking about writing from the inside, and it helped keep me in tune with the struggles the veterans were having. Better yet, as I scoured contemporary poetry for work that could teach me something, I found poems that were perfectly suited for the classroom—and some of the veterans, as they got to be more proficient writers themselves, wanted something extra, wanted to know what else they should read, wanted me to talk to them about making their language jump. And I did. And sometimes I would see wonderful things beginning inside and beyond that faded building on South Grand Avenue: ''. . . open meadows where you can spy moose if you're quiet and in a pious mood at early dawn.''

When I started teaching in the Veteran's Program, I was given limited counseling duties, mostly providing guidance for further schooling. The other counselor, the full-time counselor, was an even-keeled, soothing woman named Shulamite Ash, and by watching her at work I learned a good deal about helping people determine their educational and vocational interests. But as time went on, I found myself increasingly curious about the dark side of counseling. Men would come to us panicked about failing in college, or beaten down with inadequacy, or worried about the strains in relationships their personal redefinition was causing. They were sure they couldn't make it, they'd say; they just knew they didn't have what it takes. This was familiar stuff to me. I would tell them about some of my own uncertainties and encourage them to talk further. But I knew they needed more, that I had to get educated fast on how to help someone through this kind of crisis. I asked around and found that the Veteran's Program was fairly close to Los Angeles' pioneering Suicide Prevention Center, a place that trained lay volunteers to be crisis intervention counselors. I went through the training and began taking calls on the hot line. Before very long, I was presenting cases myself at the orientation sessions and supervising new volunteers.

My involvement with counseling was marked by continuing opportunity to learn and by a strange draw toward more and more troubled people. I hadn't been at the center six months when I began working with their most difficult population: the chronic callers. These men and women had long histories of suicide attempts and hospitalization. They were society's marginal people—sporadically employed, on some form of public assistance, alcohol or drug dependent, living alone in those desolate buildings you see nested along the freeway. I learned all I could from the center's psychologists about the chronic callers, and it seemed that the more I found out, the more involved I wanted to be with the students we had who were slowly moving away from the boundaries of such a life. They were in treatment at the VA hospital but often needed day-to-day assurance from us: support, advice, sometimes a simple check on reality. There were times when we were more social workers than teachers, and I think that dual role—following as it did the experience in the Teacher Corps—profoundly laid open the social dimension of teaching. It shaped the way I thought about the classroom.

The person I spent the most time with was Arthur. Arthur was a big man, pudgy, with a gentle, boyish face. He had been in the hospital for several years—diagnosed as paranoid schizophrenic—and had made sufficient progress to begin his reentry into society. We spoke often. His madness and his recovery were still very much present to him, and he would occasionally talk or write about both.

Arthur had always been a singular man. An isolate before he was drafted, he formed few alliances in the service, choosing to stay alone in the barracks, reading or listening to the radio. One man became his friend—a mechanic from Nebraska—and they would sometimes go to the movies. But the mechanic's time was short, and Arthur spent his last year pretty much by himself.

After he was released, he drifted through odd jobs—night watch-man, dishwasher—and moved further and further into the des-perate warmth of a megalomaniac vision:

> Day after day I fought the urge of meeting people and at
> night I walked alone fearing everything that was alive. . . .
> On the one hand I felt awe inspiring, omnipotent and
> omnipresent. . . . I took my abuses out on society, and on
> the other hand I sat or walked alone in the dark, sad,
> despairing city streets at night, a beaten, broken man.

When he was completely mad, Arthur used to roam the streets in a cape and carry a walking stick and posture and preen and strike out at passersby. One night he threw a chair through the window of a diner, and that was when the police came.

Arthur tended to turn in his papers late, and sometimes he wouldn't make it to school. But he did okay in our program, han-dling its challenges and its many potential threats. Neither mad-ness nor Mellaril had permanently damaged his thinking, and though he was a little cautious—at times halting—his critical skills were good and got better. He worked well with the tutors and finished most of his courses. When I was growing up, I didn't see many people regenerate themselves. A lot of men and women seemed lost on South Vermont, Lou Minton took his own life, and my father's health never reversed itself. Here, now, was someone emerging from the deepest misery. Slowly, slowly mov-ing out of isolating madness. The majesty of small progress. I had not seen it on South Vermont, for I was knee-high to the neighborhood's unhappiness. But I was seeing it now, and it was a powerful revelation. Even at the extreme, there is possibility.

The Veteran's Program, like many language and literacy pro-grams, paid teachers by the course. Wages were fairly low, so I had to teach a lot and over the years ended up working in a vari-ety of settings. I tutored in a community college writing center and counseled CETA workers in a summer job-training program. For a brief while, the administrators of the Veteran's Program tried offering some English, humanities, and mathematics courses right on a military facility. So every Tuesday and Thurs-day evening I drove the freeway out to an Air Force base on the southwestern edge of Los Angeles County, engaging a roomful of uniformed men and women in discussion about *The Old Man and the Sea* or a Grace Paley story or "Blackie, the Electric Rembrandt." Extension also ran a college preparation program for people in low-level law-enforcement jobs—parole aides and the like—people who came from poor backgrounds and had only high school diplomas, if that. The program was housed in the downtown center, so I would walk from the third floor to the first to teach a survey of world literature: Introductory Humanities. Each class had an intimidating range of ability. There was Domingo, a parole aide whose gang tattoos had faded along his weathered skin, whose writing was a halting scribble. But there was also Reba, who carried two notebooks and was very quiet and who, it turned out, was a more fluent and assured writer than speaker—for in writing her self-consciousness could not muffle her words.

My own higher education did not include serious study of the classics or of European literature before the twentieth century, so I didn't know much about some of the books I had to teach. I had read *Don Quixote* and Voltaire and Dostoyevski, but I knew little about Greek or Roman drama, or the epics and tales of the Middle Ages, or Dante. So I was explaining things like the origins of Greek tragedy, the evolution of its structure, and the way it was performed that I had learned in a flurry the week before: sketching out the stage on butcher paper, acting out alone in my apartment the placement of characters and the turns of the chorus, doing the things I would do later with the class to help them visualize the action. I drew maps and flowcharts of the events and stood people up and marched them through key scenes. Because the language of so much of what we were reading was difficult, I prepared lists of questions to guide the students' study, showed them how to read play dialogue, asked them to talk to me about the basic themes of the books—honor, vaulting ambition, betrayal—and relate those themes to their own lives and to the events currently in the news. I tried to humanize the distant eras we were studying—telling the class, for example, about the German burgomaster who wrote to Voltaire asking, "In confidence, is there a God or not?" (asking, too, that the philosopher answer by return mail). But still, for some, it was the wrong time and place—the reading was laborious and remote. They would need courses preliminary to this one, and they would need a dramatic change in the demands and derailing seductions and random catastrophes that their neighborhoods threw their way. Domingo, the tattooed parole aide, dropped the class after three weeks.

For others, it worked. The readings started to take hold—in a variety of ways. Blanche, who was about fifty, sat there laughing out loud as she read a prose rendering of Chaucer: "It was the best bout she'd had in years—he thrust away like a madman, hard and deep." "Hard and deep," sighed Blanche, shaking her head. She started tapping the desk: "Mmm hmm. Hard and deep. My, my." Reba, the quiet one, began spending her break asking me questions, wanting to know, in her soft voice, what her library might have that would help her. She asked me about college. Did I think she'd have a chance? I got her a catalogue from the local community college, and we started talking about courses.

And there was Olga. Olga reminded me of the tough girls I had seen in El Monte. Hair teased, heavy mascara. She was older— the lines of a hard life across her forehead, along her cheeks—but she was still rebellious. She fought me all the way on *Macbeth*. She complained about the language—"How do you expect us to *read* this stuff?"—and about the length, and about its sheer distance from us. I'd sit with her and drag her through a scene, paraphrasing a speech, summarizing a conflict. Sometimes I'd force her to direct her anger at the play, to talk at it, make her articulate exactly why she hated it, be as precise as she could about how it made her feel to sit here with this book. Finally, we finished *Macbeth*. One night in that eggshell basement lunchroom, she wrapped her hands around her cola and began to tap it on the table: "You know, Mike, people always hold this shit over you, make you . . . make you feel stupid with their fancy talk. But now *I've* read it, I've read Shakespeare, I can say I, *Olga*, have read it. I won't tell you I like it, 'cause I don't know if I do or I don't. But I like knowing what it's about."

Probably the most unusual teaching I did was through an extension program called Learning Line, a set of courses delivered by telephone conference call to people who—because of children, injury, or the infirmity of old age—were unable to leave their homes. The folks I worked with were residents of convalescent hospitals; I led a poetry class with about nine participants who were assisted, when assistance was needed, by their nurses and aides. My students were spread over Los Angeles County, from the affluent West Side south to Torrance and east to my old neighborhood in the center of the city. Once a week I would sit before a large blinking telephone console in an old storeroom and one by one get all the participants on the line: Addie and Emma in South Central, Ernest and Florence in West L.A., Lucille and Elsie in Torrance. I'd begin by reading from poems I'd selected ahead of time and sent to them, short, direct poems with sharp images and, for the most part, a meditative feel, poems, like this one from ninth-century China, that would trigger memory and reflection:

> Cold air drains down from the peaks.
> Frost lies all around my cabin.
> The trees are bare. Weak sunlight
> Shines in my window. The pond
> Is full and still. The water
> Is motionless. I watch the
> Gibbons gather fallen fruit.
> All the night I hear the deer stamping
> In the dry leaves. My old harp
> Soothes all my trouble away.
> The clear voice of the waterfall
> In the night accompanies my playing.

I'd read the poem again and ask what they thought. Addie would signal in from South Central: "It sounds real peaceful to me . . . like the man's had a good life, and now he just likes to play his music." Then Lucille: "Oh, honey, it reminds me of the little spot I grew up in, I swear it does . . . the cabin and the trees . . . and a lake. . . . I liked it very much." I'd ask Addie if the poem reminded her of any particular place, as happened with Lucille. And sometimes Addie would address Lucille directly.

Some of the participants were hard of hearing and pretty enervated, so it was difficult for them to engage in any extended exchange over temperamental trunk-line connections. But others were in decent shape and got involved via the telephone with people in other homes. They started sending me favorite poems of their own, some they had written themselves and some they had found in magazines:

> Will she ever come to my castle of dreams—
>   To those gardens of rarest bloom?
> Will she ever see the sparkling streams
>   Where gentle lights illume?

These threw me. They were sentimental as could be, and the rhymes were strained, and the diction archaic. They were the kinds of poems all my schooling had trained me to dismiss. But the intentions and feelings behind the poems were present now, couldn't be discounted, a clashing of aesthetics and human need. I wasn't quite sure what to do. I rehearsed several critical responses to the blank console. They didn't feel right—at all. The solution came indirectly. My mother called me one night to ask if I thought a card she bought for her doctor was okay. She read me the Hallmark rhyme, and I was about to tell her what I thought when it hit me. Addie and Ernest and the rest weren't sending the poems for criticism; they wanted to pass on a gift or show off a little—they wanted to participate in some fuller way. I didn't need to be the critic. There are times when it's better to let all that schooling slide. So I simply Xeroxed their poems and sent them to everybody along with my own selections. What followed was a nice surprise. The participants ended up liking both, but for different reasons: they liked the rhymes in the poems they had selected and liked the feeling of the ones I picked. And that opened the door for us to not only share the associations and memories the poems evoked, but to talk a little about technique as well. One of the women who wrote poems herself tried one without rhyme. "Here," she said in her thin voice. "Here's a poem like one of the ones Mike sends us."

◆

For all the other teaching and counseling I was doing, the Veteran's Program was still my home base: I had an assured number of classes, and I taught year-round. But programs like this come and go. Political winds shift with the seasons. Public interest in the issues that gave rise to the programs wanes and flits to a new looming threat.

"There's a job opening up on campus," Chip Anderson, my first boss in the Veteran's Program, was telling me over the phone. I was sunk down in the tattered easy chair in the counselor's office, staring out the window, absentmindedly watching the secretaries walk to the parking lot across the street. Chip's voice seemed far away: "I need someone to run the Tutorial Center in my program. You should apply. It's not teaching, it's administration . . . and supervising . . . and maybe some tutoring too. Why don't you apply . . . I don't think the Veteran's Program will be around a whole lot longer." Every so often, people come together and create in places like the Extension Building a special kind of work. From the work, a few of the helpers and a few of those being helped emerge transformed. Then money dries up, new political agendas are drawn, the people leave, new ones cease to come. The programs fade. They're written up and filed away.

Chip had left the Veteran's Program several years before to take over the directorship of UCLA's Educational Opportunity Program, known, in shorthand, as EOP. EOP programs sprung up on American college campuses in the late sixties and early seventies to recruit and assist students from low-income and minority backgrounds. The programs emerged in a variety of guises, were more often than not politically turbulent, ranged in purpose from the cynical and ineffective to the hopeful and comprehensive. Someone should write their history. The program Chip was running included counselors and tutors and provided a wide range of services. The Tutorial Center was a big operation: Around sixty seniors and graduate students were hired part time to tutor a whole range of subjects, from astronomy and Italian to mathematics and English. "I need someone to make everything systematic," Chip was saying, "someone to set up a good training, to talk about learning, to tighten this baby up. Whaddaya think?" I had hoped that something was going to come through at the Suicide Prevention Center—they had been talking about making me director of training—but a huge chunk of their funding, too, had fallen out from under them. They were cutting back rather than hiring. I was sinking fast in the mire of soft money.

My work with the children in El Monte and the veterans and, for that fact, with the old folks and the people I was counseling had taught me a lot about learning—how to foster it, what impedes it—had shaped for me a sense of human cognitive potential. The veterans had forced me to think critically about the crucial transition into college, what it is that students need to meet the intellectual demands the freshman year makes of them. And all those charged and problematic encounters with the children and the veterans and the parole aides had sharpened my ability to help people out when they felt the fear of failure and all the other emotional spasms that come with change. I would be taking all this, Chip kept pushing me to see, back to that pivotal time that was so difficult for me, back to the freshman year. "These kids need what you got. Bring it here. Teach these tutors about all you've learned." I would be going, once again, to UCLA, but this time in a position to do something. So I went out and interviewed with Chip and his staff. There would be kids like I was, I figured, young people trying to get their bearings in the unfamiliar. Maybe this should be the next place I go. UCLA. Back to where I had been before.

7

◆

The Politics
of Remediation

*The students are taking their seats in the large auditorium, moving in
two streams down the main aisles, entering from a side exit to capture
seats in the front. You're a few minutes late and find a seat somewhere
in the middle. There are a couple of hundred students around you and
in front of you, a hundred or so behind. A youngish man walks onto
the stage and lays a folder and a book on the podium. There are track
lights above him, and in back of him there's a system of huge
blackboards that rise and descend on rollers in the wall. The man
begins talking. He raises his voice and taps the podium and sweeps his
hand through the air. Occasionally, he'll turn to the moving boards
and write out a phrase or someone's name or a reference to a section of
the textbook. You begin writing these things down. He has a beard
and smiles now and then and seems wrapped up in what he's talking
about.*

*This is Introductory Sociology. It's one of the courses students can
elect to fulfill their general education requirements. The catalogue said
that Introductory Sociology would deal with "the characteristics of
social life" and "the processes of social interaction." It also said that
the course would cover the "tools of sociological investigation," but
that came last and was kind of general and didn't seem too important.
You're curious about what it is that makes people tick and curious, as
well, about the causes of social problems, so a course on social
interaction sounded interesting. You filled Sociology 1 in on some
cards and sent them out and eventually got other cards back that told
you you were enrolled.*

"These are the social facts that are reflected in the interpretations we make of them," says the man on the stage and then extends his open hand toward the audience. "Now, this is not the place to rehearse the arguments between Kantian idealists and Lockean realists, but . . ." You're still writing down, ". . . reflected in the interpretations we make of them . . . ," and he continues: "But let us stop for a moment and consider what it means to say 'social fact.' What is a fact? And in considering this question, we are drawn into hermeneutics." He turns to write that last word on the board, and as he writes you copy it down in your notes. He refers the class to the textbook, to a "controlling metaphor" and to "microanalyses"—and as you're writing this down, you hear him stressing "constructivist interpretations" and reading a quotation from somebody and concluding that "in the ambiguity lies the richness."

People are taking notes and you are taking notes. You are taking notes on a lecture you don't understand. You get a phrase, a sentence, then the next loses you. It's as though you're hearing a conversation in a crowd or from another room—out of phase, muted. The man on the stage concludes his lecture and everyone rustles and you close your notebook and prepare to leave. You feel a little strange. Maybe tomorrow this stuff will clear up. Maybe by tomorrow this will be easier. But by the time you're in the hallway, you don't think it will be easier at all.

The work space of the Tutorial Center was parceled out over three floors of Campbell Hall, a building located on the southern end of UCLA's campus, about fifty yards from the English Department where I had received graduate training nine years before. Two of the rooms were fairly large and, from the remaining pipes and sinks, looked to be defunct laboratories. One of these rooms was used to tutor mathematics, physics, and chemistry: It was called the Math Lab and was on the first floor. Humanities, social science, fine arts, and the remaining sciences were crammed into the larger second story room, but you could also find tutoring all up and down the hallway, for the rooms got crowded and, at that time, had no partitions or rugs to absorb the sound. In the basement, we had two small rooms, and those were used for group tutorials and, quite often, for English. When UCLA was still a precocious local school on the west side of town, Campbell Hall used to be the site of Home Economics, but as the university grew, that program was discarded. Now Campbell houses Linguistics, all four Ethnic Studies Centers and their libraries—Afro-American, Chicano, Asian-American, American Indian—and all the offices of UCLA's Educational Opportunity Program, whose biggest unit is the Tutorial Center.

The thing that most struck me during my first months in Campbell Hall was the level and variety of activity, the vibrancy of the place. The walls were covered with posters, flyers, and articles clipped from the newspaper: a multicolored collage of announcements from the Ethnic Studies Centers, the EOP staff, and politically active students and faculty. There were notices about American Indian dancers and Japanese watercolors and forums on labor history—one poster with a photograph of Filipino cannery workers, another with black women bent before machines in a textile mill. There were calls for legal defense funds and vigils for justice. There was news about military atrocities in Chile, CIA murders in Africa, the uprooting of the American Indian. A slow walk down the hall provided an education in culture and politics disconnected from the lives of most Americans, a reminder of culture denied, of the brazenness of power.

It was exciting to walk down the east hallways of the first or second floor, for students were everywhere, lined up for counseling appointments or scattered in groups of twos and threes working with tutors. Some images: A young woman drawing with her finger on the wall, explaining to two students the way the phases of Hegel's dialectic—thesis, antithesis, synthesis—evolve in and out of each other. A tutor listens and nods while a fellow in a sweatshirt that says "Property of UCLA Athletic Department" reads something in French. An older man is walking a girl with a pony tail through a pattern that forms a large triangle. Just as she is about to arrive at the point from which she began, she looks up and knocks her head with her knuckles and says, "Hey, I see it!" Such animation made things noisy and crowded, and it was not uncommon to find a tutor and a student in one of Campbell's stairwells or out on the lawn, seeking quiet. But for all the irritations of noise and crowding, there was an excitement in Campbell, the buzz of intellect caught on the fly, in a hallway, in old school desks jammed together.

I had reentered the bustling university, but this time with some responsibility for making it work. I was lucky in that the Tutorial Center already had a core of graduate students who were skillful teachers, and together we developed a better understanding of how we could make tutoring more effective. I had a small, makeshift office in one of the rooms on Campbell's busy first floor. We called it the fishbowl, for it was built of partitions, and the front of it was three-quarters glass. I would meet there with the tutors, listening as they described the difficulties their students were having, talking through with them ways to discover the reasoning behind poor performance. Essentially what we were trying to do was see beyond failure, develop the perception of the counselor who must look for causes of behavior rather then simply recording the behavior itself. Here's part of a tutoring session I taped and used for training.

Suzette was enrolled in a basic English class, and for her first assignment had written a personality profile of a classmate. Her teacher had placed brackets around two sentence fragments—one of the big offenses in remedial English—noted some other problems, and recommended that she come to the center. I began by asking to see the worrisome section of the personality profile:

> She was the leader who organized the class meetings and
> planned the class graduation program, and class events.
> Bringing them together as one which takes a lot of work.
> Also, worked at her sister's catering service.

"Okay," I said, "let's talk about fragments. Once your teacher put brackets around these two sentences, could you see that something was wrong?" "I see that something's wrong now," said Suzette, tapping her pencil against the table, "but I didn't see anything wrong when I was writing them."

"That's alright," I continued, "tell me more about what you see when the brackets make you focus on those two sentences."

"Well, see this sentence here?" (She pointed to "She was the leader who organized . . . ,'' the sentence that comes before the two fragments.) "I didn't want to start talking about the same thing in another sentence . . . putting . . . you know, keep repeating myself."

"Repeating yourself? That's interesting. Say some more. Tell me more about that."

"What, this?" she said, pointing back to that first sentence. "I didn't want to keep putting 'She was, she was, she was.'"

"You were trying to avoid that kind of repetition?"

"Yeah."

"Why? How did it sound to you?"

"Well, it's just not the way people write essays in college. You just don't like to see your paper with 'She . . . she . . . she . . .' You know, 'I . . . I . . . I . . .' It doesn't sound very intelligent."

"That makes sense."

I started talking to Suzette about some syntactic maneuvers that would enable her to avoid repetition. Going back over rules about sentences needing subjects and verbs would probably not do much good, for my questions revealed that Suzette's fragments were rooted in other causes. She didn't want to keep repeating the subject *she*. We worked together for about fifteen minutes, with me suggesting some general patterns and Suzette trying them out. And these were the sentences she produced:

Ronnie, having skills of organizing, brought her class
together as one. She organized the class meetings, and
planned the class graduation program and the class events.

She brought the class together with her great organizing
skills and leadership, for she prepared the class meetings,
and planned the class graduation program and the class
events.

What was interesting to me and the tutors about Suzette's fragments was that they originated from a desire to reach beyond what she considered simple, beyond the high school way. She had an idea about how college writing should sound, and she was trying to approximate her assumptions. Mina Shaughnessy, an inspired teacher, used to point out that we won't understand the logic of error unless we also understand the institutional expectations that students face and the way they interpret and internalize them. Many people respond to sentence fragments of the kind Suzette was making as though the writer had some little hole in that part of her brain where sentences are generated. They repeat a rule: "A sentence has to have a subject and a verb and express a complete thought." No matter that the rule is problematic, if they can just graft it into the fissures of the writer's gray matter, she'll start writing good sentences. But, Suzette didn't have a damaged sentence generator. What Suzette didn't have was command of some of the stylistic maneuvers that would enable her to produce the sophisticated sentences she was reaching for. The more skilled the tutors got at listening and waiting, the better they got at catching the clue that would reveal what Shaughnessy was fond of calling the intelligence of the student's mistake.

I spent most of my first year in the center creating with Chip Anderson a comprehensive training program and a large procedural manual that included everything from sample time sheets to hints on working with angry students. We improved the ways the center kept track of its payroll and the services it rendered. I earned about budgets, was exposed, without sunscreen, to academic politics. I conducted workshops and supervised tutors and counseled distressed students and did some tutoring. And I came to better understand what I had once only felt: the uncertainty and misdirection of a university freshman's life.

Some of the students I worked with were admitted to college, as I had been, under a special policy, or they had transferred in from a community college. But many, actually most, of the freshmen who visited the Tutorial Center had high school records that were different from mine; they were not somnambulant and did not have spotty transcripts. They were the kids who held class offices and saw their names on the honor roll; they went out for sports and were involved in drama and music and a variety of civic and religious clubs. If they had trouble with mathematics or English or science, they could depend on the fairness of a system that rewarded effort and involvement: They participated in class discussions, got their work in on time, helped the teacher out, did extra-credit projects. In short, they were good academic citizens, and in some high schools—especially beleaguered ones— that was enough to assure them a B. So though some of them came to UCLA aware that math or English or science was hard for them, they figured they'd do okay if they put in the time, if they read the textbook carefully and did all their homework. They saw themselves as academic successes.

These were the first students I'd worked with who did not have histories of failure. Their placement in a course designated "remedial" or the receipt of a D or an F on a midterm examination—even being encouraged by counselors to sign up for tutorial support—was strange and unsettling. They simply had little experience of being on the academic fringe. Thus it was not uncommon for visitors to the Tutorial Center at first to deny what was happening to them. People whose placement tests had indicated a need for English-as-a-second-language courses would often ask us to try to get that judgment reversed. They considered themselves to be assimilated, achieving Americans. Their names had shifted from Keiko to Kay, from Cheung to Chuck. They did not want to be marked as different. Students who were placed in Remedial English would ask us to go look at their tests, hoping there had been a mistake. Tutors often had to spend their first session working through the various emotions this labeling produced. You knew when that student walked through the door; you could sense the feeling of injustice he brought with him as he sat down alongside you. "Something's wrong," Tony blurted out soon after he introduced himself. "This class is way below my level." The tutor assured him that the class was a tough one and would soon get harder. "Well, I hope so," he said, "'cause I took Advanced English in high school. I feel kind of silly doing this stuff."

But others among these young people knew or had long suspected that their math or English needed improvement. Their placement in a remedial course confirmed their suspicions. The danger here was that they might not be able to separate out their particular problems with calculus or critical writing from their own image of themselves as thinkers, from their intellectual self-worth. The ugly truth was exposed. The remedial designation or the botched essay or the disastrous midterm ripped through their protective medals. "I'm just no good at this," said one young woman, holding her smudged essay. "I'm so stupid." Imagine, then, how they felt as they found themselves in a four-hundred-acre aggregation of libraries and institutes and lecture halls, where they could circle the campus and not be greeted by anyone who knew anything about them, where a professor who had no idea who they were used a microphone to inform them that social facts are reflected in the interpretations we make of them.

"It was so weird," said Kathy. "I was walking down the hall in the Engineering Building and suddenly I felt really strange. I felt I was completely alone here. Do you know what I mean? Like I go for days and don't see anybody I know." The huge lecture halls, the distance from the professor, the streams of students you don't know. One of the tasks facing all freshmen is to figure out ways to counter this loneliness. Some will eventually feel the loneliness as passage, as the rending of the familiar that is part of coming of age. The solitude of vast libraries and unfamiliar corridors will transform into college folklore, the bittersweet tales told about leaving home, about the crises of becoming adult. But a much deeper sense of isolation comes if the loneliness you feel is rooted in the books and lectures that surround you, in the very language of the place. You are finally sitting in the lecture hall you have been preparing to sit in for years. You have been the good student, perhaps even the star—you are to be the engineer, the lawyer, the doctor. Your parents have knocked themselves out for you. And you can't get what some man is saying in an *introductory* course. You're not what you thought you were. The alien voice of the lecturer is telling you that something central to your being is, after all, a wish spun in the night, a ruse, the mist and vapor of sleep.

I had seen Andrea before, but this time she was limping. Her backpack was stretched with books. Her collar and pleats were pressed, and there was a perfect white ribbon in her hair. She had been secretary of her high school and a gymnast, belonged to the Biology Club, and worked on the annual. Her father was a bell captain at a hotel in Beverly Hills; her mother a seamstress. They immigrated when Andrea was five, and when they were alone at home, they spoke Japanese. Andrea was fluently bilingual. She graduated fifteenth in a class of five hundred. She came to UCLA with good grades, strong letters, and an interest in science. She had not been eating well since she'd been here. The doctors told her she was making herself anemic. A week before, she had passed out while she was driving and hit a tree on a sidewalk near her home. Her backpack must have weighed twenty pounds.

All colleges have their killer courses, courses meant to screen students from science or engineering or those departments in arts and humanities that aren't desperate for enrollments. At UCLA the most infamous killer course is Chemistry 11-A, General Chemistry. The course is difficult for lots of reasons, but the primary one is that it requires students not just to understand and remember individual facts, formulas, and operations but to use them to solve problems, to recognize what kind of problem a particular teaser is and to combine and recombine facts, formulas, and operations to solve it. Andrea failed the midterm. Her tutor explained that she didn't seem to have much experience solving chemistry problems. Andrea would sit before her book for hours evening after evening, highlighting long stretches of text with a yellow marker, sketching the structure of benzene and butadiene, writing down Avogadro's law and Dalton's law, repeating to herself the differences between ionic and covalent bonds. The midterm exam hit her like a blind punch. It didn't require her to dump her memory. It gave her a short list of problems and asked her to solve them.

Andrea felt tremendous pressure to succeed, to continue to be all things to all people. She was speaking so softly I had to lean toward her. She said she was scared. Her cheek was still bruised from the accident. She missed a week of school then, and as she spoke, I had the sudden, chilling recognition that further injuries could save her, that deliverance could come in the form of another crash. I began talking to her about counseling, how helpful it can be to have someone to talk to, how I'd done it myself, how hard the sciences are for so many of us, how we all need someone to lean on. She looked up at me, and said in a voice drifting back somewhere toward childhood, "You know, I wish you had known me in high school."

James had a different reaction to failure.

He sat in my office and repeated that he was doing okay, that he'd been studying hard and would pull his grades up on his finals. "I've got my study skills perfected, and I am punctual about visiting the library." He paused and looked at his legs, placed his two hands palms down on his thighs, and then he pressed. "I will make it. My confidence was down before." James was on academic probation; he needed to pass all his courses or he would be what they called STD: subject to dismissal. "I've got the right attitude now. I took a motivation course over the break, and that helped me improve my study skills and get my priorities straight." He was looking right at me as he said all this: handsome, muscular, preppy. Dressed for success. Mechanical successfulness. I'm okay, you're okay. Jay Gatsby would have noted his poise and elocution. I sat there quietly listening, trying to decide what to do with his forced jock talk. I drifted a little, trying to conjure up the leader of James' "motivation seminar," the person delivering to him a few techniques and big promises: a way to skim a page or manage his time. James listened desperately and paid his money and went off with a positive attitude and his study skills perfected, emboldened with a set of gimmicks, holding a dream together with gum and string.

James's tutor suggested that he come see me because he was getting somewhere between a C and a D in his composition course and seemed increasingly unable to concentrate. His responses to the tutor's questions were getting vague and distracted. I asked James for his paper and could quickly see that he had spent time on it; it was typed and had been proofread. I read further and understood the C−; his essay missed the mark of the assignment, which required James to critically analyze a passage from John Berger's *Ways of Seeing*. What he did instead was summarize. This was something I had seen with students who lacked experience writing papers that required them to take an idea carefully apart. They approach the task in terms they can handle, retell the material to you, summarize it, demonstrate that, yes, they can understand the stuff, and here it is. Sometimes it is very hard to get them to see that summary is not adequate, for it had been adequate so many times before. What you have to do, then, is model step by step the kind of critical approach the paper requires. And that was what I started to do with James.

I asked him what he thought Berger's reason was for writing *Ways of Seeing*, and he gave me a pretty good answer. I asked another question, and for a brief while it seemed that he was with me. But then he stopped and said, "I should have gotten better than a C−. I think I deserve way higher than that." There it was. A brand. I said that I knew the grade was a disappointment, but if he'd stick with me he'd do better. He didn't say much more. He looked away. I had tacitly agreed with his teacher, so we were past discussing the paper: We were discussing his identity and his future. I work hard, he's really saying to me. I go to class. I

read the book. I write the paper. Can't you see. I'm not a C−.
Don't tell me I'm a C−. He was looking straight ahead past me
at the wall. His hands were still on his legs.

◆

When I was in the Teacher Corps, I saw daily the effects of background on schooling. Kids came into the schools with hand-me-
down skirts and pants, they didn't have lunch money, they were
failing. The connections between neighborhood and classroom
were striking. This was true, though in different ways, with the
veterans. The Tutorial Center also served low-income white and
low- and middle-income minority students, but because the kind
of students who make it to a place like UCLA enter with a long
history of success and, to varying degrees, have removed superficial indicators of their lineage, it's harder, at first glance, to see
how profoundly a single assignment or a whole academic career
can be affected by background and social circumstance—by interactions of class, race, and gender. But as I settled into Campbell
Hall, I saw illustrations continually, ones that complicated easy
judgment and expectation.

Sometimes issues of economics and race were brought up by
the students themselves. Such issues were also raised by the existence of the Ethnic Studies Centers, the perennial posters in the
hallways, or the lobbying of older, politically active students, and
they emerged in some of the students' classes. There was wide
variation in the students' responses. Some had grown up watching their parents deal with insult, had heard slurs in their schools
about skin color and family and language. A young woman
writes in her placement exam for Freshman English:

> I could not go into the restroom, the cafeteria, or any place of
> the high school area alone, without having some girl
> following me and calling me names or pushing me around.
> Some of their favorite names for me were "wetback,"
> "beaner," or "illegal alien." I did not pay much attention to
> the name calling, but when they started pulling my hair,
> pushing me, or throwing beans at me, I reacted.

Students like her were drawn to issues of race, read the walls
of Campbell with understanding, saw connections between the

messages on green paper and the hurt in their own past. They had been sensitized to exclusion as they were growing up.

But there were those who came to Campbell Hall with a different past and a different outlook. Some of those who grew up with the protections of middle-class life knew of the wrongs done to their people, but slavery and Nisei internment and agricultural camps seemed distant to them, something heard in their grandmothers' stories—a hazy film playing in an incomprehensible past. Their own coming of age had been shaped by their parents' hard-won assimilation, the irony of that achievement being an erasure of history for the children of the assimilated. These students had passed through a variety of social and religious clubs and organizations in which they saw people of their race exercise power. They felt at the center of things themselves, optimistic, forward-looking, the force of their own personal history leading them to expect an uncomplicated blending into campus life. I thing that many of them were ambivalent about Campbell Hall— it was good to have the services, but they felt strange about being marked as different.

"Why are we reading this junk? This is just junk!" Denise was tapping the page and looking at me, then off across the room, then back at me. Underneath the light strikes of her finger was a passage her history professor had excerpted from the Lincoln-Douglas debates:

> . . . there is a physical difference between the white and black races which I believe will forever forbid the two races living together on terms of social and political equality. And inasmuch as they cannot so live, while they do remain together there must be the position of superior and inferior, and I as much as any other man am in favor of having the superior position assigned to the white race.

"Yeah," I said, "Abraham Lincoln. Pretty upsetting, isn't it? Why do you think the professor gave it to the class?" "Well," she said, still angry, "that's not the point. The point is, why do we have to read stuff like this?" The week before, Denise and I had the following exchange. She had to write a paper for her composition class. It was built on an excerpt from Henry Roth's immigrant novel, *Call It Sleep*, and the assignment required her to write about the hardships current immigrants face. Our discussion worked its way around to attitudes, so I suggested to Denise that she write on the things she'd heard said about Hispanic immigrants in Southern California. She looked at me as though I'd whispered something obscene in her ear. "No!" she said emphatically, pulling back her head, "that's rude." "Rude," I said. "Explain to me what's—" She cut in. "You don't want to put that in a paper. That doesn't belong." Some things were better left unsaid. Decent people, Denise had learned, just don't say them. There is a life to lead, and it will be a good life. Put the stuff your grandmother lived and your father saw behind you. It belongs in the past. It need not be dredged up if we're to move on. And, in fact, Denise could not dredge it up—the flow of her writing stopped cold by an ugly historical text that was both confusing and painful for her to see.

The counselor's office was always dusky, the sun blocked by thick trees outside the windows. There was an oversize easy chair by his desk. In it sat Marita, thin, head down, hands in her lap, her shiny hair covering her face. The counselor spoke her name, and she looked up, her eyes red in the half-light. The counselor explained that the graduate student who taught her English had accused Marita of plagiarism and had turned her paper over to the director of Freshman English. He asked her to continue, to tell me the story herself.

Marita had been at UCLA for about three weeks. This was her first writing assignment. The class had read a discussion of creativity by Jacob Bronowski and were supposed to write papers agreeing or disagreeing with his discussion. What, Marita wondered, would she say? "What is the insight with which the scientist tries to see into nature?" asked Bronowski. Marita wasn't a scientist, and she didn't consider herself to be a particularly creative person, like an artist or an actress. Her father had always been absolute about the expression of opinion, especially with his daughters: "Don't talk unless you know." "All science is the search for unity in hidden likenesses," asserted Bronowski. "The world is full of fools who speak in ignorance," Marita's father would say, and Marita grew up cautious and reticent. Her thoughts on creativity seemed obvious or, worse yet, silly next to this man Bronowski. What did it mean anyway when he said: "We remake nature by the act of discovery, in the poem or in the theorem"? She wanted to do well on the assignment, so she went to the little library by her house and looked in the encyclopedia. She found an entry on creativity and used some selections from it that had to do with mathematicians and scientists. On the bottom of the last page of her paper, she listed the encyclopedia and her English composition textbook as her references. What had she done wrong? "They're saying I cheated. I didn't cheat." She paused and thought. "You're supposed to use other people, and I did, and I put the name of the book I used on the back of my paper."

The counselor handed me the paper. It was clear by the third sentence that the writing was not all hers. She had incorporated stretches of old encyclopedia prose into her paper and had quoted only some of it. I couldn't know if she had lifted directly or paraphrased the rest, but it was formal and dated and sprinkled with high-cultural references, just not what you'd find in freshman writing. I imagined that it had pleased her previous teachers that she cared enough about her work to go find sources, to rely on experts. Marita had come from a tough school in Compton—an area to the southeast of where I'd grown up—and her conscientiousness and diligence, her commitment to the academic way, must have been a great joy to those who taught her. She shifted, hoisting herself back up from the recesses of the counselor's chair. "Are they going to dismiss me? Are they going to kick me out of school?"

Marita was adrift in a set of conventions she didn't fully understand; she offended without knowing why. Virtually all the writing academics do is built on the writing of others. Every argument procedes from the texts of others. Marita was only partially initiated to how this works: She was still unsure as to how to weave quotations in with her own prose, how to mark the difference, how to cite whom she used, how to strike the proper balance between her writing and someone else's—how, in short, to position herself in an academic discussion.

I told Marita that I would talk with her teacher and that I was sure we could work something out, maybe another chance to write the paper. I excused myself and walked slowly back to my office, half lost in thought, reading here and there in the Bronowski excerpt. It was typical fare for Freshman English anthologies, the sort of essay you'd originally find in places like *The New Yorker*. Bronowski, the eminent scientist, looking back on his career, weaving poetry in with cybernetics, quoting *Faust* in German, allusive, learned, reflective.

The people who put together those freshman anthologies are drawn to this sort of thing: It's in the tradition of the English essay and reflects rich learning and polished style. But it's easy to forget how difficult these essays can be and how developed a taste they require. When I was at Loyola, someone recommended I buy Jacques Barzun's *The Energies of Art*, a collection of "fifteen striking essays on art and culture." I remember starting one essay and stopping, adrift, two or three pages later. Then another, but no go. The words arose from a depth of knowledge and a developed perception and a wealth of received ways to talk about art and a seemingly endless reserve of allusions. I felt like a janitor at a gallery opening, silent, intimidated, little flecks of knowledge—Bagehot, Stendhal, baroque ideology—sticking to the fiber of my broom.

Marita's assignment assumed a number of things: an ability to slip into Bronowski's discussion, a reserve of personal experiences that the writer herself would perceive as creative, a knowledge of and facility with—confidence with, really—the kinds of stylistic moves you'd find in those *New Yorker* essays. And it did *not* assume that someone, by family culture, by gender, would be reluctant to engage the reading on its own terms. Marita was being asked to write in a cognitive and social vacuum. I'm sure the other students in her class had a rough time of it as well. Many competent adult writers would too. But the solution Marita used marked her as an outsider and almost tripped the legal switches of the university.

At twenty-eight, Lucia was beginning her second quarter at UCLA. There weren't many people here like her. She was older, had a family, had transferred in from a community college. She represented a population that historically hadn't gained much entrance to places like this: the returning student, the single, working mother. She had a network of neighbors and relatives that provided child care. On this day, though, the cousin on tap had an appointment at Immigration, so Lucia brought her baby with her to her psychology tutorial. Her tutor had taken ill that morning, so rather than turn her away, the receptionist brought her in to me, for I had spoken with her before. Lucia held her baby through most of our session, the baby facing her, Lucia's leg moving rhythmically, continually—a soothing movement that rocked him into sleep.

Upon entrance to UCLA, Lucia declared a psychology major. She had completed all her preliminary requirements at her community college and now faced that same series of upper-division courses that I took when I abandoned graduate study in English some years before: Physiological Psychology, Learning, Perception . . . all that. She was currently enrolled in Abnormal Psychology, "the study of the dynamics and prevention of abnormal behavior." Her professor had begun the course with an intellectual curve ball. He required the class to read excerpts from Thomas Szasz's controversial *The Myth of Mental Illness*, a book that debunks the very notions underlying the traditional psychological study of abnormal behavior, a book that was proving very difficult for Lucia.

My previous encounter with Lucia had convinced me that she was an able student. She was conscientious about her studies—recopied notes, visited professors—and she enjoyed writing: she wrote poems in an old copy book and read popular novels, both in Spanish and English. But Szasz—Szasz was throwing her. She couldn't get through the twelve-and-a-half pages of introduction. I asked her to read some passages out loud and explain them to me as best she could. And as Lucia read and talked, it became clear to me that while she could, with some doing, pick her way through Szasz's sophisticated prose, certain elements of his argument, particular assumptions and allusions, were foreign to her— or, more precisely, a frame of mind or tradition or set of assumptions that was represented by a single word, phrase, or allusion was either unknown to her or clashed dramatically with frames of mind and traditions of her own.

Here are the first few lines of Szasz's introduction:

> Psychiatry is conventionally defined as a medical specialty concerned with the diagnosis and treatment of mental diseases. I submit that this definition, which is still widely accepted, places psychiatry in the company of alchemy and

astrology and commits it to the category of pseudoscience. The reason for this is that there is no such thing as "mental illness."

One powerful reason Lucia had decided to major in psychology was that she wanted to help people like her brother, who had a psychotic break in his teens and had been in and out of hospitals since. She had lived with mental illness, had seen that look in her brother's eyes, felt drawn to help people whose mind had betrayed them. The assertion that there was no such thing as mental illness, that it was a myth, seemed incomprehensible to her. She had trouble even entertaining it as a hypothesis, and thus couldn't play out its resonances and implications in the pages that followed. Szasz's bold claim was a bone sticking in her assumptive craw.

Here's another passage alongside which she had placed a question mark:

> The conceptual scaffolding of medicine, however, rests on the principles of physics and chemistry, as indeed it should, for it has been, and continues to be, the task of medicine to study and if necessary to alter, the physiochemical structure and function of the human body. Yet the fact remains that human sign-using behavior does not lend itself to exploration and understanding in these terms. We thus remain shackled to the wrong conceptual framework and terminology.

To understand this passage, you need to have some orientation to the "semiotic" tenet that every human action potentially carries some kind of message, that everything we do can be read as a sign of more than itself. This has become an accepted notion in high-powered liberal studies, an inclination to see every action and object as a kind of language that requires interpretation. The notion and its implications—the conversation within which the phrase "sign-using" situates you—was foreign to Lucia. So it was difficult for her to see why Szasz was claiming that medicine was the "wrong conceptual framework" with which to study abnormal behavior.

Here's a third passage:

Man thus creates a heavenly father and an imaginary replica of the protected childhood situation to replace the real or longed-for father and family. The differences between traditional religious doctrine, modern political historicism, and psychoanalytic orthodoxy thus lie mainly in the character of the "protectors": they are, respectively, God and the priests, the totalitarian leader and his apologists, and Freud and the psychoanalysts.

While Freud criticized revealed religion for the patent infantilism that it is, he ignored the social characteristics of closed societies and the psychological characteristics of their loyal supporters. He thus failed to see the religious character of the movement he himself was creating.

Lucia's working-class Catholicism made it difficult for her to go along with, to intellectually toy with, the comparison of Freud to God, but there was another problem here too, not unlike the problem she had with the "sign-using" passage. It is a standard move in liberal studies to find religious analogues to nonreligious behaviors, structures, and institutions. Lucia could certainly "de-code" and rephrase a sentence like: "He thus failed to see the religious character of the movement he himself was creating," but she didn't have the background to appreciate what happens to Freud and psychoanalysis the moment Szasz makes his comparison, wasn't familiar with the wealth of conclusions that would follow from the analogy.

And so it went with other key passages. Students like Lucia are often thought to be poor readers or to have impoverished vocabularies (though Lucia speaks two languages); I've even heard students like her referred to as culturally illiterate (though she has absorbed two cultural heritages). It's true there were words Lucia didn't know (*alchemy, orthodoxy*) and sentences that took us two or three passes to untangle. But it seemed more fruitful to see Lucia's difficulties in understanding Szasz as having to do with her belief system and with her lack of familiarity with certain on-going discussions in humanities and social science—with frames of mind, predispositions, and background knowledge. To help Lucia with her reading, then, I explained five or six central discussions that go on in liberal studies: the semiotic discussion, the sacred-profane discussion, the medical vs. social model discussion. While I did this, I was encouraging her to talk through opinions of her own that ran counter to these discussions. That was how she improved her reading of Szasz. The material the professor assigned that followed the introduction built systematically off it, so once Lucia was situated in that introduction, she had a framework to guide her through the long passages that followed, all of which elaborated those first twelve pages.

The baby pulled his face out of his mother's chest, yawned, squirmed, and turned to fix on me, wide-eyed. Lucia started packing up her books with a free hand. I had missed lunch. "Let's go," I said. "I'll walk out with you." Her movement distressed the baby, so Lucia soothed him with soft coos and clicks, stood up, and shifted him to her hip. We left Campbell Hall and headed southeast, me toward a sandwich, Lucia toward the buses that ran up and down Hilgard on UCLA's east boundary. It was a beautiful California day, and the jacarandas were in full purple bloom. Lucia talked about her baby's little discoveries, about a cousin who worried her, about her growing familiarity with this sprawling campus. "I'm beginning to know where things are," she said, pursing her lips. "You know, the other day some guy stopped me and asked *me* where Murphy Hall was . . . and I could tell him." She looked straight at me: "It felt pretty good!" We walked on like this, her dress hiked up where the baby rode her hip, her books in a bag slung over her shoulder, and I began to think about how many pieces had to fall into place each day in order for her to be a student: The baby couldn't wake up sick, no colic or rashes, the cousin or a neighbor had to be available to watch him, the three buses she took from East L.A. had to be on time—no accidents or breakdowns or strikes—for travel alone took up almost three hours of her school day. Only if all these pieces dropped in smooth alignment could her full attention shift to the complex and allusive prose of Thomas Szasz. "Man thus creates a heavenly father and an imaginary replica of the protected childhood situation to replace the real or longed-for father and family."

◆

During the time I was working with Denise and Lucia and the others, all hell was breaking loose in American education. The literacy crisis that has become part of our current cultural vocabulary was taking shape with a vengeance. It was in December 1975 that *Newsweek* informed America that Johnny couldn't write, and in the fall of 1976 the *Los Angeles Times* declared a "Drop in Student Skills Unequalled in History." California, the *Times* article went on to reveal, had "one of the most pronounced drops in achievement of all." Reports on the enrollment and retention of students are a long-standing tradition in the way education conducts its business, but it seemed that every month now a new document was appearing on my desk: reports from a vice-chancellor or the university president's office or from some analyst in the state legislature. What percentage of people from families below a certain income level were entering college? What were their SAT scores? What were the SAT scores of blacks? Chicanos? Asians? More locally, how many UCLA students were being held for remedial English? Remedial math? Were there differences by race or income?

This was a new way for me to look at education. My focus had been on particular students and their communities, and it tended to be a teacher's focus, rich in anecdote and observation. Increasingly, my work in the Tutorial Center required that I take a different perspective: I had to think like a policy-maker, considering the balance sheet of economics and accountability. Chip would sit with me in the late afternoon, going over the charts and tables, showing me how to use them to argue for our programs, for in an academic bureaucracy admissions statistics and test scores and retention rates are valued terms of debate. All teaching is embedded in a political context, of course, but the kind of work I had done before coming to the Tutorial Center tended to isolate me from the immediate presence of institutions: working with a group of kids in the corner of a cafeteria, teaching veterans in a dingy satellite building. I was learning from Chip and from a shrewd vice-chancellor named Chuck Ries how to work within the policy-maker's arena. And though it was, at times, uncomfortable for me and though I would soon come to question the legitimacy of the vision it fostered, it provided an important set of lessons. Probably the central value of being at the Tutorial Center was that it forced me to examine the broad institutional context of writing instruction and underpreparation.

The work in the center led to other projects, and during my four years in Campbell Hall, I would be invited to participate in them. One was the Writing Research Project, initiated by Vice-Chancellor Ries, and its purpose was to study the uses of writing and the way it was taught at UCLA. Another was the Freshman Summer Program, six intensive weeks before the freshman year during which students took a writing course linked to an introductory course in political science or psychology or history. There is a lot to tell about these ventures—the politics of evaluating a curriculum at a university, the strains of initiating a curriculum that requires people to cross departmental lines—but the most important thing about both projects was that they led me to do something rarely achieved at a research university. I had to stand on the borders of a number of disciplines and study the way knowledge is structured in the academy and, as well, detail what it means to be unprepared to participate in that disciplinary structure.

Students were coming to college with limited exposure to certain kinds of writing and reading and with conceptions and beliefs that were dissonant with those in the lower-division curriculum they encountered. And that curriculum wasn't doing a lot to address their weaknesses or nurture their strengths. They needed practice writing academic essays; they needed opportunities to talk about their writing—and their reading; they needed people who could quickly determine what necessary background knowledge they lacked and supply it in comprehensible ways. What began troubling me about the policy documents and the crisis reports was that they focused too narrowly on test scores and tallies of error and other such measures. They lacked careful analysis of the students' histories and lacked, as well, analysis of the cognitive and social demands of the academic culture the students now faced. The work I was doing in the Tutorial Center, in the Writing Research Project, and in the Summer Program was guiding me toward a richer understanding of what it meant to be underprepared in the American research university. It seemed to me there were five overlapping problem areas—both cognitive and social—that could be used to explain the difficulties experienced by students like Marita and James and Lucia. These by no means applied equally to all the students whom I came to know, but taken together they represent, better than pie charts and histograms, what it means to be underprepared at a place like UCLA.

Many young people come to the university able to summarize the events in a news story or write a personal response to a play or a movie or give back what a teacher said in a straightforward lecture. But they have considerable trouble with what has come to be called critical literacy: framing an argument or taking someone else's argument apart, systematically inspecting a document, an issue, or an event, synthesizing different points of view, applying a theory to disparate phenomena, and so on. The authors of the crisis reports got tremendously distressed about students' difficulty with such tasks, but it's important to remember that, traditionally, such abilities have only been developed in an elite: in priests, scholars, or a leisure class. Ours in the first society in history to expect so many of its people to be able to perform these very sophisticated literacy activities. And we fail to keep in mind how extraordinary it is to ask *all* our schools to conduct this kind of education—not just those schools with lots of money and exceptional teachers and small classes—but massive, sprawling schools, beleaguered schools, inner-city schools, overcrowded schools. It is a charge most of them simply are not equipped to fulfill, for our educational ideals far outstrip our economic and political priorities.

We forget, then, that by most historical—and current—standards, the vast majority of a research university's underprepared students would be considered competently literate. Though they fail to meet the demands made of them in their classes, they fail from a literate base. They are literate people straining at the boundaries of their ability, trying to move into the unfamiliar, to approximate a kind of writing they can't yet command. And as they try, they'll make all the blunders in word choice and sentence structure and discourse strategy that regularly get held up for ridicule, that I made when I was trying to write for my teachers at Loyola. There's a related phenomenon, and we have research evidence of this: As writers move further away from familiar ways of expressing themselves, the strains on their cognitive and linguistic resources increase, and the number of mechanical and grammatical errors they make shoots up. Before we shake our heads at these errors, we should also consider the possibility that many such linguistic bungles are signs of growth, a stretching beyond what college freshmen can comfortably do with written language. In fact, we should *welcome* certain kinds of errors, make allowance for them in the curricula we develop, analyze rather than simply criticize them. Error marks the place where education begins.

Asked to produce something that is beyond them, writers might also fall back on strategies they already know. Asked to take a passage critically apart, they'll summarize it. We saw this with James, the young man distressed with his C−, but as with so much else in this book, the principle applies to more than just those labeled underprepared. I was personally reminded of it when I was writing my dissertation. My chairman was an educational research methodologist and statistician; my background straddled humanities and social science, but what I knew about writing tended to be shaped by literary models. When it came time to report on the procedures I was using in my study—the methods section of the dissertation—I wrote a detailed chronology of what I did and how I did it. I wanted to relay all the twists and turns of my investigation. About a week later I got it back covered with criticism. My chairman didn't want the vagaries of my investigative life; he wanted a compressed and systematic account. "What do you think this is," he wrote alongside one long, dancing stretch of narrative, "*Travels with Charley?*"

Associated with these difficulties with critical literacy are students' diverse orientations toward inquiry. It is a source of exasperation to many freshmen that the university is so predisposed to question past solutions, to seek counterexplanations—to continually turn something nice and clean and clear into a problem. English professor David Bartholomae recalls a teacher of his suggesting that, when stuck, student writers should try the following "machine": "While most readers of ___ have said ___, a close and careful reading shows that ___." The teacher's machine perfectly expresses the ethos of the university, a fundamental orientation toward inquiry. University professors have for so long been socialized into this critical stance, that they don't realize how unsettling it can be to students who don't share their unusual background.

There is Scott sitting in an Astronomy tutorial, his jaw set, responding to another student's question about a finite versus an infinite universe: "This is the kind of question," he says, "that you'll argue and argue about. It's stupid. No one wins. So why do it?'' And there is Rene who can't get beyond the first few sentences of her essay for Speech. She has to write a critical response to an address of Ronald Reagan's. ''You can't criticize the president,'' she explains. ''You've gotta support your president even if you don't agree with him.'' When students come from other cultures, this discordance can be even more pronounced. Our tutors continually encouraged their students to read actively, to ask why authors say what they say, what their claims are, what assumptions they make, where you, the reader, agree or disagree. Hun's tutor is explaining this to him, then has him try it, has him read aloud so she can guide him. He reads a few lines and stops short. After two more abortive trials, she pulls out of Hun the explanation that what gets written in books is set in tradition, and he is not learned enough to question the authority of the book.

Remember Andrea? She was the distressed young woman who was failing chemistry. Andrea could memorize facts and formulas but not use them to solve problems—and her inability was representative of a whole class of difficulties experienced by freshmen. What young people come to define as intellectual competence— what it means to know things and use them—is shaped by their schooling. And what many students experience year after year is the exchange of one body of facts for another—an inert transmission, the delivery and redelivery of segmented and self-contained dates and formulas—and thus it is no surprise that they develop a restricted sense of how intellectual work is conducted. They are given Ancient History one year and American History the next, and once they've displayed knowledge of the Fertile Crescent and cuneiform and Assyrian military campaigns, there is little need for them to remember the material, little further opportunity to incorporate it, little reason to use these textbook facts to engage historical problems. Next year it will be American History: a new textbook, new dates and documents and campaigns, new tests—but the same rewards, and the same reasons to forget. John Dewey saw the difficulty long ago: ''Only in education, never in the life of the farmer, sailor, merchant, physician, or laboratory experimenter, does knowledge mean primarily a store of information aloof from doing.''

Students like Andrea are caught in a terrible bind. They come to the university with limited experience in applying knowledge, puzzling over solutions, solving problems. Many of the lower-division courses they encounter—their "general education" or "breadth" requirements—will involve little writing or speaking or application, will rely on so-called objective tests that, with limited exception, stress the recall of material rather than the reasoned elaboration of it. But the gatekeeper courses—the courses that determine entrance to a major—they up the intellectual ante. Courses like Andrea's bête noire, Chemistry 11-A, are placed like land mines in the uneven terrain of the freshman year. The special nature of their demands is not made the focus of attention that it should be; that is, the courses are not taught explicitly and self-consciously as courses on how to think as a chemist or a psychologist or a literary critic. And there are few opportunities for students to develop such ability before they enroll in those courses. The faculty, for the most part, do not provide freshmen with instruction on how to use knowledge creatively—and then penalize them when they cannot do so.

It is not unusual for students to come to the university with conceptualizations of disciplines that are out of sync with academic reality. Like the note taker in the lecture hall who opened this chapter, a lot of entering freshmen assume that sociology is something akin to social work, an applied study of social problems rather than an attempt to abstract a theory about social interaction and organization. Likewise, some think psychology will be a discussion of human motivation and counseling, what it is that makes people do what they do—and some coverage of ways to change what they do. It comes as a surprise that their textbook has only one chapter on personality and psychotherapy—and a half dozen pages on Freud. The rest is animal studies, computer models of thought, lots of neurophysiology. If they like to read novels, and they elect a literature course, they'll expect to talk about characters and motive and plot, but instead they're asked to situate the novel amid the historical forces that shaped it, to examine rhetorical and stylistic devices and search the prose for things that mean more than they seem to mean. Political science should be politics and government and current events—nuclear treaties, trade sanctions, the Iran-Contra scandal—but instead it's Marx and Weber and political economy and organizational and decision-making models. And so goes the litany of misdirection. This dissonance between the academy's and the students' definitions of disciplines makes it hard for students to get their bearings with material: to know what's important, to see how the pieces fit together, to follow an argument, to have a sense of what can be passed over lightly. Thus I would see notebooks that were filled—in frantic script—with everything the professor said or that were scant and fragmented, records of information without coherence.

The discourse of academics is marked by terms and expressions that represent an elaborate set of shared concepts and orientations: alienation, authoritarian personality, the social construction of the self, determinism, hegemony, equilibrium, intentionality, recursion, reinforcement, and so on. This language weaves through so many lectures and textbooks, is integral to so many learned discussions, that it's easy to forget what a foreign language it can be. Freshmen are often puzzled by the talk they hear in their classrooms, but what's important to note here is that their problem is not simply one of limited vocabulary. If we see the problem as knowing or not knowing a list or words, as some quick-fix remedies suggest, then we'll force glossaries on students and miss the complexity of the issue. Take, for example, *authoritarian personality*. The average university freshman will know what *personality* means and can figure out *authoritarian*; the difficulty will come from a lack of familiarity with the conceptual resonances that *authoritarian personality* has acquired in the discussions of sociologists and psychologists and political scientists. Discussion . . . you could almost define a university education as an initiation into a variety of powerful ongoing discussions, an initiation that can occur only through the repeated use of a new language in the company of others. More than anything, this was the opportunity people like Father Albertson, my Shakespeare teacher at Loyola, provided to me. The more comfortable and skillful students become with this kind of influential talk, the more they will be included in further conversations and given access to further conceptual tools and resources—the acquisition of which virtually defines them as members of an intellectual community.

All students require such an opportunity. But those coming to the university with less-than-privileged educations, especially those from the lower classes, are particularly in need. They are less likely to have participated, in any extended way, in such discussions in the past. They won't have the confidence or the moves to enter it, and can begin to feel excluded, out of place, put off by a language they can't command. Their social marginality, then, is reinforced by discourse and, as happened to me during my first year at Loyola, they might well withdraw, retreat to silence.

This sense of linguistic exclusion can be complicated by various cultural differences. When I was growing up, I absorbed an entire belief system—with its own characteristic terms and expressions—from the worried conversations of my parents, from the things I heard and saw on South Vermont, from the priest's fiery tales. I thought that what happened to people was preordained, that ability was a fixed thing, that there was one true religion. I had rigid notions about social roles, about the structure of society, about gender, about politics. There used to be a rickety vending machine at Manchester and Vermont that held a Socialist Workers newspaper. I'd walk by it and feel something alive and injurious: The paper was malevolent and should be destroyed. Imagine, then, the difficulty I had when, at the beginning of my senior year at Mercy High, Jack MacFarland tried to explain Marxism to us. How could I absorb the language of atheistic materialism and class struggle when it seemed so strange and pernicious? It wasn't just that Marxist terms-of-art were unfamiliar; they felt assaultive. What I did was revert to definitions of the social order more familiar to me, and Mr. MacFarland had to draw them out of me and have me talk about them and consider them alongside Marx's vision and terminology, examining points of conflict and points of possible convergence. It was only then that I could appropriate Marx's strange idiom.

Once you start to think about underprepared students in terms of these overlapping problem areas, all sorts of solutions present themselves. Students need more opportunities to write about what they're learning and guidance in the techniques and conventions of that writing—what I got from my mentors at Loyola. They need more opportunities to develop the writing strategies that are an intimate part of academic inquiry and what has come to be called critical literacy—comparing, synthesizing, analyzing—the sort of thing I gave the veterans. They need opportunities to talk about what they're learning: to test their ideas, reveal their assumptions, talk through the places where new knowledge clashes with ingrained belief. They need a chance, too, to talk about the ways they may have felt excluded from all this in the past and may feel threatened by it in the present. They need the occasion to rise above the fragmented learning the lower-division curriculum encourages, a place within a course or outside it to hear about and reflect on the way a particular discipline conducts its inquiry: Why, for example, *do* so many psychologists who study thinking rely on computer modeling? Why is mathematics so much a part of economics? And they need to be let in on the secret talk, on the shared concepts and catchphrases of Western liberal learning.

There is nothing magical about this list of solutions. In fact, in many ways, it reflects the kind of education a privileged small number of American students have received for some time. The basic question our society must ask, then, is: How many or how few do we want to have this education? If students didn't get it before coming to college—and most have not—then what are we willing to do to give it to them now? Chip and I used to talk about our special programs as attempts to create an Honors College for the underprepared. People would smile as we spoke, but, as our students would have said, we were serious as a heart attack. The remedial programs we knew about did a disservice to their students by thinking of them as *remedial*. We wanted to try out another perspective and see what kind of program it would yield. What would happen if we thought of our students' needs and goals in light of the comprehensive and ambitious program structures more often reserved for the elite?

◆

It was during one of our afternoon meetings that Chip confirmed the rumor. We had heard that some faculty members were questioning the money being spent on our programs. They were lobbying to have it shifted, Chip explained, to what they saw as "the legitimate research mission of the university." I had known for a while, for Chip had sensitized me to it, that our position in the university was a complicated one. Certain powerful administrators and some faculty were our strong supporters—for political, for pedagogical, for ethical reasons—but others were suspicious of us, even questioned our place at a prestigious university like UCLA. The kind of work we did was suspect. What exactly *did* we do? Were we qualified to do it? Did our students belong here—were we, in fact, keeping unqualified kids in school? We didn't have a faculty advisory board or any other institutional link with academic departments, so we had no systematic way to influence or gain support from the professoriat. Chip began loaning me to English free of charge to teach a few classes, seeking even the most superficial of connections.

As it turned out, Vice-Chancellor Ries applied his cunning and successfully countered this particular offensive against our budget, but the experience remained with me. When I took Chip Anderson up on his offer to come to UCLA, I had assumed that the rigorous intellectual methods of the academy would be focused on problems of student learning. But the truth was that, by and large, the research university focuses its collective intelligence on other matters. And the places designated to deal with such problems—tutorial centers and preparatory programs—are conceived of as marginal to the intellectual community. These conditions had direct effects on the young men and women who we came to know at the center.

One day, a professor of English turned to me in the food line and began telling me about an office meeting he had with one of our students. He thought that the fellow's paper on a Wordsworth poem was such a muddle that he simply wrote "see me" on the bottom of the last page. The student showed up and, in the professor's words, the meeting was a disaster. "It was as though I were talking to someone from another planet!" he exclaimed. "I showed him line by line how the poem should be explicated. I figured he just didn't know, so I'd show him. But when he said back to me what I had said to him, I could see that we were talking completely past each other." He stopped and shrugged his shoulders: "I never felt so hopeless."

Some faculty, I knew from my tutors, were especially good with our students, made attempts to understand the difficulties they were having, and seemed to enjoy working with them. But what was more striking, and I became increasingly aware of it as time went on, was the gulf that existed between so many professors and the students who frequented the Tutorial Center. A number of faculty were like the man from English: They wanted to help but didn't know how, and they found their inability very frustrating. Others were distant and aloof, didn't particularly care to help, and shunted freshmen off to teaching assistants. Of these, a small percentage had real problems with differences of class or race.

Reflecting on my own first awkward year at Loyola, I tended to explain this gulf between faculty and students in strictly social terms. Most faculty didn't share the backgrounds of our program's students, and, unless they made efforts to the contrary, they had increasingly spent time, as we all do, with people of similar persuasion. But as I became more familiar with the university, I began to see that while there certainly could be an ethnic or cultural dimension to these troubling encounters, there was something else going on as well, and it had to do with the very way people are socialized into academic life.

As young scholars progress through graduate study, they acquire more than knowledge and method: Strong allegiances are formed. It's a time of gradual yet powerful shaping of identity as a scholar, the increasing investment of self-worth in research and publication. Graduate study forces you to give a tremendous amount of thought to the development of your discipline, to its methods, exemplary studies, and central texts. People emerge from graduate study, then, as political scientists or astronomers or botanists—but not necessarily as educators. That is, though professors may like to teach, like to talk about the knowledge they've worked so hard to acquire, it is pretty unlikely that they have been encouraged to think about, say, the cognitive difficulties young people have as they learn how to conduct inquiry in physics or anthropology or linguistics, the way biological or historical knowledge is acquired, the reading or writing difficulties that attend the development of philosophical reasoning. These issues, if addressed at all in the academy, are addressed in schools of education, and most faculty hold schools of education in low regard.

I never heard in those years a professor—an anthropologist, for example—say of a poor exam, ''There's a curious failed anthropology here," or "Look at the interesting missteps this person makes in trying to articulate the concept of liminality." Rather, the work is judged as legitimate, accurate, close to the current conversations in the discipline, the received wisdom, the canonical texts, or it is inaccurate, not close, a failure. The thrust of graduate training and the professorial commitment that follows from it are toward the preservation of a discipline, not the intellectual development of young people. That English professor had neither the training nor the inclination to see in his student's vexing Wordsworth paper the wealth of clues about the way literary inquiry develops and goes awry. And he didn't seem able to set things up so the student could reveal the twists and turns in that development. Rather, he saw the student's paper as a failed attempt, alien, as if from another planet. And he saw his job as monitoring the rightness or wrongness of incursions into his discipline.

Every so often at UCLA and other similar institutions, the delicious proposal is made to move lower-division instruction—the entire first two years, all the introductory courses—to the state and community colleges. This would allow the disciplinary focus of the university to emerge full-blown: Faculty would only teach students who have already declared their apprenticeships to mathematics or French or musicology. Fortunately, the proposal never gets very far. What's troubling is that among the counterarguments—which are mostly political and economic—you rarely hear concerns about the astounding inbreeding and narrowness that would result: a faculty already conceptually isolated along disciplinary lines talking in more self-referenced ways to less and less diverse audiences. Babel talk. The final isolation of inquiry.

The homiletic nod toward the interconnection of general education and research is commonplace. Yet a variety of investigations—from Laurence Veysey's standard history, *The Emergence of the American University*, to Gerald Graff's critique of English Studies, *Professing Literature*—all suggest that the American university has yet to figure out, conceptually or institutionally, how to integrate its general education mission with its research mission. An unresolved problem: How to interweave the social dimension of knowledge with the preservation of a discipline, how to make the advancement of a discipline go on in concert with the development of young minds.

This is not to deny that research universities have some passionate teachers. They want to excite young people about their
discipline. They volunteer to teach introductory courses. But here
they meet a powerful institutional reality. Regardless of what the
university publicists say, faculty are promoted and given tenure
and further promoted for the research they publish, not for
the extent of their involvement in undergraduate, especially
introductory-level, teaching. Yes, there are unusual cases. If
someone's research record is right on the line, then student evaluations of the person's teaching are consulted: If they're exceptionally high or exceptionally low, then they might sway a decision. If the person made an extraordinary contribution to
curriculum development, that might count—a little. Such cases
are set forth as proof that undergraduate education counts, but
by their paucity, they become the exception that proves the rule.
Publish or perish. Like most universities, UCLA gives Distinguished Teaching Awards to its outstanding teachers. One very
talented professor I knew had superlative student evaluations
and was coming up for tenure; she pleaded with her department
not to advance her for the Distinguished Teaching Award, for
winning it, she thought, might bias her tenure committee, making them conclude that too much of her research time had gone
into her teaching.

Consider, in the midst of all this, the Tutorial Center and the
students who frequent it. Tutorial centers don't produce research—the coin of the realm—but, rather, provide a service. Most
of those working in them are not in the professorial ranks and
thus are not perceived as having developed the intellectual rigor
that comes from such membership. The work the center does is
not considered a contribution to a discipline; in fact, much of
what tutors do is considered "remedial," work that isn't even
part of disciplinary pursuit but preliminary to it. What emerges
in the culture's institution that most touts humane, liberal learning is a rigid intellectual class system. Certain kinds of cognitive
work are considered peripheral and tainted; those who perform
the work become an intellectual underclass. These class divisions
of the mind are so powerful that they can override and even con-
tradict one's stated beliefs about the social order. Several faculty
whose work embodied a radical critique of culture were dismis-
sive of the work we did. And I heard remarkable stories of distin-

guished Marxist academics at other schools who flat out refused
to teach undergraduate courses. In their scholarly articles, they
pursued a critique of meritocratic capitalism, yet in their dealings
with students, they replicated the very elitism they assailed in
print. One of the simple indicators of our place in the university
was the fact that, at least during my stay, not one professor visited the center. We would get occasional phone calls, some
friendly, some quizzical, but no one came by to see how we tutored, to inquire about what we were uncovering as we worked
with students, to talk about education. The deep divisions of intellectual work in the university kept all of us moving along different strata.

By not considering the kind of work tutorial centers or other preparatory programs do as being worthy of intellectual attention,
the university encouraged a kind of loose, unrigorous talk about
underpreparation and a reductive means of assessing it. Rather
than questioning the local and national crisis reports that surrounded us—subjecting their claims to close investigation, probing their assumptions—the university marched to their apocalyptic drum. It even piped in. Yet the crisis reports were both
reflecting and contributing to a set of misleading perceptions
of underpreparation. The reports varied widely but tended to
build their case on three sources of evidence: declines in scores
on various national and local tests, rising enrollments in remedial
classes, and observations from professors. These evidential
strands combined in rhetorically powerful ways to spark alarm
and anger—in legislators, in academics, in the public.

The reports listed scores from both broad national tests and
more local, specific assessments, and inferred all sorts of dire
things from them. The most famous national test is the Scholastic
Aptitude Test—the bane of the college-bound high schooler, the
SAT—and the decline in its scores was cited regularly and with
assurance, as though the test were a geiger counter of the mind.
But tests like the SAT are much more problematic than the public
is led to believe. The fairness of the test, its legitimacy as a measure of literacy and academic potential, its use as a prerequisite
for admission to college and as an indicator of the performance
of the public schools have all been seriously challenged, at times
by Educational Testing Service researchers themselves. And, as a

further complicating irony, more recent studies of SAT and other national test scores suggest that, as one research team put it, "evidence for a massive, consistent skill decline . . . is much more mixed than the school critics have claimed."

Local assessments—studies of math or writing skills conducted by specific campuses or systems—were more specific and, in some ways, more legitimate. By their very proliferation, however, and by the academic community's reliance on them, they generated problems of a different order. The data in all the reports—and the charts and graphs that displayed them—became the vocabulary, the elements of a discourse for conducting the business of underpreparation. A vast and wealthy industry of educational institutes and consultants grew up around them. Things that seemed sensible, and in other contexts would never be challenged, now became questions to be solved by quantitative evaluation. The Tutorial Center was asked to demonstrate, with numbers, that getting individual guidance with material you don't understand is helpful, that having a chance to talk about what you're learning is beneficial. The drive to quantify became very strong, a reality unto itself, and what you couldn't represent with a ratio or a chart—what was messy and social and complex—was simply harder to talk about and much harder to get acknowledged. Patricia Cline Cohen, the historian of numeracy, notes that in America there is the belief that "to measure is to initiate a cure." But a focus on quantification—on errors we can count, on test scores we can rank-order—can divert us from rather than guide us toward solutions. Numbers seduce us into thinking we know more than we do; they give the false assurance of rigor but reveal little about the complex cognitive and emotional processes behind the tally of errors and wrong answers. What goes on behind the mistakes simply escapes the measurer's rule.

The second source of evidence for decline found in the crisis reports was statistics on remedial enrollments. The reports claimed that remedial courses were a new and alarming phenomenon, the flooding of the ivy halls with the intellectually unwashed. If anything sparked fear in the general public, these numbers did. But, in fact, courses and programs that we could call remedial are older than fight songs and cheerleaders. Since the mid-1800s, American colleges have been establishing various kinds of preparatory classes within their halls—it was, and is, their way of maintaining enrollments while bringing their entering students up to curricular par. (In 1894, for example, over 40 percent of entering freshmen came from the "preparatory divisions" of the institutions that enrolled them.) If the 1970s saw an increase in remedial courses and programs, the increase was measured in terms of very recent history and reflected the fact that universities had grown rapidly in the fifties and sixties and now had to scramble to fill their classrooms. So recruitment began for populations that had not traditionally come to college—working-class whites, blacks, and Hispanics, single parents, older folks—students who had, for the most part, received dreary educations down the line. And, yes, they would need special courses, "low-level" courses, remedial courses, but this was not the first taint of curricular sin on an otherwise pristine American university.

And then there were the faculty testimonials about decline. "These are the truly illiterate among us," said the dean. And in memos and public documents and interviews you'd read the judgments, somber and dramatic: "Simple reading is beyond them." "They have ceased to care about ideas." "What we have here is cultural illiteracy." "They have abandoned the word." This was the human side of the crisis reports, the weary battle cries from the front lines—grave and disconsolate. These pronouncements are still with us; they pepper our newspapers and magazines. No matter that the commentators are rarely on the front lines at all, listening closely as students work through an essay, probing for the logic of a sentence gone awry. Ask yourself if it is accurate to say that Lucia, the older student with the baby, can't read. That she is without culture? I'm not asking for softheartedness here—the accusation so often hurled when these questions are raised. I'm simply trying to force precision. Is it accurate to say that Marita, the girl accused of plagiarism, didn't care about ideas? The teacher who thought she was cheating missed completely the intellectual underpinnings of her action and—in a telling leap—leveled a moral judgment instead. The sad thing is that the somber one-liners are accepted, even encouraged, in the very place in the society that refuses to condone easy judgment. No academic would allow such superficial assessments in his or her own discipline.

The crisis reports conveyed a sense of tough-mindedness, but, in fact, they really weren't that intellectually rigorous at all. They lacked both historical perspective and sophistication about cognition and culture, and their alarmist tone distracted people from careful study of the students they assailed. Blaming the victim allowed institutional contributions to the crisis of underpreparation to be ignored. Stressing the "deficits," "deficiencies," and "handicaps" of the students, quantitatively displayed, diverted attention from the segmented dispensary that lower-division education has become. In the candid opinion of one university administrator:

> Almost uniformly throughout the lower division in the social sciences, I am convinced that the quality of education cannot at present be described as university-level. . . . Typically, 17- and 18-year-old freshmen, many if not most underprepared for the university, are herded together into large, anonymous lecture classes. . . . [They] take, at most, two machine-scored objective tests, with no homework assignments, no opportunity or necessity to communicate orally, no written work, and no direct contact of any kind with anyone in a teaching role, and all too frequently no human contact of any kind. . . .

Because of the complex mix of cognitive and cultural factors we've seen, the EOP students felt most strongly the effects of this impersonal, fragmented education; they, truly, were the least prepared for it, though not necessarily for the reasons the crisis reports would have us believe. But their difficulties served to illuminate, to throw into relief, the problems a great number of students—not just ours—were having. The struggles of the underprepared were revealing the needs of the many.

———◆———

Not too long ago I was speaking about curriculum at another university. It was a lunchtime speech, preceded by murmurs and clinking glassware, and I was about to leave my chair for the podium when a young woman walked up to me and asked me if I remembered her. She was vaguely familiar, a little lighter or a little heavier than someone I once knew, hair longer, shorter maybe—something. "I'm Concepción Baca," she said, extending her hand. "I was in the first summer program. I'm in graduate school here. I'm in Comparative Literature." She paused. "You're surprised, aren't you? I bet I'm the last person you expected to see here." Well, not the last. But I was surprised.

After my talk, Concepción and I sat down together. She had come, it turned out, because the director of Freshman Writing at this school had asked his teaching assistants to attend. He came over and joined us. Concepción, he said, was one of his best writing teachers. She was also doing excellent work in her graduate studies. Comparative Literature is a backbreaking degree—you must be proficient in the literature of three languages—and Concepción was getting close to the dissertation stage. "So, how'd you end up here?," I asked. "Well," she shrugged, "it's a long story. Did you know that I dropped out of UCLA?" I didn't, and as she spoke, I heard an interesting and not unfamiliar story.

Concepción stayed at UCLA for almost two years, taking a range of courses, from history and psychology to English and linguistics. Her record was spotty: some A's, some C's, two incompletes that turned to F's because she failed to make them up. That put her on academic probation. In the middle of her sophomore year, she quit. "I never really got used to living away from home," she explained. "I never felt right about it." She had trouble deciding on a major. Her best grades were in Latin American Studies, American Immigrant History, and English. She had liked English in the summer program and elected three or four other English courses along the way. Her teachers said her writing was okay, told her she should work on it. But what would she do with an English major? Her parents were spending a lot of money on her. She missed them. What would she major in? How could she keep going to school when their money was so tight? She withdrew and went to work. Two years later, she entered a different University of California campus. She had made some money herself and had a lot of time to think about those two years at UCLA. She liked cultural history and English, and those interests led her to comparative literature. She blossomed. She graduated with very good grades and went on to graduate school.

People who work in tutoring centers and preparatory programs get used to spending intense bursts of time with their students. You get closely involved for a few weeks or a few months, and then you send them off. And you wonder. You know some won't make it. There's too much working against their success. They'll drift in and out of academic probation, their transcripts a listing of C's, C-minuses, a D or two, and then the fatal F that exits them. That was what happened to Andrea, the young woman who was having such a miserable time with chemistry, who I was afraid might hurt herself just to escape. She was longing to be premed when General Chemistry was insurmountable. There are some, though, who do make it. Even those you thought were doomed. There was Vincent, whose summer program teacher commented that his writing was "very poor," who was on academic probation for part of his freshman year, who kept showing up at the Tutorial Center to work on his writing, who finally had to withdraw but came back and cleared his record as a sophomore—and by the time he was a junior was getting B's, who earned an A-minus in Advanced Composition during his senior year. Vincent's parents were migrant workers in South Fresno. Neither had gone to high school. Vincent was now thinking about graduate school in urban planning. It can happen.

As I was driving home, I thought about Concepción. I thought about how long it sometimes takes to achieve a balance, how much of myself I saw in her, how easy it would have been to misperceive her as a freshman: scattershot course selection, incompletes, C's in introductory courses, probation—and finally withdrawal. She was listed, I'm sure, as one of the summer program's failures. An attrition statistic. Concepción eventually found her way; many like her aren't as fortunate. Research universities are awful places for freshmen to be adrift, to be searching, to be in need. Attrition may be a blessing, as many contend, for it naturally purges the university of those who don't belong, those who never should have come. There's a kind of harsh institutional truth to that, I suppose, but to embrace it, you'll have to limit your definition of achievement—blunt your sense of wonder. What you'll have to do, finally, is narrow your vision of the society you want to foster.

8

---◆---

Crossing Boundaries

Through all my experiences with people struggling to learn, the one thing that strikes me most is the ease with which we misperceive failed performance and the degree to which this misperception both reflects and reinforces the social order. Class and culture erect boundaries that hinder our vision—blind us to the logic of error and the everpresent stirring of language—and encourage the designation of otherness, difference, deficiency. And the longer I stay in education, the clearer it becomes to me that some of our basic orientations toward the teaching and testing of literacy contribute to our inability to see. To truly educate in America, then, to reach the full sweep of our citizenry, we need to question received perception, shift continually from the standard lens. The exploratory stories that bring this book to its close encourage us to sit close by as people use language and consider, as we listen, the orientations that limit our field of vision.

---◆---

The humanities presume particular methods of expression and inquiry—language, dialogue, reflection, imagination, and metaphor. . . . [and] remain dedicated to the disciplined development of verbal, perceptual, and imaginative skills needed to understand experience.

—*The Humanities in American Life*, Report of the Rockefeller Commission on the Humanities

Two young men have walked in late and are standing around the back of the classroom, halfheartedly looking for seats. One wears a faded letterman's jacket, the other is bundled up in a bright red sweater and a long overcoat. A third student has plopped his books by the door and is hunkering down against the wall. This is Developmental English in a state college in Ohio. It is December, and the radiators are turned up high. Occasional clanks are emitted by some distant valve. The room is stuffy with dry heat. The teacher directs the latecomers to some seats in the front, and he begins the lesson. The class is working on pronoun agreement. They have worked on it for a week and will continue to work on it for another. The windows are frosted at the edges. In the distance, a tall smokestack releases a curling black stream diagonally across the sky.

Students designated "developmental" at this school must take a year's worth of very basic English before they can move into standard Freshman Comp. Their year is broken into two semesters. During the first semester they inch through a thick workbook filled with grammar exercises: "Circle the correct pronoun in this sentence: That was her/she in the lecture hall" or "Supply the correct pronoun for the following sentence: The recruits were upset by _____ scores on the fitness tests." Some of this they do at home. Most of it they do in class. That way, the teacher can be sure they are doing it. They hand in their workbooks regularly to have the teacher check their answers.

The course involves very little writing, except for words and phrases the students must scribble in the blanks on the pages. Some class discussion is generated when the teacher has the students read their answers. Periodically he will explain a rule or illustrate its use on the blackboard. Young men along the back wall fill in a blank now and then; the rest of the time, they're eyeballing the teacher and talking softly. A girl is filing her nails. Students in the middle of the room are bent over their workbooks, penciling in answers, erasing them, looking up and out the frosted windows. A skinny boy in the front is going down the page as mechanically as Melville's pallid scrivener.

There are sentences being written in this class, but not by mandate of the dean of instruction. Two girls close to the door have been passing notes all hour; they are producing the class's most extended discourse. Students are not asked to write here because it is assumed—as it is assumed in many such basic courses—that they must first get all their workbook pronouns to agree with their workbook antecedents. When they reach the second semester, they will, for fifteen weeks, do some small amount of writing, but that writing will be limited to single sentences. At this school, and many others, the English Department and the program that coordinates remedial courses are philosophically and administratively separated. Different schools have different histories, but often—as was the case here—the separation was strongly influenced by the English Department's desire to be freed from basic instruction. The two departments at this school, though, have an unusually stringent agreement: Anything longer than the sentence (even two or three sentences strung together) is considered *writing,* and the teaching of writing shall be the province of the English Department. Anything at the sentence level or smaller (like filling words and phrases into a workbook) is to be considered grammar review, and that falls within the domain of the remedial program. For one academic year, then, students who desperately need to improve their writing will not be writing anything longer than the sentence. This particular slicing of the pedagogical pie is extreme in its execution, but the assumptions about error, remediation, and the linguistic capabilities of poorly prepared students that undergird it remain widespread in America—and they influence everything from lesson plans to the sectioning of academic territory. Given the pervasiveness of these assumptions, it would be valuable to consider, for a moment, their origins.

A good place to begin is with the encounter of educational psychology and schooling. Turn-of-the-century English education was built on a Latin and Greek-influenced grammar, primarily a set of prescriptions for conducting socially acceptable discourse. So when psychologists began investigating the teaching of writing, they found a pedagogy of memory and drill, one concentrating on the often arcane dos and don'ts of usage. They also found reports like those issuing from the Harvard faculty in the 1890s that called attention to the presence of errors in handwriting, spelling, and grammar in the writing of that university's entering freshmen. The twentieth-century writing curriculum, then, was focused on the particulars of usage, grammar, and mechanics.

Correctness became, in James Berlin's words, the era's "most significant measure of accomplished prose."

Such a focus suited educational researchers' approach to language: a mechanistic orientation that studied language by reducing it to discrete behaviors and that defined growth as the accretion of these particulars. Quantification and measurement were central to the researchers' method, so the focus on error—which seemed eminently measurable—found justification in a model of mind that was ascending in American academic psychology. This approach was further supported and advanced by what Raymond Callahan has called "the cult of efficiency," a strong push to apply to education the principles of industrial scientific management. Educational gains were defined as products, and the output of products could be measured. Pedagogical effectiveness—which meant cost-effectiveness—could be determined with "scientific" accuracy. What emerges, finally, is a combination of positivism, efficiency, and a focus on grammar that would have a profound influence on pedagogy and research.

Textbooks as well as workbooks reflected this orientation. One textbook for teachers presented an entire unit on the colon. A text for students devoted seven pages to the use of a capital letter to indicate a proper noun. Research, too, focused on the details of language, especially on listing and tabulating error. You rarely find consideration of the social context of error, or of its significance in the growth of the writer. Instead you find studies like those of W. S. Guiler's tally of the percentages of 350 students who, in misspelling *mortgage*, erred by omitting the *t* versus those who dropped the first *g*.

Despite the fact that the assumptions about language and learning informing these approaches to teaching and research began to be challenged by the late 1930s, the procedures of the earlier era have remained with us. This trend has the staying power it does for a number of reasons: It gives a method—a putatively objective one—to the strong desire of our society to maintain correct language use. It is very American in its seeming efficiency. And it offers a simple, understandable view of complex linguistic problems. The trend reemerges most forcefully in times of crisis: when budgets crunch and accountability looms or, particularly, when "nontraditional" students flood our institutions. A reduction of complexity has great appeal in institutional decision making, especially in difficult times: a scientific-atomistic approach to language, with its attendant tallies and charts, nicely fits an economic decision-making model. When in doubt or when scared or when pressed, count.

This orientation to language complements the way we conceive of remediation.

The designation *remedial* has powerful implications in education—to be remedial is to be substandard, inadequate—and, because of the origins of the term, the inadequacy is metaphorically connected to disease and mental defectiveness. The etymology of the word *remedial* places its origins in law and medicine, and by the late nineteenth century the term generally fell into the medical domain. It was then applied to education, to children who were thought to have neurological problems. But *remedial* quickly generalized beyond the description of such students to those with broader, though special, educational problems and then to those learners who were from backgrounds that did not provide optimal environmental and educational opportunities.

As increasing access to education brought more and more children into the schools, the medical vocabulary—with its implied medical model—remained dominant. People tried to *diagnose* various *disabilities, defects, deficits, deficiencies,* and *handicaps,* then tried to *remedy* them. So you start to see all sorts of reading and writing problems clustered together and addressed with this language. For example, William S. Gray's important monograph, *Remedial Cases in Reading: Their Diagnosis and Treatment,* listed as "specific causes of failure in reading" inferior learning capacity, congenital word blindness, poor auditory memory, defective vision, a narrow span of recognition, ineffective eye movements, inadequate training in phonetics, inadequate attention to the content, an inadequate speaking vocabulary, a small meaning vocabulary, speech defects, lack of interest, and timidity. The remedial paradigm was beginning to include those who had troubles as varied as bad eyes, second language interference, and shyness. The semantic net of *remedial* was expanding and expanding.

It is likely that the appeal of medical-remedial language had much to do with its associations with scientific objectivity and accuracy—powerful currency in the efficiency-minded 1920s and 1930s. Consider, as illustration, this passage from Albert Lang's

1930 textbook, *Modern Methods in Written Examinations.* The medical model is explicit:

> Teaching bears a resemblance to the practice of medicine. Like a successful physician, the good teacher must be something of a diagnostician. The physician by means of a general examination singles out the individual whose physical defects require a more thorough testing. He critically scrutinizes the special cases until he recognizes the specific troubles. After a careful diagnosis he is able to prescribe intelligently the best remedial or corrective measures.

The theoretical and pedagogical model that was available for "corrective teaching" led educators to view literacy problems from a medical-remedial perspective. Thus they set out to diagnose as precisely as possible the errors (defects) in a student's paper—which they saw as symptomatic of equally isolable defects in the student's linguistic capacity—and devise drills and exercises to remedy them. (One of the 1930s nicknames for remedial sections was "sick sections." During the next decade they would be tagged "hospital sections.") Such corrective teaching was, in the words of one educator, "the most logical as well as the most scientific method."

Though we have, over the last fifty years, developed a richer understanding of reading and writing difficulties, the reductive view of error and the language of medicine is still with us. A recent letter from the senate of a local liberal arts college is sitting on my desk. It discusses a "program in remedial writing for . . . [those] entering freshmen suffering from severe writing handicaps." We seem entrapped by this language, this view of students and learning. We still talk of writers as suffering from specifiable, locatable defects, deficits, and handicaps that can be localized, circumscribed, and remedied. Such talk carries with it the etymological wisps and traces of disease and serves to exclude from the academic community those who are so labeled. They sit in scholastic quarantine until their disease can be diagnosed and remedied.

This atomistic, medical model of language is simply not supported by more recent research in language and cognition. But because the teaching of writing—particularly teaching designated remedial—has been conceptually and, as with the Ohio program, administratively segmented from the rich theoretical investigation that characterizes other humanistic study, these assumptions have rarely been subjected to rigorous and comprehensive scrutiny. *The Humanities in American Life,* the important position paper from which the epigraph to this section is drawn, argues passionately for the wide relevance of the humanities and urges the serious engagement of humanists in teacher training, industry, and adult basic education—areas they, for the most part, have abandoned. But until the traditional orientations to error and remediation are examined to their core, until the teaching of writing and reading to underprepared students is fundamentally reconceived, then the spirited plea of the Rockefeller Commission will be, for many in America, just another empty homiletic. Consider, after all, what those students in Developmental English are really learning.

The curriculum in Developmental English breeds a deep social and intellectual isolation from print; it fosters attitudes and beliefs about written language that, more than anything, *keep* students from becoming fully, richly literate. The curriculum teaches students that when it comes to written language use, they are children: they can only perform the most constrained and ordered of tasks, and they must do so under the regimented guidance of a teacher. It teaches them that the most important thing about writing—the very essence of writing—is grammatical correctness, not the communication of something meaningful, or the generative struggle with ideas . . . not even word play. It's a curriculum that rarely raises students' heads from the workbook page to consider the many uses of written language that surround them in their schools, jobs, and neighborhoods. Finally, by its tedium, the curriculum teaches them that writing is a crushing bore. These students traverse course after remedial course, becoming increasingly turned off to writing, increasingly convinced that they are hopelessly inadequate. "Writing," one of the students tells me. "Man, I've never been any good at writing." "English," says another, "is not my thing."

This last comment comes from the latecomer in the letterman's jacket. I've caught up with him after class, and as we walk outside the building, our breath turns to steam. He carries a radio, turned on now, on which a smitten rapmaster is trying to convince someone named Roxanne that he is a "debonair doc": "There's anesthesiology," he rhythmically intones, "ophthalmology, in-ternal medicine, and plastic sur-ger-y." The young man, his name is Melvyn, is moving as we talk, and I ask him about the song. He likes rap music best, he says, because the speaker, the M.C., handles words so well, uses them to build himself up, to get women, to express his ideas about things. Three good reasons to write, I think. Good old-fashioned motives for putting pen to paper. In a 1934 report on the teaching of college English, a Nebraska professor pleaded for "ceaseless, brutal drill on mechanics. . . . Never mind imagination, the soul, literature, for at least one semester, but pray for literacy and fight for it." The twisted logic of this exasperated cry lives on—it informs Melvyn's curriculum. Literacy can be gained by brutalizing the imagination. A linguistic version of burning the village to save it. The M.C., meanwhile, has swayed Roxanne and moves on to his peroration:

> It's only customary
> to give this commentary.
> You'll never find a rap
> like this in *any* dictionary.

"The humanities presume particular methods of expression and inquiry—language, dialogue, reflection, imagination, and metaphor." The primary, even the sole, manifestation of the humanities that many lower-class and underprepared students encounter in high school, community, and state college is their English class. Considering the yearlong course of study laid out for Melvyn, his M.C. might be right. The instruction in language use he confronts strips away the vibrancy and purpose, the power and style, the meaning of the language that swirls around him. The dictionary, and all that represents written language, is rendered sterile. Literacy, as that Nebraska professor recommended, is severed from imagination. Is it any wonder that so many see school approaches to language as a source of consternation, as tedious and dulling, as a rebuff rather than an invitation?

I myself I thank God for the dream to come back to school and to be able to seek the dream I want, because I know this time I will try and make my dream come true.

Each semester the staff of the Bay Area literacy program we're about to visit collects samples of their students' writing and makes books for them. You can find an assortment on an old bookshelf by the coordinator's desk. The booklets are simple: mimeographed, faint blue stencil, stapled, dog-eared. There are uneven drawings on the thin paper covers: a bicycle leaning against a tree, the Golden Gate Bridge, an Aubrey Beardsley sketch. The stories are about growing up, raising children, returning—sadly or with anticipation—to hometowns, to Chicago or St. Louis or to a sweep of rural communities in the South. Many of the stories are about work: looking for work, losing work, wanting better work. And many more are about coming back to school. Coming back to school. Some of these writers haven't been in a classroom in thirty years.

The stories reveal quite a range. Many are no longer than a paragraph, their sentences simple and repetitive, tenuously linked by *and* and *then* and *anyway*. There are lots of grammar and spelling errors and problems with sentence boundaries—in a few essays, periods come where commas should be or where no punctuation is needed at all: "It was hard for me to stay in school because I was allway sick. and that was verry hard for me." Or, "I sound better. now that my boys are grown." Papers of this quality are written, for the most part, by newcomers, people at the end of their first semester. But other papers—quite a few, actually—are competent. They tend to come from those who have received a year or more of instruction. There are still problems with grammar and sentence fragments and with spelling, since the writers are using a wider, more ambitious vocabulary. Problems like these take longer to clear up, but the writers are getting more adept at rendering their experience in print, at developing a narrative, at framing an illustration, at turning a phrase in written language:

The kitchen floor was missing some of its tiles and had not been kissed with water and soap for a long time.

The [teacher] looked for a moment, and then said, "All the students wishing to be accounted for, please be seated."

A minute went by, then a tough looking Mexican boy got up, and walked to the teacher with a knife in his hand. When he got to the desk he said, "I'm here teacher! My name is Robert Gomez." With that he put the knife away, and walked over and found a seat.

Back in the jaws of dispair, pain, and the ugly scars of the defeated parents he loved. Those jaws he had struggled free of when he had moved out and away when he was eighteen years old.

. . . the wind was howling, angry, whirling.

A few new students also created such moments, indicators of what they'll be able to do as they become more fluent writers, as they develop some control over and confidence in establishing themselves on paper:

[I used to have] light, really light Brown eyes, like Grasshopper eyes. which is what some peoples used to call me. Grasshopper, or Grasshopper eyes. . . . I decided one Day to catch a Grasshopper. and look at its eye to be sure of the color.

It was early in the morning just before dawn. Big Red, the sun hasen't showed its face in the heaven. The sky had that midnight blue look. The stars losing their shine.

There are about eight or ten of these stapled collections, a hundred and fifty or so essays. Five years' worth. An archive scattered across an old bookcase. There's a folding chair close by. I've been sitting in it for some time now, reading one book, then another, story after story. Losing track. Drifting in and out of lives. Wondering about grasshopper eyes, about segregated schools, wanting to know more about this journey to the West looking for work. Slowly something has been shifting in my perception: the errors—the weird commas and missing letters, the fragments and irregular punctuation—they are ceasing to be slips of the hand and brain. They are becoming part of the stories themselves. They are the only fitting way, it seems, to render dislocation—shacks and field labor and children lost to the inner city—to talk about parents you long for, jobs you can't pin down. Poverty has generated its own damaged script, scars manifest in the spelling of a word.

This is the prose of America's underclass. The writers are those who got lost in our schools, who could not escape neighborhoods that narrowed their possibilities, who could not enter the job market in any ascendent way. They are locked into unskilled and semiskilled jobs, live in places that threaten their children, suffer from disorders and handicaps they don't have the money to treat. Some have been unemployed for a long time. But for all that, they remain hopeful, have somehow held onto a deep faith in education. They have come back to school. Ruby, the woman who wrote the passage that opens this section, walks unsteadily to the teacher's desk—the arthritis in her hip goes unchecked— with a paper in her hand. She looks over her shoulder to her friend, Alice: "I ain't givin' up the ship this time," she says and winks, "though, Lord, I might drown with it." The class laughs. They understand.

It is a very iffy thing, this schooling. But the participants put a lot of stock in it. They believe school will help them, and they are very specific about what they want: a high school equivalency, or the ability to earn seven dollars an hour. One wants to move from being a nurse's aide to a licensed vocational nurse, another needs to read and write and compute adequately enough to be self-employed as a car painter and body man. They remind you of how fundamentally important it is—not just to your pocket but to your soul as well—to earn a decent wage, to have a steady job, to be just a little bit in control of your economic life. The goals are specific, modest, but they mean a tremendous amount for the assurance they give to these people that they are still somebody, that they can exercise control. Thus it is that talk of school and a new job brings forth such expansive language, as soaring as any humanist's testament to the glory of the word: "I thank God to be able to seek the dream I want. . . ." For Ruby and her classmates the dream deferred neither dried up like a raisin in the sun, nor has it exploded. It has emerged again—for it is so basic—and it centers on schooling. "I admire and respect knowledge and thoes that have it are well blessed," writes another student. "My classmates are a swell group becaus they too have a dream and they too are seeking knowledge and I love them for that."

Sitting in the classroom with Ruby, Alice, and the rest, you think, at times, that you're at a revival meeting. There is so much testifying. Everybody talks and writes about dreams and goals and "doing better for myself." This is powerful, edifying—but something about it, its insistence perhaps, is a little bit discordant. The exuberance becomes jittery, an almost counterphobic boosting and supporting. It is no surprise, then, that it alternates with despair. In their hearts, Ruby and her classmates know how tenuous this is, how many times they've failed before. Somebody says something about falling down. Sally says, "I've felt that too. Not falling down on my legs or knees, but falling down within me." No wonder they sermonize and embrace. It's not just a few bucks more a week that's at stake; literacy, here, is intimately connected with respect, with a sense that they are not beaten, the mastery of print revealing the deepest impulse to survive.

When they entered the program, Ruby and Alice and Sally and all the rest were given several tests, one of which was a traditional reading inventory. The test had a section on comprehension— relatively brief passages followed by multiple-choice questions— and a series of sections that tested particular reading skills: vocabulary, syllabication, phonics, prefixes and roots. The level of the instrument was pretty sophisticated, and the skills it tested are the kind you develop in school: answering multiple-choice questions, working out syllable breaks, knowing Greek and Latin roots, all that. What was interesting about this group of test takers was that—though a few were barely literate—many could read and write well enough to get along, and, in some cases, to help those in their communities who were less skilled. They could read, with fair comprehension, simple news articles, could pay bills, follow up on sales and coupons, deal with school forms for their kids, and help illiterate neighbors in their interactions with the government. Their skills were pretty low-level and limited profoundly the kinds of things they could read or write, but they lived and functioned amid print. The sad thing is that we don't really have tests of such naturally occurring competence. The tests we do have, like the one Ruby and the others took, focus on components of reading ability tested in isolation (phonetic discrimination, for example) or on those skills that are school-oriented, like reading a passage on an unfamiliar topic unrelated to immediate needs: the mating habits of the dolphin, the Mayan pyramids. Students then answer questions on these sorts of passages by choosing one of four or five possible answers, some of which may be purposely misleading.

To nobody's surprise, Ruby and her classmates performed miserably. The tasks of the classroom were as unfamiliar as could be. There is a good deal of criticism of these sorts of reading tests, but one thing that is clear is that they reveal how well people can perform certain kinds of school activities. The activities themselves may be of questionable value, but they are interwoven with instruction and assessment, and entrance to many jobs is determined by them. Because of their centrality, then, I wanted to get some sense of how the students went about taking the tests. What happened as they tried to meet the test's demands? How was it that they failed?

My method was simple. I chose four students and had each of them take sections of the test again, asking them questions as they did so, encouraging them to talk as they tried to figure out an item.

The first thing that emerged was the complete foreignness of the task. A sample item in the prefixes and roots section (called Word Parts) presented the word "unhappy," and asked the test-taker to select one of four other words "which gives the meaning of the underlined part of the first word." The choices were *very, glad, sad, not*. Though the person giving the test had read through the instructions with the class, many still could not understand, and if they chose an answer at all, most likely chose *sad*, a synonym for the whole word *unhappy*.

Nowhere in their daily reading are these students required to focus on parts of words in this way. The multiple-choice format is also unfamiliar—it is not part of day-to-day literacy—so the task as well as the format is new, odd. I explained the directions again—read them slowly, emphasized the sample item—but still, three of the four students continued to fall into the test maker's trap of choosing synonyms for the target word rather than zeroing in on the part of the word in question. Such behavior is common among those who fail in our schools, and it has led some commentators to posit that students like these are cognitively and linguistically deficient in some fundamental way: They process language differently, or reason differently from those who succeed in school, or the dialect they speak in some basic way interferes with their processing of Standard Written English.

Certainly in such a group—because of malnourishment, trauma, poor health care, environmental toxins—you'll find people with neurolinguistic problems or with medical difficulties that can affect perception and concentration. And this group— ranging in age from nineteen to the mid-fifties—has a wide array of medical complications: diabetes, head injury, hypertension, asthma, retinal deterioration, and the unusual sleep disorder called narcolepsy. It would be naive to deny the effect of all this on reading and writing. But as you sit alongside these students and listen to them work through a task, it is not damage that most strikes you. Even when they're misunderstanding the test and selecting wrong answers, their reasoning is not distorted and pathological. Here is Millie, whose test scores placed her close to the class average—and average here would be very low just about anywhere else.

Millie is given the word "kilometer" and the following list of possible answers:

   a. thousand
   b. hundred
   c. distance
   d. speed

She responds to the whole word—*kilometer*—partially because she still does not understand how the test works, but also, I think, because the word is familiar to her. She offers *speed* as the correct answer because: "I see it on the signs when I be drivin'." She starts to say something else, but stops abruptly. "Whoa, it don't have to be 'speed'—it could be 'distance.'"

"It could be 'distance,' couldn't it?" I say.

"Yes, it could be one or the other."

"Okay."

"And then again," she says reflectively, "it could be a number."

Millie tapped her knowledge of the world—she had seen *kilometer* on road signs—to offer a quick response: *speed*. But she saw just as quickly that her knowledge could logically support another answer (*distance*), and, a few moments later, saw that what she knew could *also* support a third answer, one related to number. What she lacked was specific knowledge of the Greek prefix *kilo*, but she wasn't short on reasoning ability. In fact, reading tests like the one Millie took are constructed in such a way as to trick you into relying on commonsense reasoning and world knowledge—and thereby choosing a *wrong* answer. Take, for example, this item:

Cardio<u>gram</u>
a. heart
b. abnormal
c. distance
d. record

Millie, and many others in the class, chose *heart*. To sidestep that answer, you need to know something about the use of *gram* in other such words (versus its use as a metric weight), but you need to know, as well, how these tests work.

After Millie completed five or six items, I had her go back over them, talking through her answers with her. One item that had originally given her trouble was "<u>extra</u>ordinary": a) "beyond"; b) "acute"; c) "regular"; d) "imagined." She had been a little rattled when answering this one. While reading the four possible answers, she stumbled on "imagined": "I . . . im . . ."; then, tentatively, "imaged"; a pause again, then "imagine," and, quickly, "I don't know that word."

I pronounce it.

She looks up at me, a little disgusted: "I said it, didn't I?"

"You did say it."

"I was scared of it."

Her first time through, Millie had chosen *regular*, the wrong answer—apparently locking onto *ordinary* rather than the underlined prefix *extra*—doing just the opposite of what she was supposed to do. It was telling, I thought, that Millie and two or three others talked about words scaring them.

When we came back to "<u>extra</u>ordinary" during our review, I decided on a strategy. "Let's try something," I said. "These tests are set up to trick you, so let's try a trick ourselves." I take a pencil and do something the publishers of the test tell you not to do: I mark up the test booklet. I slowly begin to circle the prefix *extra*, saying, "This is the part of the word we're concerned with, right?" As soon as I finish she smiles and says "beyond," the right answer.

"Did you see what happened there?" I said. "As soon as I circled the part of the word, you saw what it meant."

"I see it," she says. "I don't be thinking about what I'm doing."

I tell her to try what I did, to circle the part of the word in question, to remember that trick, for with tests like this, we need a set of tricks of our own.

"You saw it yourself," I said.

"Sure did. It was right there in front of me—'cause the rest of them don't even go with 'extra.'"

I had been conducting this interview with Millie in between her classes, and our time was running out. I explained that we'd pick this up again, and I turned away, checking the wall clock, reaching to turn off the tape recorder. Millie was still looking at the test booklet.

"What is this word right here?" she asked. She had gone ahead to the other, more difficult, page of the booklet and was pointing to "egocentric."

I take my finger off the recorder's STOP button. "Let's circle it," I say. "What's that word? Say it."

"Ego."

"What's that mean?"

"Ego. Oh my." She scans the four options—*self, head, mind, kind*—and says "self."

"Excellent!"

"You know, when I said 'ego,' I tried to put it in a sentence: 'My ego,' I say. That's *me*."

I ask her if she wants to look at one more. She goes back to "cardiogram," which she gets right this time. Then to "thermometer," which she also gets right. And "bifocal," which she gets right without using her pencil to mark the prefix. Once Millie saw and understood what the test required of her, she could rely on her world knowledge to help her reason out some answers. Cognitive psychologists talk about task representation, the way a particular problem is depicted or reproduced in the mind. Something shifted in Millie's conception of her task, and it had a powerful effect on her performance.

It was common for nineteenth-century American educators to see their mission with the immigrant and native-born urban poor as a fundamentally moral one. Historian Michael Katz quotes from the Boston school committee's description of social and spiritual acculturation:

> . . . taking children at random from a great city,
> undisciplined, uninstructed, often with inveterate
> forwardness and obstinacy, and with the inherited stupidity
> of centuries of ignorant ancestors; forming them from animals
> into intellectual beings, and . . . from intellectual beings into
> spiritual beings; giving to many their first appreciation of
> what is wise, what is true, what is lovely and what is pure.

In our time, educators view the effects of poverty and cultural dislocation in more enlightened ways; though that moralistic strain still exists, the thrust of their concern has shifted from the spiritual to the more earthly realm of language and cognition. Yet what remains is the disturbing tendency to perceive the poor as *different* in some basic way from the middle and upper classes— the difference now being located in the nature of the way they think and use language. A number of studies and speculations over the past twenty-five years has suggested that the poor are intellectually or linguistically deficient or, at the least, different: They lack a logical language or reason in ways that limit intellectual achievement or, somehow, process information dysfunctionally. If we could somehow get down to the very basic loops and contours of their mental function, we would find that theirs are different from ours. There's a huge literature on all this and, originating with critics like linguist William Labov, a damning counterliterature. This is not the place to review that work, but it would be valuable to consider Millie against the general outlines of the issue.

Imagine her in a typical classroom testing situation. More dramatically, imagine her in some university laboratory being studied by one or two researchers—middle class and probably white. Millie is a strong woman with a tough front, but these would most likely be uncomfortable situations for her. And if she were anxious, her performance would be disrupted: as it was when she didn't identify *imagined*—a word she pronounced and knew— because she was "scared of it." Add to this the fact that she is very much adrift when it comes to school-based tests: She simply doesn't know how to do them. What would be particularly damning for her would be the fact that, even with repeated instruction and illustration, she failed to catch on to the way the test worked. You can see how an observer would think her unable to shift out of (inadequate) performance, unable to understand simple instructions and carry them out. Deficient or different in some basic way: nonlogical, nonrational, unable to thi   analytically. It would be from observations like this that a theory of fundamental cognitive deficiency or difference would emerge.

We seem to have a need as a society to explain poor performance by reaching deep into the basic stuff of those designated as other: into their souls, or into the deep recesses of their minds, or into the very ligature of their language. It seems harder for us to keep focus on the politics and sociology of intellectual failure, to keep before our eyes the negative power of the unfamiliar, the way information poverty constrains performance, the effect of despair on cognition.

"I was so busy looking for 'psychopathology,' . . ." says Robert Coles of his early investigations of childhood morality, "that I brushed aside the most startling incidents, the most instructive examples of ethical alertness in the young people I was getting to know." How much we don't see when we look only for deficiency, when we tally up all that people can't do. Many of the students in this book display the gradual or abrupt emergence of an intellectual acuity or literate capacity that just wasn't thought to be there. This is not to deny that awful limits still exist for those like Millie: so much knowledge and so many procedures never learned; such a long, cumbersome history of relative failure. But this must not obscure the equally important fact that if you set up the right conditions, try as best you can to cross class and cultural boundaries, figure out what's needed to encourage performance, that if you watch and listen, again and again there will emerge evidence of ability that escapes those who dwell on differences.

Ironically, it's often the reports themselves of our educational inadequacies—the position papers and media alarms on illiteracy in America—that help blind us to cognitive and linguistic possibility. Their rhetorical thrust and their metaphor conjure up disease or decay or economic and military defeat: A malignancy has run wild, an evil power is consuming us from within. (And here re-emerges that nineteenth-century moral terror.) It takes such declamation to turn the moneyed wheels of government, to catch public attention and entice the givers of grants, but there's a dark side to this political reality. The character of the alarms and, too often, the character of the responses spark in us the urge to punish, to extirpate, to return to a precancerous golden age rather than build on the rich capacity that already exists. The reports urge responses that reduce literate possibility and constrain growth, that focus on pathology rather than on possibility. Philosophy, said Aristotle, begins in wonder. So does education.

—————◆—————

You know, Mike, people always hold this shit over you, make you . . . make you feel stupid with their fancy talk. But now *I've* read it, I've read Shakespeare, I can say I, *Olga*, have read it. I won't tell you I like it, 'cause I don't know if I do or I don't. But I like knowing what it's about.

I have a vivid memory of sitting on the edge of my bed—I was twelve or thirteen maybe—and listening with unease to a minute or so of classical music. I don't know if I found it as I was turning the dial, searching for the Johnny Otis Show or the live broadcast from Scribner's Drive-In, or if the tuner had simply drifted into another station's signal. Whatever happened, the music caught me in a disturbing way, and I sat there, letting it play. It sounded like the music I heard in church, weighted, funereal. Eerie chords echoing from another world. I leaned over, my fingers on the tuner, and, in what I remember as almost a twitch, I turned the knob away from the melody of these strange instruments. My reaction to the other high culture I encountered—*The Iliad* and Shakespeare and some schoolbook poems by Longfellow and Lowell—was similar, though less a visceral rejection and more a rejecting disinterest, a sense of irrelevance. The few Shakespearean scenes I did know—saw on television, or read or heard in grammar school—seemed snooty and put-on, kind of dumb. Not the way I wanted to talk. Not interesting to me.

There were few books in our house: a couple of thin stories read to me as a child in Pennsylvania (*The Little Boy Who Ran Away*, an *Uncle Remus* sampler), the *M* volume of the *World Book Encyclope-*

dia (which I found one day in the trash behind the secondhand
store), and the Hollywood tabloids my mother would bring home
from work. I started buying lots of Superman and Batman comic
books because I loved the heroes' virtuous omnipotence—comic
books, our teachers said, were bad for us—and, once I discovered
them, I began checking out science fiction novels from my grammar school library. Other reading material appeared: the instructions to my chemistry set, which I half understood and only half
followed, and, eventually, my astronomy books, which seemed
to me to be magical rather than discursive texts. So it was that
my early intrigue with literacy—my lifts and escapes with language and rhythm—came from comic books and science fiction,
from the personal, nonscientific worlds I created with bits and
pieces of laboratory and telescopic technology, came, as well,
from the Italian stories I heard my uncles and parents tell. It
came, too, from the music my radio brought me: music that wove
in and out of my days, lyrics I'd repeat and repeat—"gone, gone,
gone, jumpin' like a catfish on a pole"—wanting to catch that
sound, seeking other emotional frontiers, other places to go. Like
rocker Joe Ely, I picked up Chicago on my transistor radio.

Except for school exercises and occasional cards my mother
made me write to my uncles and aunts, I wrote very little during
my childhood; it wasn't until my last year in high school that Jack
MacFarland sparked an interest in writing. And though I developed into a good reader, I performed from moderately well to
terribly on other sorts of school literacy tasks. From my reading I
knew vocabulary words, and I did okay on spelling tests—though
I never lasted all that long in spelling bees—but I got C's and D's
on the ever-present requests to diagram sentences and label parts
of speech. The more an assignment was related to real reading,
the better I did; the more analytic, self-contained, and divorced
from context, the lousier I performed. Today some teachers
would say I was a concrete thinker. To be sure, the development
of my ability to decode words and read sentences took place in
school, but my orientation to reading—the way I conceived of it,
my purpose for doing it—occurred within the tight and untradi-
tional confines of my home. The quirks and textures of my immediate environment combined with my escapist fantasies to draw
me to books. "It is what we are excited about that educates us,"
writes social historian Elizabeth Ewen. It is what taps our curios-

ity and dreams. Eventually, the books that seemed so distant, those Great Books, would work their way into my curiosity, would influence the way I framed problems and the way I wrote. But that would come much later—first with Jack MacFarland (mixed with his avant-garde countertradition), then with my teachers at Loyola and UCLA—an excitement and curiosity shaped by others and connected to others, a cultural and linguistic heritage received not from some pristine conduit, but exchanged through the heat of human relation.

A friend of mine recently suggested that education is one culture embracing another. It's interesting to think of the very different ways that metaphor plays out. Education can be a desperate, smothering embrace, an embrace that denies the needs of the other. But education can also be an encouraging, communal embrace—at its best an invitation, an opening. Several years ago, I was sitting in on a workshop conducted by the Brazilian educator Paulo Freire. It was the first hour or so and Freire, in his sophisticated, accented English, was establishing the theoretical base of his literacy pedagogy—heady stuff, a blend of Marxism, phenomenology, and European existentialism. I was two seats away from Freire; in front of me and next to him was a younger man, who, puzzled, finally interrupted the speaker to ask a question. Freire acknowledged the question and, as he began answering, he turned and quickly touched the man's forearm. Not patronizing, not mushy, a look and a tap as if to say: "You and me right now, let's go through this together." Embrace. With Jack MacFarland it was an embrace: no-nonsense and cerebral, but a relationship in which the terms of endearment were the image in a poem, a play's dialogue, the winding narrative journey of a novel.

More often than we admit, a failed education is social more than intellectual in origin. And the challenge that has always faced American education, that it has sometimes denied and sometimes doggedly pursued, is how to create both the social and cognitive means to enable a diverse citizenry to develop their ability. It is an astounding challenge: the complex and wrenching struggle to actualize the potential not only of the privileged but, too, of those who have lived here for a long time generating a culture outside the mainstream and those who, like my mother's parents and my father, immigrated with cultural traditions of their own. This painful but generative mix of language and story can result in clash and dislocation in our communities, but it also gives rise to new speech, new stories, and once we appreciate the richness of it, new invitations to literacy.

Pico Boulevard, named for the last Mexican governor of California, runs an immense stretch west to east: from the wealth of the Santa Monica beaches to blighted Central Avenue, deep in Los Angeles. Union Street is comparatively brief, running north to south, roughly from Adams to Temple, pretty bad off all the way. Union intersects Pico east of Vermont Avenue and too far to the southwest to be touched by the big-money development that is turning downtown Los Angeles into a whirring postmodernist dreamscape. The Pico-Union District is very poor, some of its housing as unsafe as that on Skid Row, delapidated, over-crowded, rat-infested. It used to be a working-class Mexican neighborhood, but for about ten years now it has become the con-centrated locale of those fleeing the political and economic horror in Central America. Most come from El Salvador and Guatemala. One observer calls the area a gigantic refugee camp.

As you move concentrically outward from Pico-Union, you'll encounter a number of other immigrant communities: Little To-kyo and Chinatown to the northeast, Afro-Caribbean to the southwest, Koreatown to the west. Moving west, you'll find Thai and Vietnamese restaurants tucked here and there in storefronts. Filipinos, Southeast Asians, Armenians, and Iranians work in the gas stations, the shoe-repair stores, the minimarts. A lawnmower repair shop posts its sign in Korean, Spanish, and English. A Ko-rean church announces "Jesus Loves You" in the same three lan-guages. "The magnitude and diversity of immigration to Los An-geles since 1960," notes a report from UCLA's Graduate School of Architecture and Urban Planning, "is comparable only to the New York–bound wave of migrants around the turn of the cen-tury." It is not at all uncommon for English composition teachers at UCLA, Cal-State L.A., Long Beach State—the big urban uni-versities and colleges—to have, in a class of twenty-five, students representing a dozen or more linguistic backgrounds: from Span-ish and Cantonese and Farsi to Hindi, Portuguese, and Tagalog. Los Angeles, the new Ellis Island.

On a drive down the Santa Monica Freeway, you exit on Ver-mont and pass Rick's Mexican Cuisine, Hawaii Discount Furniture, The Restaurant Ecuatoriano, Froggy's Children's Wear, Seoul Autobody, and the Bar Omaha. Turn east on Pico, and as you approach Union, taking a side street here and there, you'll start seeing the murals: The Virgin of Guadalupe, Steve McQueen, a scene resembling Siqueiros's heroic workers, the Statue of Liberty, Garfield the Cat. Graffiti are everywhere. The dreaded Eighteenth Street gang—an established Mexican gang—has marked its turf in Arabic as well as Roman numerals. Newer gangs, a Salvadoran gang among them, are emerging by the violent logic of territory and migration; they have Xed out the Eighteenth Street *placas* and written their own threatening insignias in place. Statues of the Blessed Mother rest amid potted plants in overgrown front yards. There is a rich sweep of small commerce: restaurants, markets, bakeries, legal services ("Income Tax y Amnestia"), beauty salons ("Lolita's Magic Touch—Salon de Belleza—Unisex"). A Salvadoran restaurant sells teriyaki burgers. A "Discoteca Latina" advertises "great rap hits." A clothing store has a Dick Tracy sweatshirt on a half mannequin; a boy walks out wearing a blue t-shirt that announces "Life's a Beach." Culture in a Waring blender.

There are private telegram and postal services: messages sent straight to "domicilio a CentroAmerica." A video store advertises a comedy about immigration: *Ni de Aqui/Ni de Alla*, "Neither from Here nor from There." The poster displays a Central American Indian caught on a wild freeway ride: a Mexican in a sombrero is pulling one of the Indian's pigtails, Uncle Sam pulls the other, a border guard looks on, ominously suspended in air. You see a lot of street vending, from oranges and melons to deco sunglasses: rhinestones and plastic swans and lenses shaped like a heart. Posters are slapped on posters: one has rows of faces of the disappeared. Santa Claus stands on a truck bumper and waves drivers into a ninety-nine cent outlet.

Families are out shopping, men loiter outside a cafe, a group of young girls collectively count out their change. You notice, even in the kaleidoscope you pick out his figure, you notice a dark-skinned boy, perhaps Guatemalan, walking down Pico with a cape across his shoulders. His hair is piled in a four-inch rockabilly pompadour. He passes a dingy apartment building, a *pupuseria*, a body shop with no name, and turns into a storefront social services center. There is one other person in the sparse waiting room. She is thin, her gray hair pulled back in a tight bun, her black dress buttoned to her neck. She will tell you, if you ask her in Spanish, that she is waiting for her English class to begin. She might also tell you that the people here are helping her locate her son—lost in Salvadoran resettlement camps—and she thinks that if she can learn a little English, it will help her bring him to America.

The boy is here for different reasons. He has been causing trouble in school, and arrangements are being made for him to see a bilingual counselor. His name is Mario, and he immigrated with his older sister two years ago. His English is halting, unsure; he seems simultaneously rebellious and scared. His caseworker tells me that he still has flashbacks of Guatemalan terror: his older brother taken in the night by death squads, strangled, and hacked apart on the road by his house. Then she shows me his drawings, and our conversation stops. Crayon and pen on cheap paper: blue and orange cityscapes, eyes on billboards, in the windshields of cars, a severed hand at the bus stop. There are punks, beggars, piñatas walking the streets—upright cows and donkeys—skeletal homeboys, corseted girls carrying sharpened bones. "He will talk to you about these," the caseworker tells me. "They're scary, aren't they? The school doesn't know what the hell to do with him. I don't think he really knows what to do with all that's in him either."

In another part of the state, farther to the north, also rich in immigration, a teacher in a basic reading and writing program asks his students to interview one another and write a report, a capsule of a classmate's life. Caroline, a black woman in her late forties, chooses Thuy Anh, a Vietnamese woman many years her junior. Caroline asks only five questions—Thuy Anh's English is still difficult to understand—simple questions: What is your name? Where were you born? What is your education? Thuy Anh talks about her childhood in South Vietnam and her current plans in America. She is the oldest of nine children, and she received a very limited Vietnamese education, for she had to spend much of her childhood caring for her brothers and sisters. She married a serviceman, came to America, and now spends virtually all of her time pursuing a high school equivalency, struggling with textbook descriptions of the American political process, frantically trying to improve her computational skills. She is not doing very well at this. As one of her classmates observed, she might be trying too hard.

Caroline is supposed to take notes while Thuy Anh responds to her questions, and then use the notes to write her profile, maybe something like a reporter would do. But Caroline is moved to do something different. She's taken by Thuy Anh's account of watching over the babies. "Mother's little helper," she thinks. And that stirs her, this woman who has never been a mother. Maybe, too, Thuy Anh's desire to do well in school, her driven eagerness, the desperation that occasionally flits across her face, maybe that moves Caroline as well. Over the next two days, Caroline strays from the assignment and writes a two-and-a-half-page fiction that builds to a prose poem. She recasts Thuy Anh's childhood into an American television fantasy.

Thuy Anh is "Mother's little helper." Her five younger sisters "are happy and full of laughter . . . their little faces are bright with eyes sparkling." The little girls' names are "Hellen, Ellen, Lottie, Alice, and Olie"—American names—and they "cook and sew and make pretty doll dresses for their dolls to wear." Though the family is Buddhist, they exchange gifts at Christmas and "gather in the large living room to sing Christmas carols." Thuy Anh "went to school every day she could and studied very hard." One day, Thuy Anh was "asked to wright a poem and to recite it to her classmates." And, here, Caroline embeds within her story a prose poem—which she attributes to Thuy Anh:

My name is Thuy Anh I live near the Ocean. I see the waves boisterous and impudent bursting and splashing against the huge rocks. I see the white boats out on the blue sea. I see the fisher men rapped in heavy coats to keep their bodys warm while bringing in large fishes to sell to the merchants, Look! I see a larg white bird going on its merry way. Then I think of how great God is for he made this great sea for me to see and yet I stand on dry land and see the green and hillie side with flowers rising to the sky. How sweet and beautiful for God to have made Thuy Anh and the sea.

I interview Caroline. When she was a little girl in Arkansas, she "would get off into a room by myself and read the Scripture." The "poems in King Solomon" were her favorites. She went to a segregated school and "used to write quite a bit" at home. But she "got away from it" and some years later dropped out of high school to come west to earn a living. She's worked in a convalescent hospital for twenty years, never married, wishes she had, comes, now, back to school and is finding again her love of words. "I get lost . . . I'm right in there with my writing, and I forget all my surroundings." She is classified as a basic student—no diploma, low-level employment, poor test scores—had been taught by her grandmother that she would have to earn her living "by the sweat of my brow."

Her work in the writing course had been good up to the point of Thuy Anh's interview, better than that of many classmates, adequate, fairly free of error, pretty well organized. But the interview triggered a different level of performance. Caroline's early engagement with language reemerged in a lyrical burst: an evocation of an imagined childhood, a curious overlay of one culture's fantasy over another's harsh reality. Caroline's longing reshaped a Vietnamese girlhood, creating a life neither she nor Thuy Anh ever had, an intersection of biblical rhythms and *Father Knows Best*.

Over Chin's bent head arches a trellis packed tight with dried honeysuckle and chrysanthemum, sea moss, mushrooms, and ginseng. His elbow rests on the cash register—quiet now that the customers have left. He shifts on the stool, concentrating on the writing before him: "A young children," he scribbles, and pauses. "Young children," that doesn't sound good, he thinks. He crosses out "children" and sits back. A few seconds pass. He can't think of the right way to say it, so he writes "children" again and continues: "a young children with his grandma smail . . ." "Smail." He pulls a Chinese-English dictionary from under the counter.

In front of the counter and extending down the aisle are boxes of dried fish: shark fins, mackerel, pollock. They give off a musky smell. Behind Chin are rows of cans and jars: pickled garlic, pickled ginger, sesame paste. By the door, comic books and Chinese weeklies lean dog-eared out over the thin retaining wire of a dusty wooden display. Chin has found his word: It's not *smail*, it's *smile*. "A young children with his grandma smile . . . " He reaches in the pocket of his jeans jacket, pulls out a piece of paper, and unfolds it. There's a word copied on it he has been wanting to use. A little bell over the door jingles. An old man comes in, and Chin moves his yellow pad aside.

Chin remembers his teacher in elementary school telling him that his writing was poor, that he didn't know many words. He went to middle school for a few years but quit before completing it. Very basic English—the ABCs and simple vocabulary—was, at one point, part of his curriculum, but he lived in a little farming community, so he figured he would never use it. He did, though, pick up some letters and a few words. He immigrated to America when he was seventeen, and for the two years since has been living with his uncle in Chinatown. His uncle signed him up for English classes at the community center. He didn't like them. He did, however, start hanging out in the recreation room, playing pool and watching TV. The English on TV intrigued him. And it was then that he turned to writing. He would "try to learn to speak something" by writing it down. That was about six months ago. Now he's enrolled in a community college literacy program and has been making strong progress. He is especially taken with one tutor, a woman in her mid-thirties who encourages him to write. So he writes for her. He writes stories about his childhood in China. He sneaks time when no one is in the store or when customers are poking around, writing because he likes to bring her things, writing, too, because "sometime I think writing make my English better."

The old man puts on the counter a box of tea guaranteed to help you stop smoking. Chin rings it up and thanks him. The door jingles and Chin returns to his writing, copying the word from his folded piece of paper, a word he found in *People* magazine: "A young children with his grandma smile *gleefully*."

Frank Marell, born Meraglio, my oldest uncle, learned his English as Chin is learning his. He came to America with his mother and three sisters in September 1921. They came to join my grandfather who had immigrated long before. They joined, as well, the millions of Italian peasants who had flowed through Customs with their cloth-and-paper suitcases, their strange gestural language, and their dark, empty pockets. Frank was about to turn eight when he immigrated, so he has faint memories of Calabria. They lived in a one-room stone house. In the winter, the family's scrawny milk cow was brought inside. By the door there was a small hole for a rifle barrel. Wolves came out of the hills. He remembers the frost and burrs stinging his feet as he foraged the countryside for berries and twigs and fresh grass for the cow. *Chi esce riesce*, the saying went—"he who leaves succeeds"—and so it was that my grandfather left when he did, eventually finding work amid the metal and steam of the Pennsylvania Railroad.

My uncle remembers someone giving him bread on the steamship. He remembers being very sick. Once in America, he and his family moved into the company housing projects across from the stockyard. The house was dirty and had gouges in the wood. Each morning his mother had to sweep the soot from in front of the door. He remembers rats. He slept huddled with his father and mother and sisters in the living room, for his parents had to rent out the other rooms in order to buy clothes and shoes and food. Frank never attended school in Italy. He was eight now and would enter school in America. America, where eugenicists were attesting, scientifically, to the feeblemindedness of his race, where the popular press ran articles about the immorality of these swarthy exotics. Frank would enter school here. In many ways, you could lay his life like a template over a current life in the Bronx, in Houston, in Pico-Union.

He remembers the embarrassment of not understanding the teacher, of not being able to read or write. Funny clothes, oversize shoes, his hair slicked down and parted in the middle. He would lean forward—his assigned seat, fortunately, was in the back—and ask other Italian kids, ones with some English, to tell him what for the love of God was going on. He had big, sad eyes, thick hands, skin dark enough to yield the nickname Blacky. Frank remembers other boys—Carmen Santino, a kid named Hump, Bruno Tucci—who couldn't catch on to this new language and quit coming to school. Within six months of his arrival, Frank would be going after class to the back room of Pete Mastis's Dry Cleaners and Shoeshine Parlor. He cleaned and shined shoes, learned to operate a steam press, ran deliveries. He listened to the radio, trying to mimic the harsh complexities of English. He spread Pete Mastis's racing forms out before him, copying words onto the margins of newsprint. He tried talking to the people whose shoes he was shining, exchanging tentative English with the broken English of Germans and Poles and other Italians.

Eventually, Frank taught his mother to sign her name. By the time he was in his teens, he was reading flyers and announcements of sales and legal documents to her. He was also her scribe, doing whatever writing she needed to have done. Frank found himself immersed in the circumstance of literacy.

With the lives of Mario and Caroline and Chin and Frank Marell as a backdrop, I want to consider a current, very powerful set of proposals about literacy and culture.

There is a strong impulse in American education—curious in a country with such an ornery streak of antitraditionalism—to define achievement and excellence in terms of the acquisition of a historically validated body of knowledge, an authoritative list of books and allusions, a canon. We seek a certification of our national intelligence, indeed, our national virtue, in how diligently our children can display this central corpus of information. This need for certification tends to emerge most dramatically in our educational policy debates during times of real or imagined threat: economic hard times, political crises, sudden increases in immigration. Now is such a time, and it is reflected in a number of influential books and commission reports. E. D. Hirsch argues that a core national vocabulary, one oriented toward the English literate tradition—Alice in Wonderland to zeitgeist—will build a knowledge base that will foster the literacy of all Americans. Diane Ravitch and Chester Finn call for a return to a traditional historical and literary curriculum: the valorous historical figures and the classical literature of the once-elite course of study. Allan Bloom, Secretary of Education William Bennett, Mortimer Adler and the Paideia Group, and a number of others have affirmed, each in their very different ways, the necessity of the Great Books: Plato and Aristotle and Sophocles, Dante and Shakespeare and Locke, Dickens and Mann and Faulkner. We can call this orientation to educational achievement the canonical orientation.

At times in our past, the call for a shoring up of or return to a canonical curriculum was explicitly elitist, was driven by a fear that the education of the select was being compromised. Today, though, the majority of the calls are provocatively framed in the language of democracy. They assail the mediocre and grinding curriculum frequently found in remedial and vocational education. They are disdainful of the patronizing perceptions of student ability that further restrict the already restricted academic life of disadvantaged youngsters. They point out that the canon—its language, conventions, and allusions—is central to the discourse of power, and to keep it from poor kids is to assure their disenfranchisement all the more. The books of the canon, claim the proposals, the Great Books, are a window onto a common core of experience and civic ideals. There is, then, a spiritual, civic, and cognitive heritage here, and *all* our children should receive it. If we are sincere in our desire to bring Mario, Chin, the younger versions of Caroline, current incarnations of Frank Marell, and so many others who populate this book—if we truly want to bring them into our society—then we should provide them with this stable and common core. This is a forceful call. It promises a still center in a turning world.

I see great value in being challenged to think of the curriculum of the many in the terms we have traditionally reserved for the few; it is refreshing to have common assumptions about the capacities of underprepared students so boldly challenged. Many of the people we have encountered in these pages have displayed the ability to engage books and ideas thought to be beyond their grasp. There were the veterans: Willie Oates writing, in prison, ornate sentences drawn from *The Mill on the Floss*. Sergeant Gonzalez coming to understand poetic ambiguity in "Butch Weldy." There was the parole aide Olga who no longer felt walled off from *Macbeth*. There were the EOP students at UCLA, like Lucia who unpackaged *The Myth of Mental Illness* once she had an orientation and overview. And there was Frank Marell who, later in his life, would be talking excitedly to his nephew about this guy Edgar Allan Poe. Too many people are kept from the books of the canon, the Great Books, because of misjudgments about their potential. Those books eventually proved important to me, and, as best I know how, I invite my students to engage them. But once we grant the desirability of equal curricular treatment and begin to consider what this equally distributed curriculum would contain, problems arise: If the canon itself is the answer to our educational inequities, why has it historically invited few and denied many? Would the canonical orientation provide adequate guidance as to how a democratic curriculum should be constructed and how it should be taught? Would it guide us in opening up to Olga that "fancy talk" that so alienated her?

Those who study the way literature becomes canonized, how linguistic creations are included or excluded from a tradition, claim that the canonical curriculum students would most likely receive would not, as is claimed, offer a common core of American experience. Caroline would not find her life represented in it, nor would Mario. The canon has tended to push to the margin much of the literature of our nation: from American Indian songs and chants to immigrant fiction to working-class narratives. The institutional messages that students receive in the books they're issued and the classes they take are powerful and, as I've witnessed since my Voc. Ed. days, quickly internalized. And to revise these messages and redress past wrongs would involve more than adding some new books to the existing canon—the very reasons for linguistic and cultural exclusion would have to become a focus of study in order to make the canon act as a democratizing force. Unless this happens, the democratic intent of the reformers will be undercut by the content of the curriculum they propose.

And if we move beyond content to consider basic assumptions about teaching and learning, a further problem arises, one that involves the very nature of the canonical orientation itself. The canonical orientation encourages a narrowing of focus from learning to that which must be learned: It simplifies the dynamic tension between student and text and reduces the psychological and social dimensions of instruction. The student's personal history recedes as the what of the classroom is valorized over the how. Thus it is that the encounter of student and text is often portrayed by canonists as a transmission. Information, wisdom, virtue will pass from the book to the student if the student gives the book the time it merits, carefully traces its argument or narrative or lyrical progression. Intellectual, even spiritual, growth will *necessarily* result from an encounter with Roman mythology, *Othello*, and "I heard a Fly buzz—when I died—," with biographies and historical sagas and patriotic lore. Learning is stripped of confusion and discord. It is stripped, as well, of strong human connection. My own initiators to the canon—Jack MacFarland, Dr. Carothers, and the rest—knew there was more to their work than their mastery of a tradition. What mattered most, I see now, were the relationships they established with me, the guidance they provided when I felt inadequate or threatened. This mentoring was part of my entry into that solemn library of Western thought—and even with such support, there were still times of confusion, anger, and fear. It is telling, I think, that once that rich social network slid away, once I was in graduate school in intense, solitary encounter with that tradition, I abandoned it for other sources of nurturance and knowledge.

The model of learning implicit in the canonical orientation seems, at times, more religious than cognitive or social: Truth resides in the printed texts, and if they are presented by someone who knows them well and respects them, that truth will be revealed. Of all the advocates of the canon, Mortimer Adler has given most attention to pedagogy—and his Paideia books contain valuable discussions of instruction, coaching, and questioning. But even here, and this is doubly true in the other manifestos, there is little acknowledgment that the material in the canon can be not only difficult but foreign, alienating, overwhelming.

We need an orientation to instruction that provides guidance on how to determine and honor the beliefs and stories, enthusiasms, and apprehensions that students reveal. How to build on them, and when they clash with our curriculum—as I saw so often in the Tutorial Center at UCLA—when they clash, how to encourage a discussion that will lead to reflection on what students bring and what they're currently confronting. Canonical lists imply canonical answers, but the manifestos offer little discussion of what to do when students fail. If students have been exposed to at least some elements of the canon before—as many have—why didn't it take? If they're encountering it for the first time and they're lost, how can we determine where they're located—and what do we do then?

Each member of a teacher's class, poor or advantaged, gives rise to endless decisions, day-to-day determinations about a child's reading and writing: decisions on how to tap strength, plumb confusion, foster growth. The richer your conception of learning and your understanding of its social and psychological dimensions, the more insightful and effective your judgments will be. Consider the sources of literacy we saw among the children in El Monte: shopkeepers' signs, song lyrics, auto manuals, the conventions of the Western, family stories and tales, and more. Consider Chin's sources—television and *People* magazine—and Caroline's oddly generative mix of the Bible and an American media illusion. Then there's the jarring confluence of personal horror and pop cultural flotsam that surfaces in Mario's drawings, drawings that would be a rich, if volatile, point of departure for language instruction. How would these myriad sources and manifestations be perceived and evaluated if viewed within the framework of a canonical tradition, and what guidance would the tradition provide on how to understand and develop them? The great books and central texts of the canon could quickly become a benchmark against which the expressions of student literacy would be negatively measured, a limiting band of excellence that, ironically, could have a dispiriting effect on the very thing the current proposals intend: the fostering of mass literacy.

To understand the nature and development of literacy we need to consider the social context in which it occurs—the political, economic, and cultural forces that encourage or inhibit it. The canonical orientation discourages deep analysis of the way these forces may be affecting performance. The canonists ask that schools transmit a coherent traditional knowledge to an ever-changing, frequently uprooted community. This discordance between message and audience is seldom examined. Although a ghetto child can rise on the lilt of a Homeric line—books *can* spark dreams—appeals to elevated texts can also divert attention from the conditions that keep a population from realizing its dreams. The literacy curriculum is being asked to do what our politics and our economics have failed to do: diminish differences in achievement, narrow our gaps, bring us together. Instead of analysis of the complex web of causes of poor performance, we are offered a faith in the unifying power of a body of knowledge, whose infusion will bring the rich and the poor, the longtime disaffected and the uprooted newcomers into cultural unanimity. If this vision is democratic, it is simplistically so, reductive, not an invitation for people truly to engage each other at the point where cultures and classes intersect.

I worry about the effects a canonical approach to education could have on cultural dialogue and transaction—on the involvement of an abandoned underclass and on the movement of immigrants like Mario and Chin into our nation. A canonical uniformity promotes rigor and quality control; it can also squelch new thinking, diffuse the generative tension between the old and the new. It is significant that the canonical orientation is voiced with most force during times of challenge and uncertainty, for it promises the authority of tradition, the seeming stability of the past. But the authority is fictive, gained from a misreading of American cultural history. No period of that history was harmoniously stable; the invocation of a golden age is a mythologizing act. Democratic culture is, by definition, vibrant and dynamic, discomforting and unpredictable. It gives rise to apprehension; freedom is not always calming. And, yes, it can yield fragmentation, though often as not the source of fragmentation is intolerant misunderstanding of diverse traditions rather than the desire of members of those traditions to remain hermetically separate. A truly democratic vision of knowledge and social structure would honor this complexity. The vision might not be soothing, but it would provide guidance as to how to live and teach in a country made up of many cultural traditions.

We are in the middle of an extraordinary social experiment: the attempt to provide education for all members of a vast pluralistic democracy. To have any prayer of success, we'll need many conceptual blessings: A philosophy of language and literacy that affirms the diverse sources of linguistic competence and deepens our understanding of the ways class and culture blind us to the richness of those sources. A perspective on failure that lays open the logic of error. An orientation toward the interaction of poverty and ability that undercuts simple polarities, that enables us to see simultaneously the constraints poverty places on the play of mind and the actual mind at play within those constraints. We'll need a pedagogy that encourages us to step back and consider the threat of the standard classroom and that shows us, having stepped back, how to step forward to invite a student across the boundaries of that powerful room. Finally, we'll need a revised store of images of educational excellence, ones closer to egalitarian ideals—ones that embody the reward and turmoil of education in a democracy, that celebrate the plural, messy human reality of it. At heart, we'll need a guiding set of principles that do not encourage us to retreat from, but move us closer to, an understanding of the rich mix of speech and ritual and story that is America.

Epilogue: Lilia

———◆———

I sit with Lilia, the tape recorder going. "We came from Mexico when I was four years old. When I went into school, I flunked the first grade. The first grade! I had to repeat it, and they put me in classes for slow learners. I stayed in those classes for five years. I guess there was a pattern where they put me in those really basic classes and then decided I would go through my elementary school years in those classes. I didn't learn to read or write. My parents got my cousins—they came here prior to us, so they knew English really well—and they had me read for them. I couldn't. They told my parents I didn't know anything. That's when my parents decided they would move. They moved to Tulare County. My aunt was there and told them that the schools were good and that there was work in agriculture. I picked grapes and cotton and oranges—everything—for six straight summers. I kinda liked it, out there with all the adults, but I knew it wasn't what I wanted for the future. The schools *were* good. The teachers really liked me, and I did very well. . . . Between the eighth and ninth grades I came to UCLA for six weeks in the summer. It was called the MENTE program—Migrants Engaged in New Themes of Education—I came here and loved the campus. It was like dreamland for me. And I made it my goal to come here."

The school that designated Lilia a slow learner is two miles from my old neighborhood on South Vermont. She arrived as a child about eight years after I left as an adult. The next generation. We make our acquaintance in an office of the University of California at Los Angeles. Lilia is participating in an unusual educational experiment, one developed by some coworkers of mine at UCLA Writing Programs. Lilia and fifteen other freshmen—all of whom started UCLA in remedial writing courses themselves—are tutoring low-achieving students in Los Angeles area schools. The tutoring is connected to a special composition class, and Lilia and her partners write papers on their tutorial work and on issues of schooling. Lilia is writing a paper on the academic, social, and psychological effects of being placed in the remedial track. Her teacher suggested she come to see me. I can't stop asking her questions about growing up in South L.A.

Desire gets confused on South Vermont. There were times when I wanted so much to be other than what I was, to walk through the magical gate of a television cottage. But, strange blessing, we can never really free ourselves from the mood of early neighborhoods, from our first stories, from the original tales of hope and despair. There are basic truths there about the vulnerability and power of coming to know, about the way the world invites and denies language. This is what lies at the base of education—to be tapped or sealed over or distorted, by others, by us. Lilia says the tutoring makes her feel good. "Sometimes I feel that because I know their language, I can communicate. I see these kids and I see myself like I was in elementary school." Lilia stops. She asks me what it was like in South L.A. when *I* was there, when I was going to school. Not much different then, I say. Not as tough probably. She asks me if I've ever gone back. I tell her I did, just recently. . . .

The place was desolate. The power plant was still standing, smaller than I remembered it, surrounded now by barbed wire. All the storefront businesses were covered with iron grating; about half of them, maybe more, were shut down. The ones that were open had the grating pulled back the width of the door, no further. The hair and nails shop was closed. The Stranger's Rest Baptist Church was closed. Teddy's Rough Riders—an American Legion post—was battered and closed. The Huston Mortuary looked closed. My house had been stuccoed over, a dark dirty tan with holes in the walls. 9116 South Vermont. My old neighborhood was a blighted island in the slum. Poverty had gutted it, and sealed the merchants' doors. "It's worse now," I tell Lilia, "much worse. No one comes. No one goes." At Ninety-sixth Street two men were sitting on the curb outside a minimart. East on Ninety-first a girl sat in the shadows of steps tucked back from the pavement. At Eighty-ninth Street, a woman walked diagonally in front of me, moving unsteadily in a tight dress, working the floured paper off an X-L-NT burrito. As I drove back by my house, I saw a little boy playing with two cans in the dirt. Imagination's delivery. Fantasy in cylinders and tin.

Lilia is telling me about one of her fellow classmates who had also been designated a slow learner. "She said it was awful. She had no friends because everyone called her dumb, and no one wanted to be seen with a dumb person. . . . Because they were calling her dumb, she started to believe she was really dumb. And with myself and my brother, it was the same thing. When we were in those courses we thought very low of ourselves. We sort of created a little world of our own where only we existed. We became really shy."

What we define as intelligence, what we set out to measure and identify with a number, is both in us and out of us. We have been socialized to think of intelligence as internal, fixed, genetically coded. There is, of course, a neurophysiology to intelligence, but there's a feeling to it as well, and a culture. In moving from one school to another—another setting, another set of social definitions—Lilia was transformed from dumb to normal. And then, with six powerful weeks as a child on a university campus— "opening new horizons for me, scary, but showing me what was out there"—she began to see herself in a different way, tentatively, cautiously. Lilia began the transition to smart, to high school honors classes, to UCLA. She could go back, then, to the schools, to the place where, as she says, she "knows the language."

The promise of community and equality is at the center of our most prized national document, yet we're shaped by harsh forces to see difference and to base judgment on it. The language Lilia can speak to the students in the schools is the language of intersection, of crossed boundaries. It is a rich language, filled with uncertainty. Having crossed boundaries, you sometimes can't articulate what you know, or what you know seems strange. What is required, then, is for Lilia and her students to lean back against their desks, grip the firm wood, and talk about what they hear and see, looking straight ahead, looking skyward. What are the gaps and discordances in the terrain? What mix of sounds—eerie and compelling—issues from the hillside? Sitting with Lilia, our lives playing off each other, I realize that, finally, this is why the current perception of educational need is so limited: It substitutes terror for awe. But it is not terror that fosters learning, it is hope, everyday heroics, the power of the common play of the human mind.

Notes

———◆———

CHAPTER 1
Our Schools and Our Children

PAGE

5   Merrill Sheils, "Why Johnny Can't Write," *Newsweek*, 8 Dec. 1975, pp. 58–65.

5   President of Brown: quoted in Frederick Rudolph, *Curriculum: A History of the American Undergraduate Course of Study* (San Francisco: Jossey-Bass, 1978), p. 88.

5   Professor Adams Sherman Hill: quoted in Harvey A. Daniels, *Famous Last Words: The American Language Crisis Reconsidered* (Carbondale: Southern Illinois University Press, 1983), p. 52.

5   "The Growing Illiteracy of American Boys," *The Nation* 63 (1896), p. 284.

6   On the Subject A examination see Loaz W. Johnson, "The Administrative Function of English in the University of California: The Evolution of the Examination in Subject A," *University of California Publications in Education*, 7 (September 1941):273–350; and Kim Davis, Internal Memorandum, Subject A Office, Berkeley, 25 Sept. 1980.

6   Franklyn S. Hoyt, "The Place of Grammar in the Elementary Curriculum," *Teachers College Record*, 7 (Nov. 1906):467–500.

6   The high school attendance and graduation statistics come from Thomas James and David Tyack, "Learning from Past Efforts to Reform the High School," *Phi Delta Kappan* 64 (Feb. 1983):401.

6   The shifts in definitions of functional literacy are taken from Lawrence C. Stedman and Carl F. Kaestle, "Literacy and

PAGE

Reading Performance in the United States, from 1880 to the Present," *Reading Research Quarterly* 22 (Winter 1987):23.

6–7   The international secondary school comparisons come from Ernest L. Boyer, *High School: A Report on Secondary Education in America* (New York: Harper & Row, 1983), p. 33.

7   The college statistics are cited by Russell Jacoby, *The Last Intellectuals: American Culture in the Age of Academe* (New York: Basic Books, 1987), p. 130.

7   David K. Cohen and Barbara Neufield, "The Failure of High Schools and the Progress of Education," *Daedalus*, 110 (Summer 1981):86.

CHAPTER 2
"I Just Wanna Be Average"

PAGE

26   Mr. Gross is described in Theodore Sizer, *Horace's Compromise* (Boston: Houghton Mifflin, 1985), pp. 146–148.

34   Frank Smith, *Joining the Literacy Club: Further Essays into Education* (Portsmouth, N.H.: Heinemann Educational Books, 1988).

CHAPTER 3
Entering the Conversation

PAGE

49–50   E. A. Burtt, *The Metaphysical Foundations of Modern Science* (New York: Anchor, n.d.), pp. 66–67.

51   Abraham Maslow, *Toward a Psychology of Being*, 2d ed. (New York: Van Nostrand Reinhold, 1968), p. 193.

52   Tobias Hume's line comes from his lyric "Tobacco, Tobacco"; "Pallid and pink . . ." is a line from Swinburne's self-parody, "Nephelidia."

CHAPTER 4
The Poem Is a Substitute for Love

PAGE

74   "Who knows if the moon's": e.e. cummings, *100 Selected Poems* (New York: Grove Press, 1959), p. 15.

74   "The back wings": William Carlos Williams, *Selected Poems* (New York: New Directions, 1968), p. 84.

76   The Edward Taylor line is from "Housewifery."

PAGE

76–77 Wallace Stevens, *The Palm at the End of the Mind*, ed. Holly Stevens (New York: Vintage, 1967), pp. 175–176.

78 Maslow, *Psychology of Being*, p. 61.

79 Martin Buber, *I and Thou* (New York: Scribner's, 1958), pp. 52, 95.

81 Don L. Lee (Haki Madhubuti), "But He Was Cool or: he even stopped for green lights," in *Don't Cry, Scream* (Detroit: Broadside Press, 1969), p. 21.

CHAPTER 5
Literate Stirrings

PAGE

110 "All analysis": H. I. Marrou, *A History of Education in Antiquity*. (1956; reprint, Madison: University of Wisconsin Press, 1982), p. 172.

125 Maslow, *Psychology of Being*, 127.

126 R. D. Laing, *The Divided Self* (1959; reprint, London: Penguin, 1970), p. 18.

CHAPTER 6
Reclaiming the Classroom

PAGE

142 Jerome Bruner, *The Process of Education* (1960; reprint, Cambridge, Mass.: Harvard University Press, 1977), p. 33.

143 Aimé Césaire, quoted in Frantz Fanon, *Black Skin, White Masks* (New York: Grove Press, 1967), p. 83.

143 Karl Jaspers, quoted in Fanon, p. 89.

143–144 The aboriginal creation myth comes from Jerome Rothenberg, *Technicians of the Sacred* (New York: Doubleday, 1968), p. 9.

144–145 Big bang is excerpted from George D. Abell, *Exploration of the Universe*, 3d ed. (New York: Holt, Rinehart and Winston), p. 662.

148–149 Edgar Lee Masters, *Spoon River Anthology* (New York: Macmillan, 1919), p. 26.

156 Ishmael Reed, *Yellow-Back Radio Broke Down* (1969; reprint, Chatham, N.J.: The Chatham Bookseller, 1975), p. 104.

156 Saint Joseph of Cupertino, cited in Mircea Eliade, *Shamanism* (New York: Bollingen Foundation, 1964), p. 482.

PAGE

156   Thomas McGuane, *The Bushwhacked Piano* (New York: Warner, 1973), pp. 173–174.

162   "Cold air drains": Wen T'ing Yen in Kenneth Rexroth, *Love and the Turning Year: One Hundred More Poems from the Chinese* (New York: New Directions, 1970), p. 86.

CHAPTER 7
The Politics of Remediation

PAGE

178   The Lincoln quotation is from Paul M. Angle, ed., *Created Equal? The Complete Lincoln-Douglas Debates of 1858* (Chicago: University of Chicago Press, 1958), p. 235.

179–180   Jacob Bronowski, "The Creative Mind," in *The Norton Reader, Shorter Edition*, ed. Arthur M. Eastman et al. (New York: Norton, 1965), pp. 123–134.

182–184   Thomas S. Szasz, *The Myth of Mental Illness* (New York: Harper & Row, 1974), pp. 1, 4, 7.

186   Jack McCurdy and Don Speich, "Drop in Student Skills Unequaled in History," *Los Angeles Times*, 15 Aug. 1976, part I, p. 1.

188   "Research evidence": see, for example, Brooke Nielson, "Writing as a Second Language: Psycholinguistic Processes in Composing" (Ph. D. diss., University of California at San Diego, 1979).

190   Dewey, quoted in Sizer, *Horace's Compromise*, p. 95.

199   SAT critiques: a good place to begin is Warner V. Slack and Douglas Porter, "The Scholastic Aptitude Test: A Critical Appraisal," *Harvard Educational Review* 50 (May 1980):154–175.

200   "Evidence for a massive": Lawrence C. Stedman and Carl F. Kaestle, "Literacy and Reading Performance in the United States, from 1880 to the Present," *Reading Research Quarterly*, 22 (Winter 1987):22.

200   Patricia Cline Cohen, *A Calculating People* (Chicago: University of Chicago Press, 1982), p. 225.

200–201   Preparatory divisions were in many ways like high schools placed within colleges and were necessary because college recruitment and enrollment were outpacing the growth of public secondary education. While some departments were similar to academies in the nature and quality of their curriculum, many others, according to historian David Tyack (personal communication, Dec. 1987), were more basic and "remedial" and were viewed as such by faculty and administrators. It is telling, I think, that as late as 1915—a time when the quantity and quality of secondary schools had risen sufficiently to make preparatory departments less necessary—350 American colleges still maintained them. See John S. Brubacher and Willis Rudy, *Higher Education in Transition: A History of American Colleges and Universities, 1636-1976*, 3d ed. (New York: Harper & Row, 1976), pp. 243-244; and Arthur Levine, *Handbook on Undergraduate Curriculum* (San Francisco: Jossey-Bass, 1981), pp. 54-58.

202   "Almost uniformly": quoted in "UCLA: New Standing in Academia," *Los Angeles Times*, 8 July 1984, part I, p. 25.

CHAPTER 8
Crossing Boundaries

205   Report of the Commission on the Humanities, *The Humanities in American Life* (Berkeley: University of California Press, 1980), p. 2.

207-210   The discussion of error and remediation is condensed from Mike Rose, "The Language of Exclusion: Writing Instruction at the University," *College English* 47 (April 1985), pp. 341-359.

208   James Berlin, *Writing Instruction in Nineteenth-Century American Colleges* (Carbondale: Southern Illinois University Press, 1984), p. 73.

208   Raymond Callahan, *Education and the Cult of Efficiency* (Chicago: University of Chicago Press, 1962).

208   "One textbook for teachers": see Arthur N. Applebee, *Tradition and Reform in the Teaching of English: A History* (Urbana, Ill.: National Council of Teachers of English, 1974), pp. 93-94.

208   "A text for students": see P. G. Perrin, "The Remedial Racket, " *English Journal* 22 (1933), p. 383.

208   W. S. Guiler, "Background Deficiencies," *Journal of Higher Education* 3 (1932), p. 371.

209   William S. Gray, *Remedial Cases in Reading: Their Diagnosis and Treatment* (Chicago: University of Chicago Press, 1922).

PAGE

209–210   Albert Lang, *Modern Methods in Written Examinations* (Boston: Houghton Mifflin, 1930), p. 38.

210   "The most logical": H. J. Arnold, "Diagnostic and Remedial Techniques for College Freshman," *Association of American Colleges Bulletin* 16 (1930), p. 276.

212   "Ceaseless, brutal drill": the professor is quoted in Oscar James Campbell, *The Teaching of College English* (New York: Appleton-Century, 1934), pp. 36–37.

221   Michael Katz, *The Irony of Early School Reform* (Cambridge, Mass.: Harvard University Press, 1968), p. 120.

222   Robert Coles, in Sherry Kafka and Robert Coles, *I Will Always Stay Me: Writings of Migrant Children* (Austin: Texas Monthly Press, 1982), p. 134.

224   Elizabeth Ewen, *Immigrant Women in the Land of Dollars* (New York: Monthly Review Press, 1985), p. 90.

226   "The magnitude and diversity": Edward W. Soja, Allan D. Heskin, and Marco Cenzatti, *Los Angeles: Through the Kaleidoscope of Urban Restructuring* (Los Angeles: UCLA Graduate School of Architecture and Urban Planning, 1985), p. 8.

233   E. D. Hirsch, *Cultural Literacy: What Every American Needs to Know* (Boston: Houghton Mifflin, 1987); Diane Ravitch and Chester E. Finn, Jr., *What Do Our 17-Year-Olds Know?* (New York: Harper & Row, 1987); Allan Bloom, *The Closing of the American Mind: How Higher Education Has Failed Democracy and Impoverished the Souls of Today's Students* (New York: Simon & Schuster, 1987); William J. Bennett, *To Reclaim A Legacy* (Washington, D.C.: National Endowment for the Humanities, 1984); Mortimer J. Adler, *The Paideia Proposal* (New York: Colliers, 1982), *Paideia Problems and Possibilities* (New York: Macmillan, 1983), and *The Paideia Program* (New York: Macmillan, 1984).

235   For a critical discussion of literary canon formation, see Paul Lauter, ed., *Reconstructing American Literature* (Old Westbury, New York: Feminist Press, 1983).

Bibliography

◆

For the reader who wishes to pursue the issues raised in this book, I offer a brief bibliography. The list is neither inclusive nor systematic; it is meant to be a sampler of books and articles that either have contributed to or reflect the ideas in *Lives on the Boundary*. For a comprehensive bibliographic survey of the study and teaching of writing, see the *Longman Bibliography of Composition and Rhetoric, 1984–1985* and *1986*, edited by Erika Lindemann. New York: Longman, 1987, 1988.

ADAMS, FRANK, with MYLES HORTON. *Unearthing Seeds of Fire: The Idea of Highlander.* Winston-Salem, N.C.: Blair, 1975.

ANDERSON, ALONZO B. and SHELLEY J. STOKES. "Social and Institutional Influences on the Development and Practice of Literacy." In *Awakening to Literacy*, edited by Hillel Goelman, Antoinette Oberg, and Frank Smith, pp. 24–37. Portsmouth, N.H.: Heinemann Educational Books, 1984.

APPLEBEE, ARTHUR N. *Writing in the Secondary School.* Urbana, Ill.: National Council of Teachers of English, 1981.

ARNOVE, ROBERT F. "The Nicaraguan National Literacy Crusade of 1980." *Comparative Education Review* 25 (June 1981): 244–260.

BARTHOLOMAE, DAVID. "Inventing the University." In *When a Writer Can't Write: Studies in Writer's Block and Other Composing Process Problems*, edited by Mike Rose, pp. 134–165. New York: Guilford, 1985.

BLUMER, HERBERT. "Social Problems as Collective Behavior." *Social Problems* 18 (Winter 1971): 298–306.

BOYER, ERNEST L. *High School: A Report on Secondary Education in America.* New York: Harper & Row, 1983.

BRANDT, DEBORAH. *Literacy as Involvement: The Acts of Writers, Readers, and Texts.* Carbondale: Southern Illinois University Press, 1989.

BRITTON, JAMES. *Language and Learning*. London: Penguin, 1970.

BRUFFEE, KENNETH A. "Liberal Education and the Social Justification of Belief." *Liberal Education* 68 (1982): 95–114.

CALKINS, LUCY MCCORMICK. *The Art of Teaching Writing*. Portsmouth, N.H.: Heinemann Educational Books, 1986.

CLIFFORD, GERALDINE JONCICH. *A Sisyphean Task: Historical Perspectives on the Relationship Between Writing and Reading Instruction*. Berkeley, Calif.: Center for the Study of Writing, 1987.

COE, RICHARD M. "Literacy 'Crises': A Systemic Analysis." *Humanities in Society* 4 (Fall 1981): 363–378.

COHEN, DAVID K. "Loss as a Theme in Social Policy." *Harvard Educational Review* 46 (Nov. 1976): 553–571.

COHEN, DAVID K., and BARBARA NEUFIELD. "The Failure of High Schools and the Progress of Education." *Daedalus* 110 (Summer 1981): 69–89.

COHEN, PATRICIA CLINE. *A Calculating People: The Spread of Numeracy in Early America* (Chicago: University of Chicago Press, 1982).

COLE, MICHAEL, and BARBARA MEANS. *Comparative Studies of How People Think: An Introduction*. Cambridge, Mass.: Harvard University Press, 1981.

COLLINS, ALAN, JOHN SEELY BROWN, and SUSAN E. NEWMAN. "Cognitive Apprenticeship: Teaching the Craft of Reading, Writing, and Mathematics." In *Knowing, Learning, and Instruction*, edited by Lauren B. Resnick. Hillsdale, N.J.: Erlbaum, in press.

CONNORS, ROBERT J. "The Rhetoric of Mechanical Correctness." In *Only Connect: Uniting Reading and Writing*, edited by Thomas Newkirk, pp. 27–58. Upper Montclair, N.J.: Boynton/Cook, 1986.

CUBAN, LARRY. *How Teachers Taught: Constancy and Change in American Classrooms 1890–1980*. New York: Longman, 1984.

D'ANDRADE, ROY G. "Cultural Constructions of Reality." In *Cultural Illness and Health*, edited by Laura Nader and Thomas Maretzki, pp. 115–127. Washington, D.C.: American Anthropology Association, 1973.

DANIELS, HARVEY A. *Famous Last Words: The American Language Crisis Reconsidered*. Carbondale: Southern Illinois University Press, 1983.

DONALDSON, MARGARET. *Children's Minds*. New York: Norton, 1979.

EWEN, ELIZABETH. *Immigrant Women in the Land of Dollars: Life and Culture on the Lower East Side, 1890–1925*. New York: Monthly Review Press, 1985.

FINEGAN, EDWARD. *Attitudes Toward English Usage: The History of a War of Words*. New York: Teachers College Press, 1980.

FLOWER, LINDA, and JOHN R. HAYES. "Images, Plans, and Prose: The

Representation of Meaning in Writing." *Written Communication* 1 (Jan. 1984): pp. 120–160.

FORDHAM, SIGNITHIA, and JOHN U. OGBU. "Black Students' School Success: Coping with the 'Burden of Acting White.'" *The Urban Review* 18 (1986): pp. 176–206.

FRAATZ, JO MICHELLE BELD. *The Politics of Reading: Power, Opportunity, and Prospects for Change in America's Public Schools.* New York: Teachers College Press, 1987.

FREIRE, PAULO. "The Adult Literacy Process as Cultural Action for Freedom." *Harvard Educational Review* 40 (May 1970): 205–225.

GARDNER, HOWARD. *Frames of Mind: The Theory of Multiple Intelligences.* New York: Basic Books, 1983.

———. *The Mind's New Science: A History of the Cognitive Revolution.* New York: Basic Books, 1985.

GILMAN, SANDER L. *Difference and Pathology: Stereotypes of Sexuality, Race, and Madness.* Ithaca, N.Y.: Cornell University Press, 1985.

GOODENOW, JACQUELINE. "The Nature of Intelligent Behavior: Questions Raised by Cross-Cultural Studies," In *The Nature of Intelligence,* edited by Lauren B. Resnick, pp. 168–188. Hillsdale, N.J.: Erlbaum, 1976.

GOODLAD, JOHN I. *A Place Called School: Prospects for the Future.* New York: McGraw-Hill, 1984.

GOULD, STEPHEN JAY. *The Mismeasure of Man.* New York: Norton, 1981.

GRAFF, HARVEY J. *The Literacy Myth: Literacy and Social Structure in the Nineteenth-Century City.* New York: Academic Press, 1979.

GRAVES, DONALD H. *Writing: Teachers and Children at Work.* Portsmouth, N.H.: Heinemann, 1983.

HAKUTA, KENJI. *Mirror of Language: The Debate on Bilingualism.* New York: Basic Books, 1986.

HARSTE, JEROME C., VIRGINIA A. WOODWARD, CAROLYN L. BURKE. *Language Stories and Literacy Lessons.* Portsmouth, N.H.: Heinemann Educational Books, 1984.

HEATH, SHIRLEY BRICE. *Ways with Words: Language, Life, and Work in Communities and Classrooms.* Cambridge, England: Cambridge University Press, 1983.

HOGGART, RICHARD. *The Uses of Literacy: Aspects of Working-Class Life, with Special References to Publications and Entertainments.* London: Chatto and Windus, 1957.

HULL, GLYNDA. "Acts of Wonderment." In *Facts, Counterfacts, and Artifacts: Theory and Method for a Reading and Writing Course,* edited by

David Bartholomae and Anthony Petrosky, pp. 199–226. Upper Montclair, N.J.: Boynton/Cook, 1986.

HUNTER, CARMAN ST. JOHN, and DAVID HARMAN. *Adult Illiteracy in the United States.* New York: McGraw–Hill, 1985.

JARAMILLO, MARI L. "To Serve Hispanic American Female Students: Challenges and Responsibilities for Educational Institutions." Occasional Paper Series No. 1. Claremont, CA: Tomás Rivera Center, 1987.

JOHNSTON, PETER H. "Understanding Reading Disability." *Harvard Educational Review* 55 (May 1985): 153–177.

KAMIN, LEON J. *The Science and Politics of I.Q.* Hillsdale, N.J.: Erlbaum, 1974.

KATZ, MICHAEL B. *The Irony of Early School Reform: Educational Innovation in Mid-Nineteenth Century Massachusetts.* Cambridge, Mass.: Harvard University Press, 1968.

KINTGEN, EUGENE F., BARRY M. KROLL, and MIKE ROSE, eds. *Perspectives on Literacy.* Carbondale, Ill.: Southern Illinois University Press, 1988.

KOHL, HERBERT. *Growing Minds: On Becoming a Teacher.* New York: Harper & Row, 1985.

KOZOL, JONATHAN. "A New Look at the Literacy Campaign in Cuba." *Harvard Educational Review* 48 (August 1978): 341–377.

LABOV, WILLIAM. *Language in the Inner City: Studies in the Black English Vernacular.* Philadelphia: University of Pennsylvania Press, 1972.

LANHAM, RICHARD A. "The 'Q' Question." *South Atlantic Quarterly* 87 (Fall 1988):653–699.

LIEBOWITZ, ARNOLD H. "English Literacy: Legal Sanction for Discrimination." *Notre Dame Lawyer* 45 (1969): 7–67.

LIGHTFOOT, SARA LAWRENCE. *The Good High School: Portraits of Character and Culture.* New York: Basic Books, 1983.

LIVINGSTON, JOHN C. *Fair Game? Inequality and Affirmative Action.* San Francisco: W. H. Freeman, 1979.

LYTLE, SUSAN L., THOMAS W. MARMOR, and FAITH H. PENNER. "Literacy Theory in Practice: Assessing Reading and Writing of Low-Literate Adults." Unpublished report, Graduate School of Education, University of Pennsylvania.

MCROBBIE, ANGELA. "Working Class Girls and the Culture of Femininity." In *Women Take Issue,* edited by Women's Studies Group, pp. 96–108. London: Hutchinson, 1978.

MEIER, DEBORAH. "'Getting Tough' in the Schools." *Dissent* 31 (Winter 1984): 61–70.

MYERS, MILES. "Shifting Standards of Literacy—The Teacher's Catch 22." *Language Arts* 61 (April 1984): 26–31.

NATIONAL COALITION OF ADVOCATES FOR STUDENTS. *Barriers to Excellence: Our Children at Risk.* Boston: The National Coalition of Advocates for Students, 1985.

OAKES, JEANNIE. *Keeping Track: How Schools Structure Inequality.* New Haven: Yale University Press, 1985.

OGBU, JOHN U. *Minority Education and Caste: The American System in Cross-Cultural Perspective.* New York: Academic Press, 1978.

OHMANN, RICHARD. *English in America: A Radical View of the Profession.* New York: Oxford University Press, 1976.

OXENHAM, JOHN. *Literacy: Writing, Reading and Social Organisation.* London: Routledge and Kegan Paul, 1980.

PATTISON, ROBERT. "On the Finn Syndrome and the Shakespeare Paradox." *The Nation,* 30 May 1987, pp. 710–720.

PEÑALOSA, FERNANDO. *Central Americans in Los Angeles: Background, Language, Education.* Los Angeles: Spanish Speaking Mental Health Research Center (UCLA), 1986.

PERKINS, D. N. *The Mind's Best Work.* Cambridge: Harvard University Press, 1981.

QUINN, JIM. *American Tongue and Cheek: A Populist Guide to Our Language.* New York: Pantheon, 1980.

RED HORSE, JOHN. "Editorial Commentary: Education Reform." *Journal of American Indian Education* 25 (May 1986): 40–44.

RESNICK, DANIEL P., ed. *Literacy in Historical Perspective.* Washington, D.C.: Library of Congress, 1983.

RICHARDSON, RICHARD C., JR., ELIZABETH C. FISK, and MORRIS A. OKUN. *Literacy in the Open-Access College.* San Francisco: Jossey-Bass, 1983.

ROGOFF, BARBARA and JEAN LAVE, eds. *Everyday Cognition: Its Development in Social Context.* Cambridge: Harvard University Press, 1984.

ROHLEN, THOMAS P. *Japan's High Schools.* Berkeley: University of California Press, 1983.

ROSE, MIKE. "The Language of Exclusion: Writing Instruction at the University." *College English* 47 (April 1985): 341–355.

RUDOLPH, FREDERICK. *Curriculum: A History of the American Undergraduate Course of Study Since 1636.* San Francisco: Jossey-Bass, 1978.

SCRIBNER, SYLVIA, and MICHAEL COLE. "Unpackaging Literacy." In *Writing: The Nature, Development, and Teaching of Written Communication,* vol. 1, edited by Marcia Farr Whiteman, pp. 71–87. Hillsdale, N.J.: Erlbaum, 1981.

SHAUGHNESSY, MINA P. *Errors and Expectations: A Guide for the Teacher of Basic Writing.* New York: Oxford University Press, 1977.

SHOR, IRA, and PAULO FREIRE. *A Pedagogy for Liberation: Dialogues on Transforming Education.* South Hadley, Mass.: Bergin and Garvey, 1987.

SIZER, THEODORE. *Horace's Compromise: The Dilemma of the American High School.* Boston: Houghton Mifflin, 1985.

SMITHERMAN-DONALDSON, GENEVA. "Toward a National Public Policy on Language." *College English* 49 (Jan. 1987): 29–36.

SPIVEY, NANCY NELSON. "Construing Constructivism: Reading Research in the United States." *Poetics* 16 (1987): 169–192.

STEDMAN, LAWRENCE C., and CARL F. KAESTLE. "The Test Score Decline is Over: Now What?" *Phi Delta Kappan* 67 (Nov. 1985): 204–210.

STUDY GROUP ON THE CONDITIONS OF EXCELLENCE IN AMERICAN HIGHER EDUCATION. *Involvement in Learning: Realizing the Potential of American Higher Education.* Washington, D.C.: National Institute of Education, 1984.

TYACK, DAVID B. "The High School as a Social Service Agency: Historical Perspectives on Current Policy Issues." *Educational Evaluation and Policy Analysis* 1 (1979): 45–57.

———. *The One Best System: A History of American Urban Education.* Cambridge, Mass.: Harvard University Press, 1974.

U.S. SENATE. *Indian Education: A National Tragedy—A National Challenge.* 91st Congress, 1st Session, 1969. Report #91-501. (Also known as the Kennedy Report.)

VALDÉS, GUADALUPE. *Identifying Priorities in the Study of the Writing of Hispanic-Background Students.* Berkeley, Calif.: Center for the Study of Writing, 1988.

VEYSEY, LAURENCE R. *The Emergence of the American University.* Chicago: University of Chicago Press, 1965.

WEIS, LOIS. *Between Two Worlds: Black Students in an Urban Community College.* Boston: Routledge and Kegan Paul, 1985.

WELLS, GORDON. *The Meaning Makers: Children Learning Language and Using Language to Learn.* Portsmouth, N.H.: Heinemann Educational Books, 1986.

WILLIAMS, RAYMOND. *Keywords: A Vocabulary of Culture and Society.* London: Croom Helm, 1976.

WILLIE, CHARLES V. *Effective Education: A Minority Policy Perspective.* Westport, Conn.: Greenwood Press, 1987.

WILLIS, PAUL. *Learning to Labor: How Working Class Kids Get Working Class Jobs.* New York: Columbia University Press, 1981.

VALLI, LINDA. "Gender Identity and the Technology of Office Education." In *Class, Race, and Gender in American Education*, edited by Lois Weis, pp. 87–105. Albany: State University of New York Press, 1988.